39.00
4/13/09

COSTA RICA

COSTA RICA
Quest for Democracy

JOHN A. BOOTH

Westview
PRESS
A Member of the Perseus Books Group

NATIONS OF THE MODERN WORLD:
LATIN AMERICA

Ronald Schneider, *Series Editor*

Costa Rica: Quest for Democracy,
John A. Booth

Cuba: Dilemmas of a Revolution,
Third Edition, Juan M. del Aguila

Nations of the Modern World: Latin America

Copyright © 1998 by Westview Press, A Member of the Perseus Books Group.

Published in 1998 in the United States of America by Westview Press, 5500 Central Avenue, Boulder,
Colorado 80301-2877, and in the United Kingdom by Westview Press, 12 Hid's Copse Road, Cumnor
Hill, Oxford OX2 9JJ

Library of Congress Cataloging-in-Publication Data
Booth, John A.
   Costa Rica : quest for democracy / John A. Booth.
      p.   cm.—(Nations of the modern world. Latin America)
   Includes bibliographical references and index.
   ISBN 0-8133-7631-9 (hardcover)   ISBN 0-8133-3714-3 (paperback)
   1. Costa Rica—Politics and government. I. Title. II. Series.
JL1450.B66   1998
320.97286—dc21   98-9707
                                                                            CIP

The paper used in this publication meets the requirements of the American National Standard for
Permanence of Paper for Printed Library Materials Z39.48-1984.

10   9   8   7   6   5   4   3   2   1

For
Catherine, my younger daughter

Contents

List of Illustrations   xiii
List of Acronyms   xvii
Preface   xxi

1   LATIN AMERICAN DEMOCRACY AND COSTA RICA   1

Democracy Defined, 3
Measuring Democracy, 4
Problems with Democracy, 5
Democratization, 7
The Consolidation of Democracy, 8
Conclusions, 12
Notes, 12

2   CONTEMPORARY COSTA RICA IN CENTRAL AMERICA   17

Central American History, 17
Contemporary Central America, 22
Commonalities with the Rest of Central America, 26
Differences from the Rest of Central America, 28
"Costa Rica Es Diferente": National Myths, 29
Notes, 30

3   THE HISTORICAL DEVELOPMENT OF COSTA RICAN DEMOCRACY   32

1502–1821: Discovery, Conquest, and Colonization, 32
1821–1905: Early National Life, 35
1906–1945: Turbulence and Transition, 42

1946–the Present: Crisis and Consolidation, 47
Conclusions, 52
Notes, 53

4 THE POLITICAL FRAMEWORK OF DEMOCRACY   56

The 1949 Constitution, 56
Political Parties, 66
Suffrage and Election Administration, 71
Campaigns and Elections, 72
Conclusions, 76
Notes, 78

5 SOCIAL STRUCTURE AND CIVIL SOCIETY   82

Social Structure and Cleavages, 82
Communications Media, 91
Education, 93
Organizations and Political Mobilization, 95
Conclusions, 98
Notes, 100

6 POLITICAL PARTICIPATION   103

Exploring Participation, 103
Civil Society, 122
Summary and Conclusions, 124
Notes, 125

7 POLITICAL CULTURE   129

Latin American Political Culture and Costa Rica, 129
Overview, 130
Mass Political Culture, 130
Elite Political Culture, 147
Conclusions, 150
Notes, 151

8 POLITICAL ECONOMY IN TRANSITION 154

Evolution of the Political Economy, 155
Policy Implications of Neoliberalism, 166
Conclusions: Political Economy and Democracy, 172
Notes, 174

9 COSTA RICA IN THE WORLD 177

General Characteristics of Foreign Policy, 178
Foreign Economic Policy, 179
Geopolitics, 183
Conclusions, 192
Notes, 192

10 ANALYSIS AND CONCLUSIONS: CAN DEMOCRACY SURVIVE? 195

Democratization, 196
Operation of Democracy, 199
Political Participation and Culture, 201
External Strains and Democracy, 203
Evaluation and Prospects, 205
Lessons, 206
Notes, 208

Appendix   211
Index   219

Illustrations

Tables

3.1 Key Costa Rican electoral developments, 1825–1905   40
3.2 Characteristics of Costa Rican presidencies, 1824–1998   41
3.3 Key Costa Rican electoral developments, 1906–1946   45
3.4 Evolution of the Costa Rican electorate and turnout,
     selected presidential elections, 1919–1998   46
3.5 Key Costa Rican electoral developments, 1947–1979   48

4.1 Costa Rican Legislative Assembly elections
     and representation, 1953–1998   62
4.2 Costa Rican presidential elections, 1948–1998   67

5.1 Estimated income distribution among
     Costa Rican households, 1961–1992   84

6.1 Political participation levels, 1973 and 1995 (percent involved)   104
6.2 Urban Costa Rican participation compared to
     other Central American countries   111
6.3 Demographic factors and participation in Costa Rica, 1995   113
6.4 Mean levels of political capital by levels of
     civil society, urban Costa Rica   123

7.1 General political culture of Costa Rican citizens,
     1995 urban sample   131
7.2 Attitudes toward government, 1995 urban sample   133
7.3 Democratic and authoritarian values, 1995 urban sample   136
7.4 Urban Costa Rican democratic norms compared to other
     Central American countries   138
7.5 Correlates of political culture variables,
     1995 urban sample   139
7.6 Searching for antidemocratic Ticos,
     1995 urban sample (mean scores)   142
7.7 Characteristics of elite subsample compared
     to other urban Costa Ricans, 1995   149

8.1   Economic and population growth of Costa Rica, 1920–1996   158
8.2   Selected Costa Rican economic sectors as
          percentage of GDP, 1920–1995   159
8.3   Unemployment, consumer prices, and real wages, 1970–1996   160
8.4   Costa Rican deficit and external debt, 1970–1996   161
8.5   Impact of neoliberal reforms in Costa Rica, 1980–1990   167

A.1   Selected economic data for Central America,
          by country, 1950–1994   211
A.2   Selected social data for Central America,
          by country, 1950–1995   213
A.3   Real working-class wage indices,
          Central American countries, 1963–1994   214
A.4   Mean annual U.S. military assistance to
          Central America, 1946–1992 (in millions of dollars)   215
A.5   Mean annual U.S. economic assistance to
          Central America, 1946–1992 (in millions of dollars)   216
A.6   Growth of the Costa Rican public sector, 1920–1995
          (value added to GDP by government, in thousands of dollars) 216
A.7   Attitudes and participation, urban Costa Rica, 1995   217
A.8   Intercorrelations among modes of political participation, 1973   218
A.9   Intercorrelations among modes of political participation, 1995   218

Figures

      Costa Rica   xxiii

2.1   Central America and Panama   18

Photos

3.1   Coffee workers and coffee plants laden with beans   37
3.2   José Figueres Ferrer, leader of the National Liberation
          movement and president, 1953–1958 and 1970–1974   50
3.3   Capital city of San José, with view of the Central Park   51

4.1   Youthful supporters of Rafael Angel Calderón Fournier   74
4.2   A presidential election ballot, 1990   77

5.1   Costa Rican faces   87
5.2   Peasants' and farmers' organizations rally, 1995   99

6.1   Political participation: voting   106
6.2   Political participation: a Monge campaign rally, 1982   106

6.3 Unconventional participation: a COPAN housing protest 117
6.4 Unconventional participation: street vendors chain
    themselves together to protest efforts to regulate them, 1991 119

8.1 Traditional export coffee remains strong despite efforts
    to promote new products 171
8.2 Environmental damage from deforestation 173

9.1 Rodrigo Carazo Odio, president, 1978–1982 184
9.2 Luis Alberto Monge Alvarez, president, 1982–1986 185
9.3 Oscar Arias Sánchez, president, 1986–1990,
    and Nobel Peace laureate 188

Acronyms

ACOGE	Asociación Costarricense de Gerentes de Empresas (Costa Rican Association of Business Managers)
ANAVI	Asociación Nacional de Vivienda (National Association for Housing)
ANDE	Asociación Nacional de Educadores (National Association of Teachers)
ANFE	Asociación Nacional de Fomento de la Empresa (National Association for the Promotion of Enterprise)
APRA	Alianza Popular Revolucionaria Americana (American Popular Revolutionary Alliance)
APSE	Asociación de Profesores de Segunda Enseñanza (National High School Teachers Association)
CACM	Central American Common Market (Mercado Común Centroamericano)
CATD	Confederación Auténtica de Trabajadores Democráticos (Authentic Confederation of Democratic Workers)
CCSS	Caja Costarricense de Seguro Social (Costa Rican Social Security Institute)
CCTD	Confederación Costarricense de Trabajadores Democráticos (Costa Rican Confederation of Democratic Workers)
CCTR	Confederación de Trabajadores de Costa Rica (Confederation of Workers of Costa Rica)
CEDAL	Centro de Estudios Democráticos de América Latina (Latin American Center for Democratic Studies)
CEPAS	Centro de Estudios para la Acción Social (Center for Studies of Social Action)
CGT	Confederación General de Trabajadores (General Confederation of Workers)
CIA	U.S. Central Intelligence Agency
CNP	Consejo Nacional de Producción (National Production Council)
CNT	Confederación Nacional de Trabajadores (National Workers Confederation)

CODESA	Corporación Costarricense de Desarrollo (Costa Rican Development Corporation)
CONAI	Comisión Nacional de Asuntos Indígenas (National Commission for Indian Affairs)
COPAN	Comité Patriótico Nacional (National Patriotic Committee)
CPT	Consejo Permanente de los Trabajadores (Permanent Council of Workers)
CSJ	Supreme Court of Justice (Corte Supremo de Justicia)
CSUCA	Consejo Superior Universitario de Centro America (Superior University Council of Central America)
CTCR	Confederación de Trabajadores de Costa Rica (Confederation of Costa Rican Workers)
CUT	Confederación Unitaria de Trabajadores (Unitary Confederation of Workers)
DINADECO	Dirección Nacional de Desarrollo de la Comunidad (National Community Development Directorate)
EDUCA	Editorial Universitaria Centroamericana (Central American University Press)
EEC	European Economic Community
FCV	Frente Costarricense de Vivienda (Costa Rican Front for Housing)
FDV	Frente Democrática de Vivienda (Democratic Front for Housing)
FLACSO	Facultad Latinoamericano de Ciéncias Sociales (Latin American Social Science Faculty)
FMLN	Frente Farabundo Martí para la Liberación Nacional (Farabundo Martí National Liberation Front)
FSLN	Frente Sandinista de Liberación Nacional (Sandinista National Liberation Front)
GATT	General Agreement on Tariffs and Trade
GCE	Gran Consejo Electoral (Grand Electoral Council)
GDP	Gross domestic product
GNP	Gross national product
IADB	Inter-American Development Bank
ICE	Instituto Costarricense de Electricidad (Costa Rican Electrical Institute)
IDA	Instituto de Desarrollo Agrario (Institute of Agrarian Development)
IMF	International Monetary Fund
INVU	Instituto Nacional de Vivienda y Urbanismo (National Urbanization and Housing Institute)
ISI	Import substitution industrialization

ITAC	Instituto Teológico de America Central (Central American Theological Institute)
ITCO	Instituto de Tierras y Colonización (Institute of Land and Colonization)
MCRL	Movimiento Costa Rica Libre (Free Costa Rica Movement)
NAFTA	North American Free Trade Agreement
OAS	Organization of American States
OIJ	Judicial Investigation Organism (Organismo de Investigaciónes Judiciales)
OPEN	Organización para Emergencias Nacionales (Organization for National Emergencies)
PAE	Programa de ajuste estructural (structural adjustment program)
PLN	Partido de Liberación Nacional (National Liberation Party)
PPU	Partido Pueblo Unido (United People's Party)
PR	Partido Reformista (Reformist Party)
PUN	Partido Unión Nacional (National Union Party)
PUSC	Partido Unidad Social Cristiana (Social Christian Unity Party)
PVP	Partido Vanguardia Popular (Popular Vanguard Party)
RECOPE	Refinadora Costarricense de Petroleo (Costa Rican Petroleum Refinery)
SES	Socioeconomic status
SINART	Sistema Nacional de Radio y Televisión (National System of Radio and Television)
TNE	Tribunal Nacional Electoral (National Electoral Tribunal)
TSE	Tribunal Supremo de Elecciones (Supreme Electoral Tribunal)
UAC	Unión Agrícola Cartaginesa (Carthaginian Agricultural Union)
UPA-Nacional	Unión de Pequeños y Medianos Agricultores (Union of Small and Medium Farmers)
USAID	U.S. Agency for International Development
UTG	Unión de Trabajadores de Golfito (Golfito Workers Union)

Preface

This book is the product of a long love and admiration for Costa Rica. The object of such strong emotions has at times proven both rewarding and vexatious, both more and less than one might have hoped. Costa Rica has seduced me again and again with its beauty, its democracy, its institutionalized pacifism, and its scrappily egalitarian people. But its bureaucracy, inefficiency, pride of self, and intolerance have also sometimes driven me to distraction. Perhaps an anecdote can illustrate my point.

In August 1972 I entered Costa Rica for my first long stay driving a Volkswagen camper packed to the rafters with household goods. I had just had a weeklong intensive course in Latin driving and Mesoamerican customs and immigration practices. Of the passage through Mexico and three of Central America's four military dictatorships, I most recall the continuously unfolding physical beauty of lowland and highland tropics contrasted with the ugliness and fear of man-made poverty and repression. But when I entered the Costa Rican border station at Peñas Blancas, things changed. After being ordered to completely unload the car, I sighed and complied, expecting yet another meticulous search for guns or contraband or solicitation of a bribe to grease the bureaucratic wheels. But suddenly, without so much as a glance at our mounds of boxes and bags or our vehicle, the Costa Rican customs inspector said, "You are free to go." I repacked and left Peñas Blancas in a state of bewildered ambivalence—irritated at having had to unload for nothing yet happily relieved at the absence of soldiers and petty corruption.

In the few feet between the Nicaraguan and Costa Rican border stations, I had passed into a different, far freer, and more open place. Over the ensuing year and a half living in Costa Rica, another year's residence there in 1979–1980, and during many shorter trips through Central America, the striking contrast between the liberty and stability of democratic Costa Rica and the turbulence, repression, and tensions in Guatemala, Honduras, El Salvador, and Nicaragua remains my most vivid impression of the region. This book explores and attempts to explain this essential uniqueness of Costa Rica—its strong democracy and its striking stability.

In twenty-five years of studying Costa Rica, I have had hundreds of conversations and interviews and prevailed upon the time and generosity of many, many people. I could never begin to thank them all. Several Ticos (as the Costa Ricans call themselves), both native and adopted, I do wish to thank explicitly, however, and to ask their forgiveness if I have gotten some of it wrong: Fresia Muñoz Castro, Sonia Herrera Obando, Roberto de la Ossa, José Retana, Colón Bermúdez,

Alvaro Hernández Carvajal, Jorge Cáceres, Cristina Eguizábal, Jorge Rovira M., Héctor Pérez Brignoli, Miguel Gómez B., Manuel Araya Incera, and Astrid Fischel. Thanks, too, to Will Wilson and to the *Tico Times* for their fine photographs.

Americans whose knowledge and experience of Costa Rica have also contributed significantly to this book, whether they know it or not, include Mitch Seligson, John Hammock, Lowell Gudmundson, Fred Morris, Jack Bell, John Peeler, and Cynthia Chalker. My colleague David Leblang made helpful suggestions on Chapter 8.

My wife, Patricia Bayer Richard, Latin Americanist in training, election observer extraordinaire, and the great love of my life, has helped keep my interest in the Central American region fresh and lively and collaborated on several projects that have contributed to the manuscript. My friend and workout partner Keith Shaeffer faithfully and regularly pestered me for years to finish the book so he could read it. Thanks to my friend and editor Barbara Ellington, to her successors Karl Yambert and Jennifer Chen, and to Westview Press for their patience on the long-delayed project. Alice Colwell did an excellent job of copyediting.

Support for travel and research time in Costa Rica, for which I am most grateful, has come from the Latin American Teaching Fellows program, the Commission for the International Exchange of Scholars (Fulbright Program), the North-South Center of the University of Miami, the Howard Heinz Endowment–Center for Latin American Studies of the University of Pittsburgh Research Grants on Current Latin American Issues, and the University of North Texas. Institutional collaboration has come at different times from the School of International Relations of the Universidad Nacional Autónoma de Costa Rica, Acción Internacional Técnica (AITEC), the Dirección Nacional de Desarrollo de la Comunidad (DINADECO), and the Instituto de Fomento y Asesoría Municipal (IFAM). I extend my most sincere thanks to them all.

John A. Booth

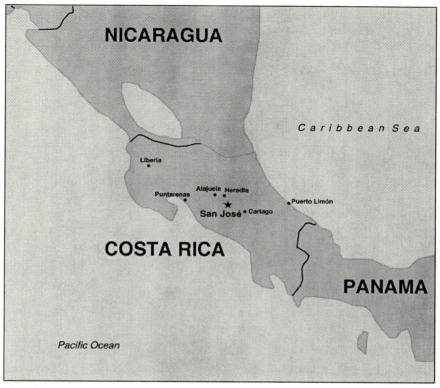

Costa Rica

1

LATIN AMERICAN DEMOCRACY AND COSTA RICA

Costa Rica is famed and important beyond its size and numbers . . . as a verdant oasis of democracy and political maturity in a desert of dictatorship and political violence.[1]

A tidal wave of military dictatorship swept Latin America in the 1970s, crushing both the Chilean and Uruguayan constitutional regimes in 1973. These democratic breakdowns of two older Latin democracies left Costa Rica as the region's longest surviving democratic regime.[2] Many feared then that Costa Rica's civilian, representative, constitutional regime might have become the last survivor of a soon to be extinct species.

Costa Rican democracy survived, however, in spite of the revolutions, military dictatorships, political upheaval, and geopolitical meddling that engulfed Central America over the next two decades. Today this tiny nation of approximately 3.7 million people has as neighbors several fledgling democracies where many reasonable observers expected none.[3] Indeed, as the twentieth century ends, the exceptions to this recent wave of democratization in Latin America, such as Cuba, now seem glaringly anomalous.[4]

Despite recent improvements, pessimism about the prospects for democracy in Latin America has long been widespread among students of the region. Scholars cite many well-known cultural and institutional features of Ibero-

American societies—including elite authoritarianism, bureaucratic centralism, corporatism, militarism, and repression—as powerful barriers to democratic rule.[5] Writing of Central America in particular, Glen Dealy forcefully states this view:

> Unlike liberal democrats . . . those both in and out of power in Central America agree that particularistic and opposing factions invariably disrupt public order and are insufficiently restrained by countervailing power centers. . . . Central Americans still pursue monolithic accord. . . . While human rights in general are defended throughout the area, individual rights are not. . . . Central Americans perceive constitutionally prescribed elections to be yet one more divisive threat to the community.[6]

Given such powerful cultural obstacles to democracy, it seems a wonder that civilian, constitutional, electoral regimes could exist at all in Latin America, much less in Central America. Although Costa Rica is often (and sometimes incorrectly) argued to deviate sharply from these regional traditions, the country is nevertheless a Latin American nation and the heir to Ibero-American traditions. Costa Rica has in fact experienced most of the cultural, historical, political, and economic forces that have affected the rest of Central America. Yet despite scholarly skepticism about the prospects for Latin democracy in general, and despite recent decades of economic crisis and political upheaval in Central America, Costa Rican democracy not only exists but persists.

This book seeks to explain why political democracy arose in Costa Rica and how it survives. Although it is beyond the scope of this work to explore democratization in Central American in general, Costa Rica cannot be appropriately understood apart from its regional context and the forces that act upon it. Some of the discussion that follows, therefore, will examine Costa Rica as part of a region of rather similar nations shaped by similar experiences and geopolitical and economic forces. This comparative strategy should help highlight both Costa Rica's commonalities with the region and its true distinctiveness.

The early institutional roots of Costa Rican democracy go back a century, and its social origins are older still (see Chapter 3), but experts generally date the present democratic regime from the 1948 civil war. Civilian, constitutional, representative government evolved gradually in Costa Rica before 1948. The regime defined by the 1949 constitution is today the most consolidated and stable in Latin America. Other Latin American experiences with democracy have been shorter, more interrupted, or less conclusive than Costa Rica's, even though recent trends have seen the dawn of hope for a regional consolidation of democracy.[7]

How so many other countries joined Costa Rica in the democratic ranks in recent years need not detain us long here but is of considerable interest to scholars and policymakers.[8] What may be more important to ask is whether Costa Rica offers a model or useful lessons for other aspiring Latin American democracies. I return to this issue in the concluding chapter.

Democracy Defined

Before we examine Costa Rican society and its system of governance, we need to define the term "democracy." Politicians often abuse this evocative word for political purposes, but political scientists also misuse the term. Those who style themselves the "scientists" of politics would, one might hope, agree on what constitutes democracy. But, alas, they do not. Although it is not any of the following things per se, democracy is nonetheless often equated by scholars with the holding of elections, constitutional rule, or any one of dozens of particular types of regimes.[9]

The main elements of democracy in its purest sense are easily seen in the word's Greek roots—*demos*, "the people," and *kratos*, "to rule": rule by the people. In its various treatments during the nearly three millennia prior to the onset of pluralist-elitist theorizing after World War II,[10] the essential characteristic of democracy—for good or ill—has been participation in the governing of a society by its people. One convenient expression of this idea is *participation by the general population of a community in its rule (the making and carrying out of decisions)*. Because democracy is defined by citizen participation, an equal right to engage in political activity is essential for all noncriminal, sane adults.

For Aristotle, democracy was the constitutional arrangement by which free, poor citizens constitute a sovereign majority and take part in making decisions and adjudicating disputes.[11] Thomas Jefferson's most preferred type of democracy was "government by its citizens in mass, acting directly and personally, according to rules established by the majority."[12] For John Stuart Mill, the "ideally best form of government" was one in which each citizen is, "at least occasionally, called on to take an actual part in the government by the personal discharge of some public function."[13]

Classical democratic theorists argued that a major function and the greatest benefit of democracy is the developmental or educative impact that participation has upon individuals and the whole community.[14] J. S. Mill, for instance, expected participation to bring about "that education of the intelligence and the sentiments which is carried down to the very lowest ranks of the people."[15] Jean-Jacques Rousseau believed that as a participant in governance, the citizen must "consult his reason. . . . By dint of being exercised, his faculties will develop, his ideas take on a wider scope, his sentiments become ennobled, and his whole soul be . . . elevated. . . . [He would turn] from a limited and stupid animal into an intelligent being and a man."[16]

Another important function of participation and benefit of democracy is the protection of the rights and interests of citizens. The social contract theorists agreed that should a government formed by the consent of its citizens fail its duty to defend their safety, freedom, and property, then citizens would have a right and an obligation to reform or replace it.[17] One of democracy's major drawbacks for some classical theorists was precisely this prospect for unrest, but Jefferson saw such "turbulency" as beneficial: "It prevents the degeneracy of a government and nourishes a general attention to the public affairs."[18] Thus via participation citizens communicate their desires to government and help keep it responsive.

Measuring Democracy

The classical approach to democracy has several implications: First, democracy involves public participation in decisionmaking and administration, and this participation can vary in amount and quality. Thus *democracy is not a constant but a variable.* There may be more or less democracy, depending upon the amount and quality of public participation in decisionmaking and implementation in any particular system.[19]

Because democracy is variable, it is theoretically (and at least in part practically) possible to determine how much or how little of it there is in a particular society at a given moment. This can be done by measuring and evaluating the amount and quality of political participation that goes on. One helpful approach to assess the amount and nature of democracy has been formulated by Carl Cohen, who identifies three dimensions of democracy.[20] The first is the *breadth* of democracy, or the fraction of the citizenry participating in the making and carrying out of decisions. Breadth may vary according to the type of participation, from wide in the case of voting, for example, to rather narrow (few participating) in holding public office in most representative systems.

A second dimension is the *range* of democracy, the array of issues and decisions over which the public exercises decisions (e.g., leader selection, areas subject to legislation, dispute resolution). Classical liberal polities have relatively small ranges of democracy because much economic decisionmaking is reserved for the private sector. Socialist regimes, in contrast, have a much wider range of economic activity governed by public decisions because their economies are subject to public ownership and regulation.

The third of Cohen's dimensions of democracy is its *depth*, or the potential to influence decisions and the autonomy of popular participation. Participation is deep when it truly has the potential to shape public policy and when it is not manipulated or controlled by actors other than those participating. The individuals or groups taking part need not achieve their goals to have deep participation; they must merely have had the chance to influence policy.

One critical problem of democracy is the size of the community being governed. A very small community (such as a Swiss commune, a New England town, or a Central American cooperative) may be easily ruled by direct popular action, but the larger the community the more unwieldy direct participation becomes. Larger systems require representative government in order to function efficiently.

There is, however, a necessary loss in the breadth of democracy when a small number of representatives make and administrative specialists carry out decisions on behalf of a much less involved mass of citizens. Democratic depth also declines when political parties and other elites mediate between government and citizens by selecting candidates for public office and setting the public agenda.

Representative forms of democracy, by theoretical and arithmetic necessity, permit less participation and are thus less democratic than governance by direct citizen involvement in rule. This makes it somewhat difficult to evaluate democracy in large, modern political communities. How can one determine whether there is sufficient citizen participation in a representative system to warrant calling it a democracy? Is there a "democratic threshold" of some sort?

In fact, however, these questions may be the wrong ones. It appears more helpful to think of democracy as an ideal type of polity with full citizen participation—as a standard against which to evaluate particular nations. If we view democracy this way, there is no particular magic formula, threshold, or regime type that automatically earns the label "democratic." Particular polities merely approach, more or less, the ideal.

Is there some practical standard that might help us classify representative governments as having democratic tendencies? Anthony Birch supplies a helpful outline: "It is . . . fundamental to all democratic theories, that private citizens should have the opportunity to vote in elections, to organize political parties and pressure groups, and to give public expression to their views on political issues without fear of reprisals if their views happen to be unpopular with the government of the day."[21] Under these conditions, a formally democratic regime would be civilian, popularly elected, and constrained by a constitution. It would follow democratic decisionmaking rules and would accommodate citizen organization, mobilization, and communication with the government. Of course, one may also evaluate such a structurally "democratic" regime in terms of Cohen's suggested standards of breadth, range, and depth of participation.

So many observers label Costa Rica a "democracy" because, as both supporters and critics of the system agree, its regime has clearly met these structural standards ever since the early 1950s.[22] This volume simply takes Costa Rica's membership in the club of democratic nations as a given, then tries to answer several significant questions suggested by the previous discussion. What is the breadth of participation in Costa Rica? What is the range of participation—on what public policy matters does the popular voice actually have a meaningful impact? What is the depth of participation in Costa Rica—how autonomously and freely may Costa Ricans take part? Are the breadth, depth and range of Costa Rican democracy changing, and if so, how?

Problems with Democracy

In referring to "turbulency," Jefferson recognized a certain negative potential in pure democracy, a problem acknowledged by most democratic theorists. Indeed, at a fundamental level there is nothing either more turbulent or more democratic than a lynch mob—a crowd of people deciding a person's guilt of a crime and spontaneously murdering their prisoner with a rope and a handy tree. For the advocate of democracy, this scenario raises alarming difficulties. Although a lynching may, in Jefferson's words, "epitomize attention to public affairs," it hardly achieves Rousseau's ideal of "ennobling the soul" or "elevating the spirit." Since it was probably not mob rule that moved so many to praise democracy, something must still be missing from our treatment.

One strong current of political thought has long and deeply suspected that in every crowd of citizens there lurks a potential lynch mob.[23] Aristotle, for example, attributed the perversion of democracy to the people's inability to resist demagoguery, the manipulation of popular will by unscrupulous leaders.[24] Similarly, Alexander Hamilton asked: "Are not popular assemblies frequently subject to the impulses of rage, resentment, jealously, avarice, and other irregular and violent propensities?"[25]

Indeed, this very concern about masses' propensity to tyrannize and their weakness for demagogues prompted mid-twentieth-century theorists and political scientists known as pluralist-elitists to attempt a major revision of democratic theory.[26] This school argued that most political decisions should be made by allegedly more enlightened, competent, and tolerant competing elites. The pluralist-elitists redefined democracy as an elite-governed system with minimal citizen involvement.[27]

Other solutions to the problematic aspects of democracy exist. Classical theorists' argue for the educative effects of citizen participation, suggesting that both the individual and collective capacity and wisdom of citizens—albeit limited initially—improve through participation. John Mueller contends that whether such education of mass publics occurs or not, democracies work anyway: "The amazing thing about democracy is that [its citizens] *are* substantially incompetent, but the process nevertheless generates able, even superior leaders and tends to keep them responsive and responsible. The system seems to work for the same reason that demagogues are kept in check: You cannot fool all of the people all of the time."[28]

For democracy to ennoble citizens rather than to debase them through mob rule, a society needs to restrain the worst impulses of elites and the public until the common sense of self-interest prevails and participation improves citizens' capabilities and regard for the common good. The usual proposals to solve these problems involve constitutions and citizens' rights.

A constitution provides for rights and their protection.[29] First, for there to be any democracy at all within a society, its citizens must be able to participate in making and carrying out public decisions. Second, it therefore follows that the principal reason for limiting any one citizen's right to participate must be to ensure the right of other citizens also to participate. Ultimately, such basic participatory rights will be best protected by two things: The first is a constitution—a set of rules for political interaction agreed upon among the citizens. To promote and protect democracy, a constitution must guarantee majorities and minorities alike the right to participate and protect each from abuse by the other. Subgroups require protected and equal participation rights, as do the winners and losers in particular conflicts.

Practically speaking, such constitutionally guaranteed rights translate into rather simple, elegant, and familiar concepts: the right to public political opinion and to speak out freely; the right to assemble peacefully and to associate freely for political purposes; the right peaceably to oppose incumbent officeholders and to remain free and safe while so doing; the right to free and fair elections of office-holders; the right to petition government and public officials; and the right to pursue and obtain redress from errors or abuses of authority by public officials.

Some argue further that public funding of elections, workplace democracy, and some redistributive efforts to ensure equal political opportunity are also essential for the effective exercise of political rights.[30] Their point is not to argue in favor of economic equality for its own sake but as a necessary means of empowering a polity's least advantaged citizens so as to give their participation real potential for influence.

Democratization

Now that we have defined and discussed democracy, we are left with a critical question: How does democracy arise as a functioning political system? The change from some nondemocratic form of government to representative democracy is known as democratization. With the exception of classical Greek city-states, democracy is a rather new form of governance. Representative democracy in nation-states has existed for only a couple of centuries, with the vast majority of its current examples having developed only in recent decades. Why and how does democratization occur? Why did it occur in Costa Rica?

Political scientists, once surprisingly little concerned with democratization, have recently expended enormous energy on the subject. They have formulated four contending theories about why democracy occurs, based on political culture, political processes, sociopolitical structures, and elite behavior.

Political culture approaches argue that democracy arises from a process of cultural change that leads to widely shared democratic norms. The major exponent of this school is Ronald Inglehart, who argues that the path to democracy in Western societies took the following steps: Protestantism challenged Catholicism and helped bring about economic development and prosperity, which promoted higher levels of interpersonal trust that eventually led to citizens' developing a democratic political culture. At that point, systemic democracy was able to emerge.[31]

The process theories of democratization contend that undemocratic power holders will share power with the people only when forced to do so. They identify several forces capable of provoking such change: breakdown of the coalition supporting authoritarian rule, collapse of the political order due to war or economic crisis, external imposition, and "demonstration effects" (imitation of other models).[32] On a global scale, some of these occur in cycles that cause many nations to liberalize or democratize almost simultaneously.

The structural theorists agree that authoritarian elites would not relinquish power willingly but contend that socioeconomic structures are the main causes of democratization. Noting that most democracies have attained certain levels of per capita wealth and literacy, they conclude that citizens' resources give them power to force democratization. Especially likely to cause authoritarians to democratize are the widespread distribution of education, income, wealth, and popular organization (associations), sometimes reflected in new or newly political mobilized economic classes. Distributed structural resources thus permit the mobilization of demands for democratic reform that authoritarians sometimes cannot resist.[33]

Finally, elite theorists contend that the small minority of influential individuals who manage key resources in all societies control democratization. Ironically, in order for popular participation in rule to occur, powerful minorities must limit their own behavior and accept citizen involvement. Many democracies appear to arise from an accord, formal or informal, among the leaders of important social, political, and economic forces to accommodate each other in politics, tolerate some citizen involvement, and play the political game by democratic rules.[34]

For Costa Rica, these theories raise several questions. Did popular culture evolve toward democracy and eventually lead national elites to adopt democratic rules? Did the previous regime experience a crisis or breakdown that brought democracy, or was there a demonstration effect? Did socioeconomic resources or civil society become sufficiently decentralized that popular forces were able to force ruling elites to include them in the political game? Or did elites merely elect, for whatever reason, to adopt new rules that admitted the masses into the political arena? Chapter 3 examines the Costa Rican case and evaluates the relative merit of these theories in explaining what happened there. It stresses a combination of structural forces, civil society, and elite actions in shaping Costa Rica's democratization.

The Consolidation of Democracy

Whatever the path by which societies arrive at civilian, constitutional rule, another critical question is whether they can survive.[35] Many democracies fail, especially in Latin America. The long-term stability of a democratic regime may depend upon several things: the nature of the elite settlement, the political culture of elites and masses, the structures of the political system, the role of the state, socioeconomic factors, and external influences.[36]

Elite Settlement

One apparent key to the survival of stable democracy at the scale of the nation-state is the development of a persistent working agreement among elites, or *elite settlement*.[37] An elite settlement that includes a wide array of the most significant social and political forces tends to be stable because it will be challenged less by disgruntled outside elites. Many such regime-consolidating settlements have stabilized constitutional democracies through pacts among the leaders of critical political and economic groups. The adoption of formal political constitutions has often accompanied such pacts, laying out essential, consensual rules for the political game.

The drafting and ratification of the U.S. Constitution (1787–1789) is a good example of an elite settlement. Two Latin American examples are the 1958 National Front constitutional accord between Colombia's Liberal Party and Conservative Party and the Venezuelan three-party accord of the late 1950s.[38] Each settlement included many social forces and adopted liberal democratic political rules, and each has since contributed to stable regimes. More recent examples may include negotiated settlements (with formal democratic rules of the game) of the Nicaraguan, Salvadoran, and Guatemalan civil wars.

But accords among elites need not be formal. Settlements may develop slowly and less dramatically, as in Costa Rica. As Chapter 3 reveals, despite important antecedents in earlier decades, Costa Rica's current settlement among party and economic leaders evolved over roughly a decade after the 1948 civil war. It grew out of decisions by the social democratic victors in the war to accommodate other political groups; those groups later decided to return the favor. From this beginning, continued mutual tolerance eventually cemented a democratic settlement.

Political Culture

Another factor that can restrain minority or majority tyranny is political culture. Certain attitudes, beliefs, and expectations about governance among both elites and masses can help stabilize democratic rule.

Other things equal, the more of a society's top political, social, and economic leaders who favor citizen participation, civil liberties, and a restrained interelite competition for power, the stronger and more stable will be democracy. An elite political culture committed to restricted competition by democratic rules of the game can promote the consolidation and survival of a stable democratic regime. When great social stress arises, elites' commitment to accommodate each other, popular participation, and constitutional rules become essential for democratic stability. This is so because, especially in times of crisis, elites' economic, institutional, and coercive power would tempt them to repress mass participation or violate democratic rules, thus undermining democracy.

For the general mass of citizens, the relationship of political culture to the long-term stability of the regime is similar to that of elites, if perhaps not quite so essential at moments of crisis. The stronger the support in the common political culture for the democratic regime, participation in public affairs, key civil liberties, and democratic rules, the better sustained will be democracy. The more the populace participates and expects to do so, the more interests will be articulated to government and the more attention government will have to pay to the citizens' demands.[39] Robert Putnam has recently suggested that among the aspects of mass participation most essential to democracy is *civil society*, the involvement of citizens in organizations, which builds public trust and strengthens democratic norms.[40]

Chapters 6 and 7 explore how citizen participation and mass and elite political culture in Costa Rica impinge on democratic governance, both positively and negatively. Of particular interest are such factors as popular commitment to civil government, civil liberties, and the alternation of parties in power, as well as elites' penchant to accommodate each other and working-class pressures and elite consensus on democratic political rules.

Like quitting smoking, establishing democracy in Latin America has historically proven easier to begin than to complete successfully. Indeed, some countries—including Costa Rica—have "become democratic" several times. Samuel Huntington traces the cycles of democratization and democratic breakdown in Latin America and elsewhere since the nineteenth century.[41] But despite some temporary reversals, no other Latin nation has had Costa Rica's success at remaining in the democratic mode for such a long period.

Governmental and Political Structures

Other than those obvious structural features implicit in democratic rules of the game already mentioned above, the variety of governmental structures possible within a democracy is great. Most Latin American nations, however, have followed the constitutional model originally adopted by the United States: republican, presidential, representative systems (a few of them also federal). There have been a few experiments such as the revolutionary regimes of Cuba and Nicaragua, but these are marked exceptions.[42]

Observers of Latin American democracy concur that certain structural traits have contributed toward the stability of representative, constitutional governments in the region:

1. A presidential (rather than a parliamentary) form of government, checked by significant legislative power, to focus elite and mass political competition upon elections and to restrain executive authority.
2. A party system that is competitive but centrist (not sharply polarized), and in which parties are institutionally strong (i.e., are flexible, capable, and adaptable).
3. Strong, independent electoral agencies to establish and maintain voter roles and to oversee elections, thus curtailing election fraud.[43]

Role of the State

Civilian, representative, constitutional government in Latin America has enjoyed greater stability in nations in which

1. The state has developed significant strength and autonomy (an effective bureaucracy, significant extractive capacity, and legitimacy) so that its regimes may govern without excessive use of repression.[44]

2. Civilian politicians have contained the size of the national armed forces and have avoided appearing to threaten military corporate self-interest.[45]

Chapters 4 and 5 examine various aspects of the formal structure of Costa Rican government, its relation to the Costa Rican economy, and the overall role of the state in Costa Rica. Social democratic economic strategies of the Costa Rican state, established in the wake of the 1948 democratic revolution, prevailed for several decades through governments of both the National Liberation Party (Partido de Liberación Nacional, or PLN) and several, more conservative Unity coalition governments. A combination of recession, massive foreign debt, and neoliberal economic pressures from the international lending community has recently altered the contemporary political economy. The state has reduced its scope and economic role and curtailed its programs, raising questions about the range of democracy in Costa Rica and whether government resources remain adequate to sustain political stability.

Socioeconomic Factors

Democratic stability in Latin America appears to theorists and observers likely to be enhanced to the degree that

1. A society is homogeneous, that is, its citizens are more alike than different.[46]
2. Social cleavages (divisions by wealth, race, ethnicity, language, and so forth) are crosscutting rather than mutually reinforcing.[47]
3. Where significant inequalities do exist, such as very great and persistent inequalities of wealth and income, governments help ameliorate poverty among the most poor.
4. Economic growth has been relatively steady over a long period, and the negative effects of recessions appear to be shared broadly throughout society.

Costa Rica's great national myth holds that the nation was and today remains a homogeneous and egalitarian society, and that these factors gave rise to the nation's modern democracy. Costa Rica, however, is not so homogeneous as it is often perceived. Although a core of the nation's population was mainly Spanish and there were relatively few indigenous people, Costa Rica has experienced periods of heavy immigration from many sources. A large mestizo[48] population was annexed with Guanacaste in the nineteenth century. Today there are significant minority populations, and Protestantism is rapidly growing in the predominantly Roman Catholic nation. The national myth of relative social equality also warrants close examination. Evidence suggests that income inequality in Costa Rica has always been greater than commonly believed and may have become substantially more unequal in recent years.

To evaluate how certain socioeconomic and class phenomena either reinforce or limit Costa Rican democracy, Chapters 5 and 8 explore the relationship of the state to social and economic structures and examine various social strata, including religious and racial minorities.

External Pressures

It has clearly been helpful to their survival for Latin American democracies to remain on the friendly side of the United States. Constitutional, civilian regimes suspected by Washington of tendencies toward communist influence were either overthrown (Guatemala in 1954, Chile in 1973), or attacked, subverted, and undermined with the active participation of the United States (Nicaragua 1979–1990). In contrast, in Venezuela, Colombia, and Costa Rica the radical left has been kept on the margins of politics. This has helped assure continued goodwill from Washington. Latin American democracies must also cope with the related problems of regional conflict and revolution in neighboring countries. Chapters 5 and 8 discuss how, during the decades of the 1970s and 1980s, Costa Rica's international economic and political environment became vastly more complex and threatening and thus provided significant challenges to stability.

Conclusions

Costa Rica's remarkable democratic regime has deep historical roots that in many ways make it an unusual case in Latin America despite the recent wave of democratization in the region. The nation has developed a stable system of civilian, constitutional rule sustained by checks on executive power, low levels of repression, democratic elite and mass culture, crosscutting social cleavages, policies that have promoted economic growth and somewhat ameliorated poverty, and generally good relations with the United States. The following chapters explore the patterns and relationships that define both the strengths and weaknesses of Costa Rican democracy.

This study is not solely about Costa Rican politics and the nation's democracy. Its goal is to examine the larger society in many of its facets and dimensions. The nation's great national myth roots the nation's contemporary democracy in its economic and social history. As with many myths, there are inaccuracies in this one, but democracy in Costa Rica is indeed linked to social and economic forces that cannot be disregarded.

Notes

1. Charles D. Ameringer, *Democracy in Costa Rica* (New York: Praeger, 1982), p. vii.
2. Costa Rica had preceded into constitutional civilian rule by nearly a decade what were the region's other oldest remaining democracies—Colombia and Venezuela. See John A.

Peeler, *Latin American Democracies: Colombia, Costa Rica, Venezuela* (Chapel Hill: University of North Carolina Press, 1985).

3. Population estimate for 1998 based upon the Inter-American Development Bank (IADB), *Socio-Economic Progress in Latin America: Annual Report 1997* (Washington, D.C.: IADB, 1997), table A-1.

4. Samuel Huntington, *The Third Wave: Democratization in the Late Twentieth Century* (Norman: University of Oklahoma Press, 1990); Mitchell A. Seligson and John A. Booth, eds., *Elections and Democracy in Central America, Revisited* (Chapel Hill: University of North Carolina Press, 1995); Guillermo O'Donnell, Philippe C. Schmitter, and Laurence Whitehead, eds., *Transitions from Authoritarian Rule: Prospects for Democracy* (Baltimore: Johns Hopkins University Press, 1986); Larry Diamond, Juan J. Linz, and Seymour Martin Lipset, eds., *Democracy in Developing Countries,* vol. 4: *Latin America* (Boulder: Lynne Rienner Publishers–Adamantine Press, 1989).

5. See, for instance, Guillermo O'Donnell, *Modernization and Bureaucratic Authoritarianism: Studies in South American Politics* (Berkeley: Institute of International Studies–University of California, 1973); Howard J. Wiarda, *The Democratic Revolution in Latin America* (New York: Holmes and Meier, 1990); and several contributors to Wiarda's edited volume *Politics and Social Change in Latin America: Still a Distinct Tradition?* (Boulder: Westview Press, 1992), especially Charles Wagley, "A Framework for Latin American Culture," pp. 25–30; Glen C. Dealy, "The Tradition of Monistic Democracy in Latin America," pp. 40–69, and "Pipe Dreams: The Pluralistic Latins," pp. 281–294; Richard M. Morse, "Claims of Political Tradition," pp. 70–107, and "Toward a Theory of Spanish American Government," pp. 125–145. Other arguments along this line include Emilio Willems, *Latin American Culture* (New York: Harper and Row, 1975), chs. 5 and 14; Glen C. Dealy, *The Latin Americans: Spirit and Ethos* (Boulder: Westview Press, 1992).

6. Dealy, "Pipe Dreams," pp. 282–283, 287–288.

7. Terry Karl, "Imposing Consent? Electoralism vs. Democratization in El Salvador," pp. 9–36; and Wayne A. Cornelius, "The Nicaraguan Elections of 1984: A Reassessment of Their Domestic and International Significance," in Paul Drake and Eduardo Silva, eds., *Elections and Democratization in Latin America: 1980–1985* (San Diego: University of California–San Diego, Institute for Iberian and Latin American Studies and Center for U.S.-Mexican Studies, Institute of the Americas, 1986), pp. 61–71; John A. Booth, "Elections and Democracy in Central America: A Framework for Analysis," pp. 7–35, and John Peeler, "Democracy and Elections in Central America: Autumn of the Oligarchs?" pp. 185–198, both in John A. Booth and Mitchell A. Seligson, eds., *Elections and Democracy in Central America* (Chapel Hill: University of North Carolina Press, 1989); John A. Booth, Anne L. Howard, Lord Kennet, David Pfrimmer, and Margaret Ellen Roggensack, *The 1985 Guatemalan Elections: Will the Military Relinquish Power?* (Washington, D.C.: International Human Rights Law Group, Washington Office on Latin America, 1985); David Carliner, John A. Booth, Joseph Eldridge, Margaret Ellen Roggensack, and Bonnie Teneriello, *Political Transition and the Rule of Law in Guatemala* (Washington, D.C.: International Human Rights Law Group, Washington Office on Latin America, 1988); Wiarda, *The Democratic Revolution*; Huntington, *The Third Wave.*

8. See, for instance, Drake and Silva, *Elections and Democratization*; James M. Malloy and Mitchell A. Seligson, eds., *Authoritarians and Democrats: Regime Transition in Latin America* (Pittsburgh: University of Pittsburgh Press, 1987); Booth and Seligson, *Elections and Democracy in Central America*; O'Donnell et al., *Transitions from Authoritarian Rule*; Diamond et al., *Democracy in Developing Countries*; Enrique A. Baloyra, ed., *Comparing*

New Democracies: Transition and Consolidation in Mediterranean Europe and the Southern Cone (Boulder: Westview Press, 1987).

9. Anthony H. Birch, *The Concepts and Theories of Modern Democracy* (London: Routledge, 1993), pp. 45–49. The discussion in this section is based heavily upon Booth, "Elections and Democracy in Central America: A Framework for Analysis," pp. 1–10.

10. The most widespread misconception of the meaning of democracy in modern political science is that of the pluralist-elitists, whose approach is well synthesized in Robert Dahl's *Polyarchy* (New Haven: Yale University Press, 1971). For a version of this theory applied to the Third World and in particular to Latin America, see Larry Diamond and Juan Linz, "Introduction," in Diamond et al., *Democracy in Developing Countries*. Paul Cammack skewers this approach from a Marxist perspective in "Democratization and Citizenship in Latin America," in Geraint Parry and Michael Moran, eds., *Democracy and Democratization* (London: Routledge, 1994), pp. 174–194.

The pluralist-elitists, fearing mass participation, deemphasize popular participation in politics in favor of limited competition among elites that resembles the practice of liberal constitutionalism in large, modern industrial countries. Critics of pluralist-elitism attack it for excessive narrowness and for distorting the classical definition of democracy. See Carole Pateman, *Participation and Democratic Theory* (Cambridge: Cambridge University Press, 1970), pp. 1–44; Peter Bachrach, *The Theory of Democratic Elitism* (Boston: Little, Brown, 1966); Benjamin Barber, *Strong Democracy: Participatory Politics in a Strong Age* (Berkeley: University of California Press, 1984), pp. 3–114.

11. Aristotle, *Politics*, Richard Robinson, trans. (Oxford: Oxford University Press, 1962), pp. 74–81.

12. Thomas Jefferson, Letter to John Taylor (May 28, 1816), in *The Jeffersonian Tradition in American Democracy*, Maurice Wiltse, ed. (Chapel Hill: University of North Carolina Press, 1935), p. 83.

13. John Stuart Mill, *Considerations on Representative Government* (Indianapolis: Bobbs-Merrill, 1958), p. 42.

14. Ibid., pp. 82–92.

15. Ibid., p. 128.

16. Jean-Jacques Rousseau, *The Social Contract*, excerpted in Carl Cohen, ed., *Communism, Fascism, and Democracy* (New York: Random House, 1962), p. 478. Thomas Jefferson similarly claims that where men participate maximally their innate sense of morality will be "strengthened by exercise, as may any particular limb of the body." See Jefferson's letter to Peter Carr (August 10, 1787), in Wiltse, *Jeffersonian Tradition*, p. 67.

17. See, for instance, John Locke, *Second Treatise on Government*, excerpted in Cohen, *Communism, Fascism, and Democracy*, pp. 452–469; Rousseau, *The Social Contract*, excerpted in Cohen, *Communism, Fascism, and Democracy*, p. 474; and Jefferson, Letter to Madison (January 30, 1787), in Wiltse, *Jeffersonian Tradition*, pp. 79–80.

18. Jefferson, Letter to Madison, in Wiltse, *Jeffersonian Tradition*, pp. 79–80. An excellent recent formulation of these virtues is that of John Mueller, "Democracy and Ralph's Pretty Good Grocery: Elections, Equality, and the Minimal Human Being," *American Journal of Political Science* 36 (November 1992): 983–1003.

19. This section draws heavily on Booth, "Elections and Democracy in Central America: A Framework for Analysis."

20. Carl Cohen, *Democracy* (New York: Free Press, 1971), pp. 8–36. For an alternative formulation, see Barber, *Strong Democracy*, pp. 117–311.

21. Birch, *Concepts and Theories*, p. 82.

22. See, for instance, Cynthia H. Chalker, "Elections and Democracy in Costa Rica," in Seligson and Booth, *Elections and Democracy, Revisited*, pp. 103–122; Charles D. Ameringer, *Democracy in Costa Rica* (New York: Praeger, 1982); Chester Zelaya, Oscar Aguilar Bulgarelli, Daniel Camacho, Rodolfo Cerdas, and Jacobo Schifter, *Democracia en Costa Rica? Cinco opiniones polémicas* (San José, Costa Rica: Editorial Universidad Estatal a Distancia, 1978).

23. Mueller, "Democracy," pp. 993–997.

24. Aristotle, *Politics,* book 4, ch. 4.

25. Alexander Hamilton, *The Federalist Papers,* no. 6 (New York: Mentor, 1961), pp. 56–57.

26. The theorists of this group are numerous; for citations to and a discussions of their work see Pateman, *Participation and Democratic Theory,* ch. 1.

27. Barber, in *Strong Democracy,* pp. 3–25, derides this approach as "zookeeping." Others have attacked the pluralist-elitists' reasoning as excessively pessimistic about mass publics, empirically inaccurate, based upon an erroneous reading of democratic theory, and offering a flawed solution; see Pateman, *Participation and Democratic Theory,* ch. 1, Bachrach, *The Theory of Democratic Elitism,* and Mueller, "Democracy."

28. Mueller, "Democracy," p. 997.

29. See Cohen, *Democracy,* pp. 120–155; Joshua Cohen and Joel Rogers, *On Democracy* (Middlesex, England: Penguin Books, 1984), pp. 149–161; Mueller, "Democracy"; Birch, *Concepts and Theories,* ch. 11; and Cammack, "Democratization and Citizenship."

30. See Adam Przeworski, *Capitalism and Social Democracy* (Cambridge: Cambridge University Press, 1985); John Dunn, *The Politics of Socialism* (Cambridge: Cambridge University Press, 1984); Cohen and Rogers, *On Democracy,* pp. 154–166.

31. Ronald Inglehart, "The Renaissance of Political Culture," *American Political Science Review* 82 (November 1988): 1203–1230; and *Culture Shift in Advanced Industrial Society* (Princeton: Princeton University Press, 1990). Of great influence on Inglehart were Gabriel Almond and Sidney Verba, *The Civic Culture* (Boston: Little, Brown, 1963).

32. See, for instance, Huntington, *The Third Wave,* ch. 2; O'Donnell et al., *Transitions from Authoritarian Rule;* and Georg Sorensen, *Democracy and Democratization* (Boulder: Westview Press, 1993), ch. 2.

33. See Sorensen, *Democracy and Democratization,* ch. 2; Tatu Vanhanen, *The Process of Democratization* (New York: Crane and Russak, 1990); Dietrich Rueschemeyer, Evelyne Huber Stephens, and John D. Stephens, *Capitalist Development and Democracy* (Chicago: University of Chicago Press, 1992); Robert D. Putnam, *Making Democracy Work: Civic Traditions in Modern Italy* (Princeton: Princeton University Press, 1993); and Robert D. Putnam, "Bowling Alone: America's Declining Social Capital," *Journal of Democracy* 6, 1 (January 1995): 65–78. Deborah J. Yashar, *Demanding Democracy: Reform and Reaction in Costa Rica and Guatemala, 1870s–1950s* (Stanford: Stanford University Press, 1997), takes a strongly structuralist approach to Costa Rica's democratization but includes an elite component (pp. 1–25).

34. Michael Burton, Richard Gunther, and John Higley, "Introduction: Elite Transformations and Democratic Regimes," in John Higley and Richard Gunther, eds., *Elites and Democratic Consolidation in Latin America and Southern Europe* (Cambridge: Cambridge University Press, 1992); Terry Lynn Karl, "Dilemmas of Democratization in Latin America," *Comparative Politics* 23, 1 (1990): 1–21; John Peeler, *Latin American Democracies: Colombia, Costa Rica, Venezuela* (Chapel Hill: University of North Carolina Press, 1985).

35. Rueschemeyer et al., *Capitalist Development and Democracy*; Enrique Baloyra, "Conclusion: Toward a Framework for the Study of Democratic Consolidation," in Baloyra, *Comparing New Democracies*, p. 299; Adam Przeworski, "Some Problems in the Study of the Transition to Democracy," pp. 58–62; Alfred Stepan, "Paths Toward Redemocratization: Theoretical and Comparative Considerations," pp. 68–84, and Guillermo O'Donnell, "Introduction to the Latin American Cases," pp. 3–18, all in O'Donnell et al., *Transitions from Authoritarian Rule*; John A. Booth and Mitchell A. Seligson, "Paths to Democracy and the Political Culture of Costa Rica, Mexico, and Nicaragua," in Larry Diamond, ed., *Political Culture and Democracy in Developing Countries* (Boulder: Lynne Rienner Publishers, 1994), pp. 99–130; Mitchell A. Seligson and John A. Booth, "Political Culture and Regime Type: Evidence from Nicaragua and Costa Rica," *Journal of Politics* 55 (August 1993): 777–792.

36. The organization of the following discussion is distilled mainly from two sources: Peeler, *Latin American Democracies*, pp. 104–128, and Diamond and Linz, "Introduction," in Diamond et al., *Democracy in Developing Countries*, pp. 9–47.

37. Peeler, *Latin American Democracies*; Burton et al., "Introduction: Elite Transformations."

38. Peeler, *Latin American Democracies*, pp. 43–93; John Peeler, "Elites and Democracy in Central America," in Seligson and Booth, *Elections and Democracy Revisited*, pp. 244–263; see also Peeler's "Elite Settlements and Democratic Consolidation: Colombia, Costa Rica, and Venezuela," pp. 81–111, and Burton et al., "Introduction: Elite Transformations," pp. 1–37, in Higley and Gunther, *Elites and Democratic Consolidation*; Rafael López Pintor, "Mass and Elite Perspectives in the Process of Transition to Democracy," in Baloyra, *Comparing New Democracies*, pp. 99–101; Terry Lynn Karl, "Petroleum and Political Pacts: The Transition to Democracy," in O'Donnell et al., *Transitions from Authoritarian Rule*, pp. 196–219.

39. Diamond and Linz, "Introduction," pp. 35–37.

40. Putnam, "Bowling Alone," pp. 65–83; Putnam, *Making Democracy Work*.

41. Huntington, *The Third Wave*.

42. Note that even revolutionary Nicaragua, via its 1987 constitution, adopted a republican, representative, presidential regime quite similar to the regional norm.

43. Diamond and Linz, "Introduction," pp. 22–23, 35–37; Peeler, *Latin American Democracies*, 104–109, 112–114, 124–127.

44. Diamond and Linz, "Introduction," pp. 27–28; Peeler, *Latin American Democracies*, pp. 127–128.

45. Diamond and Linz, "Introduction," pp. 32–35; Peeler, *Latin American Democracies*, pp. 115–117.

46. Diamond and Linz, "Introduction," pp. 38–42; Peeler, *Latin American Democracies*, p. 127.

47. For example, if social class (prosperity vs. poverty) and race (white and black) were mutually reinforcing so that most of the white were wealthy and most of the black were poor, the whites might be much more committed to preserving their advantages, whereas the grievances of poor blacks for their disadvantages due to race would be reinforced by economic grievances. In contrast, were wealth and poverty randomly distributed without correlation to race, that might lower the pressures for politicized conflict over class, whether to reinforce or exacerbate conflict between races.

48. Mixed Spanish and Indian race but predominantly Hispanic in culture.

2

CONTEMPORARY COSTA RICA IN CENTRAL AMERICA

This chapter examines Costa Rica in Central American perspective. It reviews the region's history of military intervention in politics, political instability, human rights abuse, extreme poverty and inequality, and economies heavily dependent upon agricultural exports. The chapter then analyzes what contemporary Costa Rica has in common with its isthmian neighbors, and what about Costa Rica is most different. The chapter concludes with a presentation of Costa Rica's national democratic myths.

Central American History

Almost from the outset Costa Rica's development stood somewhat apart from that of its neighbors.[1] The Mesoamerican isthmus (Figure 2.1) was conquered and colonized by the Spanish in the early sixteenth century, but the Costa Rican area, far to south on the isthmus, was settled only late in that century. Spanish colonial life was organized under the bureaucratic authority of the Kingdom of Guatemala, a subunit of the Viceroyalty of New Spain, which had its seat in Mexico. The kingdom included six separate colonies: Chiapas (later lost to Mexico), Guatemala, Honduras, El Salvador, Nicaragua, and Costa Rica.[2] Despite the rapid decimation of the original Indian populace by disease, displacement, abuse, enslavement, and some outright extermination, significant Indian populations survived. Considerable racial mixing, or *mestizaje*, took place; the Spanish

FIGURE 2.1   Central America and Panama

language and much of its culture eventually became dominant. Two main deviations from this pattern occurred: In Guatemala Indians remained racially and culturally distinct from mestizos and numerically preponderant. In the Costa Rican colony, few Indians survived, so that despite the extensive intermarriage there the populace retained rather more European traits than in the other colonies.

The Spanish seized most resources, including the best land, and forced most indigenous people into captive labor in mines and plantations. They produced gold, silver, timber, beef and hides, dyes, and cacao for local or regional consumption and, increasingly, for export to Spain. Spanish crown trusts of land eventually converted into grants of private property, establishing the *criollo* heirs of the conquerors and important early colonists as owners of immense tracts of land known as haciendas. A new class structure developed, marked by extreme inequality between the wealthy largeholders and the poorer, lower-status mestizos and the abused Indians. Because the surviving Indians often resisted, the crown and hacienda owners subdued them with military force. Upper-class culture rationalized violent coercion of the poor to preserve the economic order.

Costa Rica, in contrast, had much less wealth in exportable resources, fewer Indians to exploit, and was geographically isolated. It thus failed to develop the same rapacious elite culture as its northern neighbors and remained somewhat more socially homogeneous than the northern colonies.

In 1821 Mexico declared its independence from Spain, taking the colonies of the Kingdom of Guatemala with it. After briefly joining the Mexican empire in 1822 and 1823, the five southern former colonies broke away from Mexico. They established the five-province Central American Federal Republic, with its capital in Guatemala. Almost immediately internal strife developed within the federation—between new elite political factions known as Liberals and Conservatives, among Guatemala and the other provinces, between centrists and local nationalists, and among key personalities. Civil war soon broke out among these camps, and military figures quickly became heavily involved in political affairs. In 1839 the Central American Republic collapsed into the five separate nations of modern Central America, leaving a persistent but frustrated dream of Central American unity.

From 1838 to 1945, the five Central American nations, by then independent of each other, shared many historical trends and developed many common features. Dependency upon export agriculture grew steadily as the Central American nations produced ever more coffee and then bananas. Following independence, Central America's tiny, privileged elites used their control of government to keep power and repress popular demands. These elites perpetuated an essentially unregulated, externally oriented economic system for their own benefit.

Except in Costa Rica, continued Liberal-Conservative factionalism, forced indigenous labor, and the hacienda system all contributed to a strong political role for the region's armies. Militaries (at first belonging to individual caudillos from the landholding elite) fought in the civil wars and suppressed resistance by workers and those deprived of their land. "This heavy military involvement in economic and political life retarded the development of civil political institutions and spawned both military rule and considerable political violence. Except for Costa Rica, Central American nations spent most of the period from 1838 until 1945 under either civilian or military dictatorships."[3]

Costa Rica was isolated enough and sufficiently dominated by Conservatives at the time of independence to escape most civil war and the resultant militarization of politics. However, even Costa Rica experienced periods of military rule and dictatorship in the late nineteenth and early twentieth centuries. Although initially without the striking extremes of social and economic inequality seen to its north, Costa Rica did have significant economic inequalities that grew over time. Costa Rica's economy eventually became more like its neighbors' as coffee production increased the concentration of landownership. Later bananas became another key export crop. New railroads and ports built to support agricultural exports further integrated the region into the world economy.

In the twentieth century, continued expansion of Central America's coffee and banana industries accelerated both the concentration of wealth and economic dependency upon export prices. World War I and the Great Depression of the 1930s both reduced exports and lowered commodity prices, which in turn spawned political unrest. El Salvador's oligarchical political system experienced a reform movement and an abortive revolution in 1931 and 1932, crushed by the gratuitous massacre of some 30,000 people. This began direct military rule of the country until 1979. Guatemala and Nicaragua also experienced protracted periods of military rule. Costa Rica's fledgling civilian, electoral government was interrupted by military rule from 1917 to 1919, threatened by significant labor and political turbulence in the 1930s, abused by a conservative-communist coalition from 1942 to 1948, and torn by civil war in 1948.

Political turbulence roiled the isthmus in the early twentieth century. U.S. forces intervened in Nicaragua to help rebel Conservatives in 1909, then occupied Nicaragua from 1912 to 1925 to suppress a Liberal uprising. In 1927 U.S. troops again entered Nicaragua because of a Liberal rebellion, then stayed to fight a six-year war against anti-interventionist rebels led by Augusto Sandino. The main legacy of U.S. intervention was the U.S.-trained Nicaraguan national guard. Its commander, Anastasio Somoza García, in 1936 overthrew the constitutional government and established a forty-three-year dynastic dictatorship. Guatemala, ruled by a series of tyrants during the 1930s, experienced serious unrest that the government ferociously repressed. By the end of World War II, however, the struggle for democracy in Guatemala could no longer be contained. A new civilian, democratic, "revolutionary" government came to power, but it ruled for a scant decade before being overthrown by a U.S.-backed conspiracy in 1954.

Honduras, less party-polarized, less integrated into the world economy, and with less concentration of wealth than elsewhere in Central America, also experienced less turmoil in the early twentieth century than its neighbors. Labor organization took place early and rapidly in the large banana enclaves of Honduras but was heavily repressed in the 1940s. Civilian rule predominated, although it was sometimes dictatorial; the rather weak Honduran armed forces began to intervene in politics regularly only in the 1950s.

External Intervention

Foreign meddling in Central America has been extensive from its earliest days. Britain occupied Belize and established the Mosquito Protectorate in Atlantic Nicaragua for mining and logging and to promote transit routes across the isthmus. In the mid-nineteenth century, U.S. intervention in Central America and competition with Britain grew rapidly. Both nations were interested in a possible canal, and in 1850 agreed in the Clayton-Bulwer Treaty to share a canal and not to establish colonies in Central America. Britain nevertheless occupied Honduras's Bay Islands in 1852 and retained both Belize and Mosquitia. A U.S. filibusterer, William Walker, invited to Nicaragua by Liberal insurgents in a complex political and business conspiracy, seized power in Nicaragua in 1856 and declared that he would annex Nicaragua to the United States. Conservatives from around Central America rallied to their Nicaraguan counterparts in the 1857 National War. Walker, ousted by the Central Americans, escaped under U.S. protection.

U.S. private investment in Central America grew sharply in the late nineteenth century. By 1900 the United States had become the dominant power in the region, using its embassies and armed forces to promote business for U.S. firms and to advance American strategic interests. President Theodore Roosevelt could not persuade Colombia or Nicaragua to agree on a lease to build a transisthmian canal. In 1903 Roosevelt landed marines to help insurgents win "independence" for Colombia's province of Panama and got his canal treaty that way. A major U.S. interest in Nicaragua then became conservation of the U.S. monopoly on the canal in Panama. U.S. troops occupied Nicaragua for most of the three decades after 1912. U.S. agents supervised elections, ran Nicaragua's customshouse, and established and trained its national guard. U.S. troops also intervened briefly in Honduras.

Fearing rising German and Japanese power and possible war, presidents Herbert Hoover and Franklin Roosevelt pursued better relations with Latin America during the 1930s, eventually removing U.S. soldiers from Nicaragua and several Caribbean nations. However, when World War II broke out the United States established a heavy military presence in Central America to protect the Panama Canal and the southern U.S. flank. Central American armed forces were trained and upgraded in support of hemispheric security, which eventually facilitated the containment of feared communist influence after World War II.

Costa Rica, though not completely stable between 1900 and 1945, was less politically turbulent than its neighbors. U.S. economic interests, especially the booming United Fruit Company, were heavily involved in the rapidly expanding banana industry, but this aroused no fundamental national security concerns for the United States. Indeed, Costa Rica held little geopolitical interest for the United States because its mountainous terrain made a competing canal impossible. Costa Rican relations with the United States remained tranquil.

Contemporary Central America

After the 1940s social change in Central America accelerated rapidly. External meddling in Central American affairs has varied but at times has had nearly cataclysmic impact on the region. The post–World War II decades in Central America have been marked by nearly continuous struggles for economic growth and political stability and for contending visions of democratization.

In the late 1940s and early 1950s, the United States had begun heavily to emphasize containment of communism in the region; its new goals and behaviors soon destabilized the area. Prodemocracy movements or conflicts broke out in Nicaragua, Honduras, Costa Rica, and Guatemala in the mid- and late 1940s but failed in Nicaragua and Honduras.

In Guatemala and Costa Rica, the democratic forces actually captured power, but only one of them survived. In 1948 the government of Teodoro Picado (a coalition between the conservative Republican Party [Partido Republicano] and the Popular Vanguard Party [Partido Vanguardia Popular, or PVP] and its unions) attempted to have the Costa Rican Legislative Assembly (Asamblea Legislativa) nullify the 1948 election results. Contending political forces rebelled against Picado, his communist allies, and the election manipulation. They won, and for a year and a half an *anticommunist* revolutionary government, the National Liberation junta, led by José Figueres Ferrer, ruled Costa Rica. The United States did not challenge the revolutionary government at least in part because it had unseated a coalition with communist participation and thus did not threaten U.S. security interests. Costa Rica's revolutionaries presided over the redrafting of the national constitution and in 1949 turned over power to the 1948 election's victor, Otilio Ulate Blanco.

Although the United States tolerated the Costa Rican revolution and supported the new regime there, the Central Intelligence Agency (CIA) helped overthrow the elected civilian government of Guatemala in 1954. This was done on suspicion that this constitutional, elected Guatemalan government of president Jacobo Arbenz tolerated and even included (rather than suppressing) communist elements. The new U.S.-backed Guatemalan government heavily and violently repressed thousands of citizens associated with the democratic government, parties, and unions. In 1957 the military took over the regime; by 1960 Guatemala's first guerrilla movements had formed, soon to be followed by horrifically escalated repression by the regime.

Elsewhere in Central America the Somoza family dictatorship survived the assassination of its founder in 1956 as Anastasio Somoza García's sons assumed power. The Salvadoran polity continued under military rule as it had since the

1930s. The Honduran military became increasingly involved in directly ruling the country in the 1950s and 1960s.

Declining commodity prices and a recession in the late 1950s caused a wave of political unrest. This, plus the rise to power of Fidel Castro's revolutionary government in Cuba, prompted Central American leaders to revisit Central American unity to promote economic development and political stability. They wanted economic modernization and growth in the capitalist mode that would increase the well-being of rich and poor alike. Such growth, they thought, would mollify the poor and keep malcontents from embracing radical political doctrines. The five nations thus formed the Central American Common Market (CACM; Mercado Común Centroamericano) in 1960 to promote investment, industrialization, and economic cooperation. The CACM's goals coincided with those of the U.S. Alliance for Progress, which directed considerable aid into the region for infrastructure development.

The CACM and Alliance for Progress investments profoundly affected Central America, but with consequences often dramatically different from those intended—especially in politics. Industrial production boomed, above all in the capital-intensive production of consumer goods, which led to a marked increase in manufacturing employment and production (see Appendix, Table A.1). Industrial growth combined with the diversification and modernization of agricultural export production (cotton, sugar, oils) in the 1950s and 1960s to produce a 35 percent increase in per capita gross domestic product (GDP), a measure of overall economic activity, regionwide between 1960 and 1970 (see Appendix, Table A.1). Agricultural employment declined markedly in all countries, and the service sectors expanded dramatically in the 1960s and 1970s. Central America's urban populations grew everywhere, as rural dwellers were pushed from the land or drawn to cities by new industry, better public services, and hopes for a better life. Improved public health let the region's population shoot up 80 percent, from 11 million to more than 20 million, between 1960 and 1980. Literacy, university enrollment, and life expectancy rose throughout Central America (Appendix, Table A.2).

This rapid socioeconomic change, however, proved not the answer to Central America's dreams but a worsening nightmare. The worst poverty, one target of the development strategy, did not diminish. Rather, poverty increased throughout the region because capital-intensive industrialization generated high profits for investors but few new jobs for workers. Rural and urban unemployment rose markedly in the 1960s and 1970s. A severe new recession began in the mid-1970s because of oil price increases and problems within the by then stagnating CACM. In Nicaragua, El Salvador, and Guatemala, the governments protected investors' profits by holding wages well below rising costs of living. In those three countries, real wages declined sharply beginning in the late 1960s and generally continued to fall throughout the next decade (see Appendix, Table A.3). Only in Honduras and Costa Rica did governments implement real wage increases or modest land distribution programs to let workers maintain or recover their incomes. The mid- and late 1970s were particularly hard: Rising energy prices pushed inflation extremely high, unemployment rose, regional markets shrank, and the CACM effectively collapsed.

Declining popular living standards and growing inequality of wealth and income in Nicaragua, El Salvador, and Guatemala brought rising labor mobilization and political unrest—precisely what the CACM's architects had hoped to avoid.[4] The governments answered demands for reform and labor unrest with ferocious repression. In each nation disparate social and political forces began to radicalize and gradually unify into a revolutionary coalition linked to armed rebels. Small Marxist-Leninist guerrilla groups had begun in the early 1960s in Guatemala and Nicaragua and in the 1970s in El Salvador in hopes of imitating Castro's success in Cuba. Weak for many years, the guerrillas began to draw new support as regime repression escalated. A broad rebel front formed first in Nicaragua. Led by the Sandinista National Liberation Front (Frente Sandinista de Liberación Nacional, or FSLN), it overthrew the Somoza regime in 1979. U.S. economic and military assistance prevented a similar coalition from winning in El Salvador in the early 1980s and eventually resulted in a stalemated civil war. In Guatemala rebel activity that had begun in 1960 was violently suppressed in the 1970s. Guerrilla violence boiled up again in the 1980s, unleashing a wave of repression by Guatemala's military regimes. In contrast, Honduras and Costa Rica, although quite distinct regimes, responded much less violently to unrest and thus avoided radicalizing their opponents.[5]

Patterns of aid from the United States to Central America illustrate graphically how U.S. interest in Central America has changed since the end of World War II (Appendix, Tables A.4 and A.5). The United States at first paid little attention to the region after World War II, providing no military assistance and an average of only $630,000 per year in economic aid to the entire region from 1946 through 1952. But as U.S. administrations and Congress worried more about containing communist influence in the isthmus, U.S. military aid escalated. For 1953–1961, military assistance went mainly to Guatemala and Nicaragua. In the 1960s and 1970s, the United States clearly directed its military aid toward perceived threats of Marxist influence (Appendix, Table A.4). Concern about human rights abuses in El Salvador and Guatemala led to U.S. military aid cutbacks to both nations in the late 1970s, the only real exception to the pattern of rapidly rising U.S. military aid.

With the onset of the Sandinista revolution in Nicaragua and El Salvador, U.S. aid to combat insurgencies skyrocketed. Leftist Nicaragua was cut off from aid, but El Salvador, Honduras, and even Costa Rica drew hugely increased military aid contributions. U.S. military aid to the region for 1981–1988 reached almost $1.3 billion as the administration of Ronald Reagan labored to align the rest of the region's countries against the Sandinistas in Nicaragua and provided aid to help defeat rebellions in El Salvador. Guatemala's terrible human rights record blocked most U.S. military aid there.

Economic aid (Appendix, Table A.5) followed patterns similar to those of military assistance except that the United States found it easier to provide nonmilitary assistance regardless of human rights abuses. The Reagan administration heavily pressured Honduras and Costa Rica to assist the U.S.-backed anti-Sandinista *contra* forces by providing sanctuary, political, and logistical support. The reward for their cooperation was U.S. assistance, especially during the early and mid-1980s. For 1985–1988, U.S. economic aid to Costa Rica averaged about $171 million per year, roughly 7 percent of that country's GDP. Combined military and economic assistance to Honduras (1985–1988) averaged nearly $237 million per year, also around 7 percent of GDP. U.S. military and economic aid to El Salvador's regime, fighting to defeat the rebels of the Farabundo Martí National Liberation Front (Frente Farabundo Martí para la Liberación Nacional, or FMLN), combined to an average of $392 million per year from 1981 through 1988, roughly equal to one-twelfth of the country's GDP.

Increased U.S. attention to Central America accompanied the region's transformation in the 1980s from an often ignored backwater of U.S. interest into a major theater of U.S.–Soviet bloc geopolitical conflict. Soviet interest in Central America had been rather low until the 1980s, and except for Cuba the Eastern bloc was only nominally involved in the area. Cuba's revolutionary regime had supported Marxist insurgent groups in Guatemala, El Salvador, and Nicaragua to a limited extent in the 1960s and early 1970s, often to the displeasure of the USSR. However, after the Sandinista victory in Nicaragua in 1979, the Soviet Union and other Eastern bloc nations began stepped-up aid to Nicaragua, especially military assistance. When the United States started and steadily escalated the *contra* war, Soviet military aid to Nicaragua rose rapidly to fund a large counterinsurgency army. When the United States embargoed trade with Nicaragua and curtailed Western credit and aid in the mid-1980s, Eastern bloc economic aid replaced the losses.

Nicaragua's Marxist-led revolution, its growing dependence upon the Soviet Union and Cuba, and its rapidly growing military capability caused alarm in Costa Rica, Honduras, and El Salvador. Tensions within the region, exacerbated by East-West competition, escalated tremendously. Only with the Iran-*contra* scandal's weakening of U.S. resolve to overthrow the Sandinista government of Nicaragua and the beginning of *perestroika* and improved U.S.-Soviet relations in the late 1980s did tensions begin to subside in Central America.[6] However, in one of the two last great acts of intervention in the region, U.S. troops invaded Panama in December 1989 and replaced the military regime of Manuel Noriega with the civilian government that had been fraudulently denied power in the 1989 election. In the second case, even though the cold war was by then virtually over, the United States interfered extensively in Nicaragua's 1990 election to help Violeta Barrios de Chamorro defeat the FSLN.

After these events the United States' fear of the expansion of communist influence in Central America abated. The administration of George Bush thus acquiesced to the settlement of the Salvadoran civil war in 1992 and began to disengage both geopolitically and in terms of U.S. assistance (Appendix, Tables A.4 and A.5). The Guatemalan civil war eventually ended in late 1996. Thus if the 1980s was a decade of rapidly increasing foreign intervention in Central America, the 1990s saw the pendulum swing in quite the other direction. Settlements were reached in the region's civil wars. Civilian, constitutional governments ruled in all six nations of the isthmus.[7] For the administration of Bill Clinton, Mexico and the North American Free Trade Agreement had assumed first place in U.S. concerns about Latin America.

Commonalities with the Rest of Central America

As noted above, Central America since World War II has experienced rapid social change, political turmoil, and external interference that included direct and indirect armed intervention and massive military and economic assistance programs. Costa Rica has experienced all of these problems, albeit in some cases less intensely than its neighbors.

Like the other Central American societies, Costa Rica is small and generally lacking in mineral wealth. Such small economies are necessarily interdependent with the rest of the world and only partly successful at promoting change. Although through the CACM they struggled to diversify, reduce external dependency, and become more self-sufficient, all Central American nations nevertheless continued to specialize in agricultural export commodities such as coffee, bananas, cotton, and beef. These they sell abroad for the currency necessary to purchase those foreign goods and services upon which much of the rest of their economies depend. In recent decades, terms of trade (relative prices of imports and exports) have generally been disfavorable for Central American nations. For instance, the price of vital imported petroleum has risen greatly since 1973, whereas the value of exports from the region has declined overall.[8] The collapse of the Central American Common Market and a severe regional recession marked the 1980s. Central American countries borrowed massively abroad, mostly from other governments or from intergovernmental lenders, in order to keep their economies from slowing down even more. External debt and the servicing of that debt became an economic ball and chain because they competed with imports needed to keep the economies working (see Appendix, Table A.1).

Because of their location, economic structures, traditions, and communications, Central American nations are heavily subject to external influences. The Central American nations have often meddled in each other's affairs, a practice that reached a fever pitch during the 1980s. Their proximity and relative ease of communication with each other (due to modern roads, air transport, and mass media) make the events and problems of one nation quickly known to and often influential in the rest of the isthmus.

There has long been considerable international labor migration within the region. Political and economic refugees in large numbers move to neighboring countries; Honduras and Costa Rica received hundreds of thousands of Salvadorans, Guatemalans, and Nicaraguans in the 1980s. Political exiles from one nation lived, conspired, and sometimes built guerrilla armies and bases in neighboring nations. The broadcast zones of at least some of each nation's radio and television stations overlap neighboring territory, a fact sometimes manipulated by governments or other interests to influence public opinion next door. Nations so integrated into the world economy and so indebted as those of Central America have been particularly vulnerable to political and economic pressures from wealthy potential donors or lenders, particularly (but not exclusively) the United States. Central America's dependence on U.S. aid gave the United States enormous influence over each of its ally nations. Revolutionary Nicaragua experienced something much worse—U.S. financing of the *contra* war that helped demolish the nation's economy and unseat the Sandinistas.

Central American countries also have in common rapid population growth rates, averaging around 3 percent in recent decades (Appendix, Table A.2). A decline in the regional rate of population growth to around 2.8 percent for the period 1981–1995 stems from several factors, including urbanization, improved education, and heavy outmigration because of a decade of war in Nicaragua, El Salvador, and Guatemala.[9] Between 1960 and 1995, the region's population increased by 272 percent. Despite the rapid population growth, Central American nations are not particularly densely populated, except for El Salvador, which has about six times as many people per square kilometer as the average of the other four nations. Central America's population is becoming more and more urban (Appendix, Table A.2); almost half the region's populace lived in urban areas in 1990, up about 50 percent from 1960.

In general, health and public welfare in the region have improved since the 1940s, but Table A.2 shows that Central America as a whole still manifests many significant problems. Only about 70 percent of the region's populace is literate. Life expectancy in 1993 was about sixty-seven years, an increase of seven years since the early 1980s. Infant mortality averaged about fifty-five per 1,000 in 1993. One obvious reason for low life expectancy and poor infant mortality rates in Central America may also be seen in Table A.2, where average income figures are presented for the two poorest segments of the populace of each nation. The poorest 20 percent of the population averaged only about $95 per year in 1980 and the next poorest 30 percent only $235. People who earn so little cannot eat enough or well enough, house or clothe themselves decently, or afford adequate medical care. "Hunger and malnutrition are the fate for an increasing number of Central Americans. At least three out of four children in Honduras, Guatemala, and El Salvador are malnourished. Malnutrition causes mental deficiencies in four out of every five children born in rural Honduras. Malnutrition is not limited to the young: at least 50 percent of Central Americans do not eat enough food to meet the minimal nutritional requirements."[10]

The poorest Costa Ricans are poor indeed and probably as bad off as the poor anywhere in Central America. Although there is such abject poverty in Costa Rica, it afflicts relatively fewer people. Costa Rica does not escape Central America's worst social problems, but it experiences them less severely.

Differences from the Rest of Central America

Despite the many similarities cited above, Costa Rica differs from the rest of Central America in several ways. Although Costa Rica industrialized more slowly than other Central American nations, eventually 16 percent of its workforce was employed in manufacturing, a greater proportion than that in any other Central American country. In the late 1980s, Costa Rica ranked second in the region in the percent of GDP produced in manufacturing (Appendix, Table A.1). Costa Rica's agricultural sector has shrunk substantially below that of the rest of the Central American nations, falling to only 29 percent of the workforce in 1980.

Despite the severe recession of the early 1980s, Costa Rica's economic performance has been substantially better than that of the rest of the region. Its GDP per capita, $2,283 in 1994, exceeded the next highest (Guatemala's) by 55 percent (Appendix, Table A.1). Costa Rica's growth rate per capita was the region's highest during the second decade of the CACM (1971–1980). Costa Rica's overall production did not falter nearly so badly as did the production of the other nations of the isthmus with the decline of the CACM in the late 1970s. Costa Rica experienced a sharp recession (9 percent decline in GDP 1981–1987), but this was the least severe of the region, which suffered an average GDP decline of 17 percent. For 1990–1994, Costa Rica's GDP per capita recovered 10 percent—double the regional mean (Appendix, Table A.1).

Distribution of income in Costa Rica is more equitable than in the rest of Central America. Table A.2 indicates that in 1980 the average income of the poorest fifth of Costa Ricans was $176.70 per year, 85 percent above the regional average. (Although difficult to estimate, the average income for the poorest fifth of U.S. citizens in 1980 was probably twelve to fifteen times greater than that in Costa Rica.)[11] For the next poorest 30 percent of Costa Ricans, the mean annual income of $500.80 was 213 percent above the regional mean. Such income levels are very poor in comparison to mean income levels in the United States or Europe, but they do provide Costa Rica's poor people modestly better standards of welfare than those prevalent anywhere else in Central America.

In social characteristics Costa Rica stands out from the rest of the region in several areas (Appendix, Table A.2). Costa Rica has the lowest percentage of indigenous population (0.6 percent) of any nation of the region. Costa Rica's literacy rate, close to 90 percent, is almost 23 percent higher than the regional average. University enrollment per capita is nearly four times higher than the Central American average. Infant mortality per 1,000 live births in 1993 was fourteen; the mean for the isthmus was fifty-five. Life expectancy of Costa Ricans was seventy-six years, nine years longer than the regional average.

How has Costa Rica, though still a poor nation, accomplished such relatively high standards of health, education, and welfare despite its similarities to the rest of Central America, Latin America, and the Third World? Such attainments are at least in part the direct product of public policy. Costa Rica began investing in education in the nineteenth century. It abolished its armed forces in 1949 and has devoted the savings to education, public health, and health care. To illustrate, Costa Rica's ratio of human service spending to defense spending in the 1970s and 1980s ranged around twenty to one in favor of human services. In the other isthmian countries, these ratios ranged from one to one to no higher than four to one.[12] A second source of these exceptionally good social indicators and achievements in education and literacy may be found in the income distribution figures cited in Table A.2. Poor Costa Ricans are obviously better off than their peers in other Central American countries. Their modest additional incomes provide a margin of support for survival and welfare.

"Costa Rica Es Diferente": National Myths

Many of these traits that distinguish Costa Rica from its neighbors have over time become woven into the country's national political mythology. Two clichés about Costa Rica embody much of the truth as well as its paradoxes. The first, seen on everything from travel brochures to T-shirts and often even heard from the lips of Ticos themselves, is "*Costa Rica es diferente*" (Costa Rica is different). Indeed, no one who has ever visited elsewhere in Latin America would deny it. The second is Costa Rica's self-description as the "Switzerland of the Americas," an allusion to both the nation's beautiful mountainous geography and its democracy. But as we have seen, Costa Rica—despite its real differences from its neighbors—paradoxically has many more things in common with Central America in the form of shared history, economy, and contemporary problems.

Costa Rica's great national myth, the one that most concerns us here, is a widely shared explanation of the evolution of the nation's democratic institutions and practices.[13] Like many myths, this one has sufficient grounding in history and in social reality to seem valid to Costa Ricans and to scholars both native and foreign. As with many myths, it ignores much contrary evidence and may serve particular interests.

Lowell Gudmundson convincingly argues that the most influential version of the Costa Rican national political myth was developed by economists and historians associated directly with the National Liberation movement and junta of 1948–1949 and that it served their political goals.[14] As a more recent example of myth building, one may cite Costa Rica's celebration of the centennial of its democracy in 1989. To affirm officially that democracy in Costa Rica began in 1889, though not entirely without historical basis (see Chapter 3), clearly served both the foreign policy and domestic interests of the administration of President Oscar Arias Sánchez. The claim, however, overlooked several facts: Most citizens could not vote in the early years of Costa Rican "democracy"; a 1914 coup d'état resulted in military rule until 1917; and a civil war in 1948 was followed by a year and a half of de facto rule by the victorious junta. Political myths, then, should be examined with some care.

Costa Rica's great myth contends that democracy arose and persists because of high degrees of social equality, equality of land distribution, racial homogeneity, and a tradition of nonviolence.[15] Through its first 300 years, the society was an agrarian democracy of families of mainly European stock. Costa Ricans were subsistence smallholders who lived isolated from each other and from the rest of Central America and the world. Egalitarian conditions and democratic values developed among early Costa Ricans, who resolved their conflicts peacefully and had little use for soldiers and armies. From this base evolved the culture, values, and institutions of modern Costa Rican democracy.

As we will see in the following chapters, some elements of the Costa Rican national myth are true or substantially so and do help us understand democracy there. Other aspects of the myth, however, are not true and require considerable demystification. Costa Rica is indeed distinct from the rest of Central America and Latin America in important ways, but it is far less different than either its myth or an uncritical first look might suggest. Democracy in Costa Rica is thus more complex—and more paradoxical—than the national myth would lead us to believe.

Notes

1. For more detailed histories, see John A. Booth and Thomas W. Walker, *Understanding Central America* (Boulder: Westview Press, 1993), pp. 17–51; Ralph Lee Woodward Jr., *Central America: A Nation Divided* (New York: Oxford University Press, 1976); Miles L. Wortman, *Government and Society in Central America: 1680–1840* (New York: Columbia University Press, 1982); Ciro F. S. Cardoso and Héctor Pérez Brignoli, *Centroamérica y la economía occidental (1520–1930)* (San José: Editorial Universidad de Costa Rica, 1977); Héctor Pérez Brignoli, *Breve historia de Centroamérica* (Madrid: Alianza Editorial, 1985); and Deborah J. Yashar, *Demanding Democracy: Reform and Reaction in Costa Rica and Guatemala, 1870s–1950s* (Stanford: Stanford University Press, 1997).

2. Panama, though on the Mesoamerican isthmus, was part of Colombia, and I will not include it in discussing the region unless I explicitly refer to it.

3. Booth and Walker, *Understanding Central America*, p. 21.

4. Ibid., pp. 61–115. For further discussion of the Nicaraguan revolution, see John A. Booth, *The End and the Beginning: The Nicaraguan Revolution* (Boulder: Westview Press, 1985). On El Salvador, see Tommie Sue Montgomery, *Revolution in El Salvador* (Boulder: Westview Press, 1982). On Guatemala, see Susanne Jonas, *The Battle for Guatemala* (Boulder: Westview Press, 1991).

5. Booth and Walker, *Understanding Central America*, pp. 117–127.

6. Ibid., pp. 68–115.

7. Mitchell A. Seligson and John A. Booth, eds., *Elections and Democracy in Central America, Revisited* (Chapel Hill: University of North Carolina Press, 1995).

8. John Weeks, *The Economies of Central America* (New York: Holmes and Meier), pp. 80–88.

9. Nicaragua's population growth also slowed in the late 1980s because of war and a bad economy. See Inter-American Development Bank (IADB), *Latin America After a Decade of*

Reforms: Economic and Social Progress in Latin America, 1997 Report (Baltimore: Johns Hopkins University Press, 1997), table A-1.

10. Tom Barry and Deb Preusch, *The Central America Fact Book* (New York: Grove Press, 1986), p. 140.

11. Estimate based upon the International Bank for Reconstruction and Development, *World Development Report 1983* (New York: Oxford University Press, 1983), tables 1, 27.

12. Booth and Walker, *Understanding Central America,* appendix, table 11.

13. For explication and analysis of elements of the Costa Rican myth, see Charles D. Ameringer, *Democracy in Costa Rica* (New York: Praeger, 1982), pp. 1–20; Elizabeth Fonseca, *Costa Rica Colonial: La tierra y el hombre* (San José, Costa Rica: Editorial Universitaria Centroamericana, 1984); and Lowell Gudmundson, *Costa Rica Before Coffee: Society and Economy on the Eve of the Export Boom* (Baton Rouge: Louisiana State University Press, 1986); and Mavis Hiltunen de Biesanz, Richard Biesanz, and Karen Zubris de Biesanz, *Los costariccenses* (San José, Costa Rica: Editorial Universidad Estatal a Distancia, 1979), pp. 30–39. There is an excellent English version of *Los costariccenses,* albeit abridged by almost half: Richard Biesanz, Karen Zubris Biesanz, and Mavis Hiltunen Biesanz, *The Costa Ricans* (Englewood Cliffs, N.J.: Prentice-Hall, 1982).

14. Gudmundson, *Costa Rica Before Coffee,* pp. 1–24.

15. For an example of key elements of the myth applied, see John Patrick Bell, *Crisis in Costa Rica: The Revolution of 1948* (Austin: University of Texas Press, 1971), pp. 3–10.

3

THE HISTORICAL DEVELOPMENT OF COSTA RICAN DEMOCRACY

This chapter begins with a historical sketch of the colonial era.[1] Subsequent sections focus on key factors and events in Costa Rican democratization, including important economic and social forces driving change, the development of elite politics, evolution of electoral institutions and processes, and popular participation in politics. This discussion is divided into three major periods: 1821–1905, 1906–1945, and 1946 to the present. This division emphasizes the dramatic transformation of Costa Rican politics from its turbulently undemocratic early national life to its current system of institutionalized constitutional rule consolidated after the 1948 civil war. During the nineteenth century, elite rule, militarism, dictatorship, and instability predominated, with occasional exceptions that suggested democratic potential. After 1906 democratization developed in several stages broken by setbacks and considerable conflict. The 1948 civil war and its aftermath gave birth to the modern democratic regime.

1502–1821: Discovery, Conquest, and Colonization

Christopher Columbus made landfall in Costa Rica in 1502 at what is today Puerto Limón. The small indigenous population consisted mainly of the Gran

Nicoyas of northwestern Costa Rica and smaller tribes of Chibcha origin in the southern and Atlantic zones. Columbus and later Spanish explorers saw Indians wearing gold jewelry and concluded that this signified potential wealth. Greedily inspired, they named this territory "Costa Rica" (Rich Coast). They soon discovered that except for a quickly exhausted alluvial deposit and the jewelry acquired through trade, the area had no gold. The name nevertheless stuck, giving the mineral-poor country its great national joke—that it should have been called instead "Costa Pobre" (Poor Coast).

From 1502 to 1560, expeditions explored both coasts and conquered the Nicoyas. Around 1560 the Spanish established a first settlement in the *meseta central,* the elevated valleys of the central mountains. Juan Vázquez de Coronado explored the *meseta* and in 1564 moved the first settlement to the newly founded capital city of Cartago. Between 1560 and 1610, sixteen other Spanish settlements were established in Costa Rica, but most failed. "The hostility of the Indians, the isolation of the settlements established, the rigors of the tropical climate, and the difficulty of making the new cities self-sufficient rapidly forced the abandonment of all but two, Cartago and Esparza."[2] From Cartago the population gradually spread to other *meseta* villages and to near the Pacific Coast and around the Gulf of Nicoya, then part of the Nicaraguan colony.[3] San José, eventually the capital and largest city, was not established until 1755.[4]

For the first century of colonization, the Spanish who came to Costa Rica consisted mainly of minor, untitled nobility (*hidalgos*) from Andalucía, Castilla, and Extremadura, many of them possibly of Sephardic Jewish origin. Because of the poverty and isolation of the colony, in-migration was slow. For example, the 1611 census counted only 330 Spaniards, and by 1700 the number rose only to 2,146 (including the criollos born in Costa Rica).[5] Some colonists came with considerable personal capital, and most were assigned extensive *encomiendas* (trusts of land) by the crown that eventually evolved into private property. Efforts to cultivate cacao and tobacco for export failed. Compared to more mineral-rich and accessible colonies, Costa Rica "has been called the Cinderella of the Spanish colonies, because it was in great measure abandoned to its own resources; taxes were imposed upon it; it was repressed, ignored, and miserably poor."[6] The paucity of valuable minerals, a chronic shortage of labor, and early export crop debacles forced even those with considerable land or high social status to live modestly.

Costa Rica's indigenous people reacted in three ways to the Spanish incursion.[7] Some fled outside the Spanish-dominated *meseta;* others resisted encroachment for decades. Certain Indians succumbed to Spanish control, some of them willingly and others conquered. The early *encomienda* effectively transformed most of the indigenous into serfs for Spanish land grantees. Later colonists illegally appropriated common lands once set aside for indigenous communities. Most of Costa Rica's Indians, however, simply died out from new European diseases, from the disruption of the economies by colonization, and from slaving (especially prevalent in the Nicoya peninsula). Intermarriage eventually assimilated many of the surviving, incorporated Indians into the emergent mestizo population.

Costa Rican colonists at first acquired few African slaves because there were very few mines in which to use them. Later they imported slaves to work the cattle haciendas of Guanacaste and the Atlantic zone cacao plantations because the small indigenous population could not support the large haciendas that developed elsewhere in the region.[8] The paucity of Indians and slaves kept agricultural labor scarce and fairly expensive. Aggravating the labor shortage and retarding the growth of largeholdings was the landless mestizo peasantry's easy access to common or open crown lands on the colony's periphery. Further obstacles to Costa Rica's growth included the *meseta* population's relative isolation from the coasts by terrain that made shipping difficult and costly.

Costa Rica's myth describes colonial society as essentially poor, isolated, and so rural that it virtually lacked towns and social differentiation. The colony was indeed poor and isolated, which restrained Spanish immigration after the early seventeenth century. But recent studies have shown that towns and sharp social differentiation, though less than in neighboring colonies, always existed.[9] The colony's creole aristocracy originated among the descendants of the conquerors and *hidalgo* land grantees. Trading and commercial activity provided sources of wealth for a few. Church and tax records reveal that some colonists owned fairly large landholdings but had trouble extracting much income from them because of the lack of cheap, coercible labor. Lower in the status hierarchy were the descendants of common soldiers, mestizos, the remaining indigenous people, and slaves. Many poorer Ticos owned no land and thus farmed or grazed common lands. Most colonial Costa Ricans were subsistence farmers, but there were also artisans, miners, drovers, boatmen, fishermen, and dockworkers.[10]

The myth of racial and cultural homogeneity has several flaws. Nobility, race, ethnicity, and wealth intertwined to define a status hierarchy headed by a self-conscious criollo aristocracy. Despite the postconquest decline of the native population, as late as 1700 four of five Costa Ricans were indigenous. But by the 1800 census, of the 52,591 people counted only one in six was indigenous and two-thirds were "Spanish [creole] and mestizo." During the eighteenth century, enough slaves were imported to raise the black population from one-fourteenth of the colony's total in 1700 to one-sixth in 1800.[11] "It is evident that during the seventeenth and eighteenth centuries there was no equality, and despite the proximity [of the Creoles] with other human groups, segregation by race always prevailed. . . . One might say that they lived 'nearby each other but not mixed up together' [*juntos pero no revueltos*]."[12]

These social patterns left legacies of a racial bias that strongly valued light skin and hair[13] and another national myth that Costa Ricans were largely of "pure" Spanish extraction. It is true that the *meseta central* had fewer indigenous people and slaves than other Central American colonies and thus had a higher ratio of European to Indian traits. However, the populace of Guanacaste had a much greater admixture of indigenous and African traits. Thus the Costa Rican population overall is mestizo, with a wide range of phenotypes.

Certain aspects of colonial life may well have contributed to the eventual development of democracy. First, unlike other Latin American colonies, Costa Rica never developed an extensive quasi-feudal hacienda system controlled by a creole aristocracy, with highly concentrated landownership and operated with labor coerced by the army and police. Civil life in Costa Rica thus evolved with much less recourse to the armed forces that became so common (and troublesome) elsewhere in Latin America. Militarism would arise in Costa Rica, but civilian rule played an important early historical role.

Second, although social and economic inequality always existed, the Costa Rican colony's low levels of economic differentiation (when compared to neighboring Spanish colonies) probably contributed to the development of egalitarianism in the social culture. Costa Rica had many free peasant cultivators (yeomen), and because of the labor shortage even extensive landownership did not automatically generate concentrated wealth. With much of the population involved in family farming and free rural wage labor, Costa Rican peasants remained relatively free and prosperous.

Third, Costa Rica's isolation gave the political elite some experience with self-government. The colonial bureaucracy in Guatemala had ultimate authority in most matters, but within Costa Rica local *cabildos* (municipal councils) developed. The first *hidalgos* elected the *cabildo* of Cartago, which, because of its distance from Guatemala, enjoyed considerable influence over policy. As new towns developed other cabildos formed and most apparently operated fairly freely from the colonial administration.[14] "This autonomy partially explains the way in which Costa Rica slowly acquired its own experience in the development of its government, eventually enjoying a political maturity that the other countries of the region could not achieve. [The autonomy] appears to have been the principal factor that permitted [Costa Rica], after Independence, to govern itself more efficaciously than its neighbors."[15]

Fourth, late in the colonial era aristocratic factions of Conservatives and Liberals emerged within the civilian political class active in the *cabildos*; these factions were prototypes of later political parties. Conservatives tended to predominate among the aristocracy of Cartago and Heredia; they were more loyal to the crown and supportive of the Catholic Church. San José and Alajuela, in contrast, had more Liberals, many of whom had been banished from Cartago for trading tobacco outside the tight restrictions of the colonial system.[16] Costa Rica's protoparties remained relatively civil with each other after independence.

1821–1905: Early National Life

Costa Rica's foundation myth holds that after independence the nation's rural, protodemocracy developed further with the expansion of the sector of small coffee-producing yeoman farmers. This was aided by the continuing civilian political tradition, a weak military, and modest levels of political conflict, so that democracy would begin to consolidate by the 1889 election. However, evidence reveals that elite political dominance, conflict, instability, and militarism all played a far greater role between 1821 and 1905 than is usually known. Wealthy, largeholding coffee barons usually dominated a national political scene in which the armed forces eventually interfered. Indeed, militarism, conflict, and dictatorial rule became increasingly common as the nineteenth century advanced.

Economic and Social Forces

Coffee cultivation, practiced in the colony as early as 1740 and resulting in modest early exports via Chile by the 1820s, was enthusiastically promoted by postindependence Costa Rican governments.[17] Coffee boomed with the opening of direct export to Europe in 1845 and the hard currency it earned. This earning capacity made coffee the principal engine of national economic growth and social change for a century.

The coffee boom quickly increased the number of small coffee farmers. Landpoor and landless peasants (and even landless upper-class Costa Ricans) moved to the agricultural frontiers and established small coffee farms. Like the growth rings of a tree, the agricultural frontier, especially for coffee, expanded concentrically for well over a century.[18] This created a growing class of yeoman farmers who could live decently, producing coffee with family labor (Photo 3.1). The large yeomanry, the absence of Indians, and the abolition of slavery in 1821 kept the agricultural labor supply scarce and wages high during much of the nineteenth century.

A contrasting effect of the coffee boom was increased economic inequality. A strong class of larger coffee planters and importer-exporters developed among the aristocracy. Larger producers' greater earnings permitted them to invest in coffee milling and gave them a strategic advantage in the marketplace through leverage over prices and credit. They began to purchase or assume smaller coffee farms through bad debts, creating a new class of landless agricultural workers. Some of the dispossessed moved to the coffee frontier and started over, but good wages persuaded others to remain as laborers on the larger plantations. The labor shortage that persisted until the 1880s kept rural wages high enough that landless Ticos did not become impoverished. The big coffee producers and the landless peasantry became interdependent. "Because peasants and artisans . . . were not mere servile employees or passive instruments of exploitation, . . . it was therefore necessary to elaborate a series of subtle psychosocial, symbolic, and normative ('soft') mechanisms in order to guarantee that [the peasants] could be *persuaded* to work."[19]

The emergent coffee grower (*cafetalero*) elite that dominated politics never adopted the military-guaranteed forced labor schemes employed elsewhere in Central America.[20] Such arrangements likely would have been quite difficult to

PHOTO 3.1   Coffee workers and coffee plants laden with beans (photo courtesy *Tico Times*)

enforce given the wide availability of uncolonized land to which free peasants might flee. Rather than coercing peasants to work for them, the social and political aristocracy (most of them soon converted into coffee growers) simply paid the high wages needed to attract workers.

During the nineteenth century, Costa Rican society diversified, the population grew, and the economy linked itself to the external world through trade. Importing and exporting led to the growth of urbanization, government and regulation, financial institutions, and occupational specialization. Increased social differentiation gave birth to interest groups and labor organizations.[21] To protect societal interests, between 1830 and 1865 the government required workers in key trades to join guilds (*gremios*). The government also chartered guilds of doctors and lawyers in the 1850s. Workers themselves formed numerous independent mutual aid societies in the last quarter of the nineteenth century as the economy became increasingly dependent upon international markets and Costa Rica experienced the novelty (for Ticos) of unemployment.[22]

The aristocracy, led by the *cafetaleros,* maintained its dominion in politics and largely excluded the general public and new social forces from national affairs. Costa Rica's armed forces grew and became politically more powerful after the Central American National War of 1857, expanding enormously during the Liberal era after 1870.[23] Officers connived with factions of the coffee aristocracy to depose or impose president after president.

To facilitate coffee exports, Tomás Guardia's government in 1871 contracted for the construction of a railroad from the capital, San José, to the Atlantic port of Limón. The government paid for it mainly with land in the Atlantic coastal region that later provided the main resources of the banana industry. Railroad construction attracted to Costa Rica Italians, Spaniards, English-speaking Caribbean blacks, and Chinese, diversifying Costa Rican society. The Chinese and blacks in particular experienced racial discrimination, and the exploitation of these groups by the railroad construction company led to Costa Rica's earliest recorded labor unrest. Chinese railroad workers struck in 1874, Jamaicans in 1879, and Italians in 1888. Native Costa Rican telegraph workers staged their first strike in 1883.

Railroad construction also gave birth to the banana industry near the end of the nineteenth century. Fruit companies, especially United Fruit, arose when railroad companies discovered foreign markets for bananas. Foreign capital soon established economic enclaves in the Atlantic zone that drained swamps and industrialized production, packing, and shipping. This created a timely need for new agricultural workers just as coffee's expansion had slowed.

The banana boom spurred labor organization among banana workers, who toiled under terrible conditions. Foreign-owned fruit companies also aggravated political corruption by using their wealth to secure government cooperation in keeping taxes low and in controlling workers.

By 1900 Costa Rica's population of 270,000 had roughly quintupled since 1800 and had spread over much more of the national territory. The growth of the coffee industry had simultaneously expanded the yeoman peasantry (small farm owners), concentrated landownership, and increased the rural proletariat (rural wageworkers). Increased trade had diversified the society and economy, brought improved transportation and communications, and further integrated Costa Rica into the world economy as a commodity exporter.

Politics

One distinctive feature of Costa Rica's early national history was that it largely escaped the independence struggles and subsequent Liberal-Conservative wars that afflicted much of the rest of Latin America. As Guatemala's most distant region, Costa Rica's colonial status ended without any local combat in 1821 when Mexico won independence. Conservatives tended to support participation in Agustín de Iturbide's Mexican empire, whereas the Liberals favored republican government.

The two factions temporized, jointly declaring via the *cabildos* their intention to wait until the situation in Mexico clarified. The *cabildos* met, elected a series of governing juntas from 1821 to 1824, and drafted an interelite pact that declared Costa Rican sovereignty. In 1823 the Liberal-republicans won the single small battle with the Conservative-imperialists at Ochomogo, ironically a month after the Mexican empire had collapsed.[24]

In 1823 the other four Central American colonies formed the Central American Federal Republic, which Costa Rica soon joined. Before long, conflict between Conservatives and Liberals ripped the four northern provinces, but with the Liberal triumph at Ochomogo Costa Rica generally remained on the margin of the internecine struggle. Indeed, civil conflict in neighboring Nicaragua became so severe that the residents of Guanacaste sought annexation to Costa Rica in 1824. Costa Rica agreed, and the Central American congress ratified the annexation. Neither Costa Rica's infrequent Liberal-Conservative conflict nor its early civilian rule brought political stability. The turbulent first quarter century of Costa Rican independence contained ambiguous portents for the political future. There were interelite elections, constitutional rule, state building, and interparty accommodation, but these were interspersed with militarism, coups d'état, dictatorship, and armed conflict.[25]

From 1823 through 1838, Costa Rica was part of the Central American federation. A congress elected in 1824 chose Liberal educator Juan Mora Fernández as Costa Rica's first chief of state. The congress also wrote a "fundamental law," or constitution, establishing a bicameral legislature and weak executive. Formal rules for governing the province of Costa Rica set patterns that would prevail for most of the next eight decades. Liberal and Conservative politicians, drawn from the social and economic elite who had dominated the *cabildos*, made political rules that guaranteed elite domination of the polity. Table 3.1 details common provisions of the constitutions in force from 1821 through 1844: indirect election of the president and legislature by a college of electors; public rather than secret voting; and property, education, and sex qualifications for voting that limited suffrage to wealthy, literate males. Electors were typically coffee-farming aristocrats, because to qualify for the post typically required substantial property holdings and education. Electors then chose the officeholders, who had to meet still stiffer capital and property ownership qualifications.[26] Liberal and Conservative factions among the *cafetalero* aristocracy contested for power; they often manipulated elections by fraud and even by military force. The system of indirect elections among the economic elite restricted voting to one-tenth or less of Costa Rican men.

President Mora's successors were often violent and dictatorial. Braulio Carrillo Colina seized power in a coup in 1838, declared himself "dictator for life," and took Costa Rica out of the failing Central American federation.[27] Carrillo's enemies invited the former president of the Central American Federal Republic, General Francisco Morazán Quesada, to overthrow Carrillo in 1842. Soon after-

TABLE 3.1   Key Costa Rican Electoral Developments, 1825–1905

	Constitutional Provision or Law
1821	Election of president and legislature by indirect election (citizens choose electors, who elect officials). Presidential election by absolute majority of electors; runoffs generally by congress rather than electors.
	Property and education qualifications for voting (generally increasing from 1821 through 1848, declining thereafter until 1913).
	No female suffrage (prohibition is implicit through 1847, explicit until 1949).
	Voting is public.
1844	Voting mandatory (practice lapses in subseqent constitutions).
1859	Absolute no reelection of president (modified to no immediate reelection in 1969).
1889	First opposition party victory over incumbent in an election.

sour ces: Bernhard Thibaut, "Costa Rica," in Dieter Nohlen, ed., *Enciclopedia electoral latinoamericano y del Caribe* (San José, Costa Rica: Instituto Interamericano de Derechos Humanos, 1993), pp. 185–187; Fabrice Edouard Lehoucq, "The Origins of Democracy in Costa Rica in Comparative Perspective," Ph.D. dissertation, Duke University, 1992; and Fabrice Edouard Lehoucq, "Institutional Change and Political Conflict: Evaluating Alternative Explanations of Electoral Reform in Costa Rica," *Electoral Studies* 13, 4 (December 1994).

ward a widespread popular revolt in turn toppled Morazán, who was captured and executed.

For many decades afterward, Costa Rica remained politically unstable, as one may see in the fate of Costa Rican presidencies. As Table 3.2 reveals, from 1824 through 1905, 17 percent of Costa Rica's presidents were toppled by a coup, 24 percent served a year or less in office, and 36 percent of the period was spent under military rule. Military presidents averaged 4.8 years in office but civilians only 2.3 years. Between 1835 and 1899, Costa Rica was ruled by generals—usually *cafetaleros*—over half the time.[28] "During this period there were six different constitutions, and there were numerous changes of government with military support. Civilian governments, generally of short duration, were usually elected indirectly."[29]

Despite all this turmoil, certain antecedents of eventual democracy appeared. Most notably, elections—indirect and elite-dominated—became an important facet of Costa Rican politics. There was one brief and anomalous period of expanded popular suffrage and direct elections from 1844 to 1847. Laws establishing electoral rolls were passed in 1848 and 1861.[30]

In 1870 Colonel Tomás Guardia Gutiérrez, a Liberal and commander of the Alajuela barracks, seized power. Guardia's modernizing dictatorship from 1870 to 1882 had various important effects: His 1871 constitution established a unicameral legislature and a strong executive. Other reforms strengthened the state and rationalized the national bureaucracy. Guardia raised taxes and invested heavily in education, public health, and transportation, beginning the construction of the

TABLE 3.2   Characteristics of Costa Rican Presidencies, 1824–1998

	1824–1905	*1906–1949*	*1950–1998*
Mean presidency length in years	2.7	3.1	4.0
Civilian only	2.3	3.2	4.0
Military only	4.8	1.5	0.0
Percentage of period under military rule	36	7	0
Percentage of presidents serving less than one year	24	14	0
Percentage of presidencies ended by coup	17	14	0
Mean voter turnout as percent of population	—[a]	14.5	40.3

[a]Not available; estimated at consistently below 10 percent.

sour ces: Harold H. Bonilla, *Los presidentes,* vols. 1 and 2 (San José: Universidad Estatal a Distancia–Editorial Costa Rica, 1979), and Tribunal Supremo de Elecciones.

Atlantic Railway. He substantially strengthened the armed forces by contracting Prussian officers and purchasing several warships. Guardia regularly violated the constitution and human rights and repressed his opponents.

Ironically, however, Tomás Guardia's dictatorship also contributed to the subsequent democratization of Costa Rica by its long-run effects upon the coffee barons' political power, education, and social and economic forces. First, by concentrating power in his own hands Guardia greatly curtailed the influence of the *cafetaleros.* By the late nineteenth century, the Conservative movement per se had largely disappeared. Interelite politics had therefore evolved mainly into competition among personalistic *cafetalero* factions that generally supported the policies of agroexport liberalism. After Guardia's death in 1882, coffee planter politicians, frustrated by their loss of power to the dictator, reasserted themselves in politics.[31]

Second, Guardia's expansion of public education increased literacy and thus eventually expanded the citizen population. Third, growth of the state and bureaucracy augmented the tiny middle class. Finally, construction of the Atlantic Railway gave rise to the banana industry and economic diversification, attracted immigrants, activated new economic forces, and stimulated labor mobilization.

Guardia's Liberal successors enacted anticlerical policies to counteract the growing political and educational strength of the once weak Catholic Church. The Liberal laws of 1884 provided for secular, compulsory, and free education, expelled Archbishop Bernardo Thiel and the Jesuit order from the country, secularized marriage and cemeteries, and legalized divorce. In response, the Catholic Church encouraged unprecedented popular mobilization in politics, driven both by religious concerns and by social problems caused by recession and unemployment. Despite the indirect election system, in the 1889 presidential vote—sometimes incorrectly celebrated as the birth of Costa Rican democracy—political parties for the first time appealed broadly for public support. The newly formed Catholic Union Party stirred voters' fears of anticlericalism so much that electors voted against the incumbent Liberals by a four-to-one ratio. The military then rebelled to prevent opposition victor José J. Rodríguez from taking office. But urban Costa Ricans, incited by the church, rioted in favor of Rodríguez. Liberals and the army, stunned by the popular mobilization, backed down and ceded him the presidency.

The 1889 opposition victory and successful transfer of power represented a historical first in Costa Rica. However, that election had little short-run import because the Liberals recaptured power in 1893 and suppressed the Catholic Union Party. Indeed, regimes from 1894 through 1905 were consistently authoritarian and elections fraudulent. Nevertheless, the 1889 election had marked important innovations in Costa Rican politics. First, the mobilization of ordinary citizens around a call for social justice anticipated future church political activism and social Christian and social democratic movements. Second, the virtual popular uprising in favor of Rodríguez in 1889 compelled the military to respect an opposition election victory, presaging the future contribution of popular forces to democratization.[32]

1906–1945: Turbulence and Transition

The development and consolidation of democracy are the hallmarks of Costa Rican history since 1906. Along the road to democracy, however, lay several difficult obstacles. From 1906 through World War II, coffee and banana exports predominated and world economic and political turbulence repeatedly buffeted Costa Rica. The rise of new working- and middle-class forces eventually destabilized the *cafetalero* regime and provoked a systemic crisis.

Economic and Social Forces

Costa Rica in the early twentieth century experienced several recessions driven by its export dependency and world markets. The lengthy recession that had begun in the 1880s continued until 1909. The next four decades saw more boom-and-bust cycles in both coffee and bananas, products that had come to dominate national economic fortunes. Coffee revenues went through several price cycles, and banana production peaked around 1910 then plunged during the 1930s. These dramatic export volume and price changes for Costa Rica's main crops dramatically affected the nation's economic health. Gross national product (GNP) per capita contracted during the first decade of the century, grew for almost two decades, then again slumped badly during the Great Depression of 1929 through the mid-1940s.[33]

This economic turbulence generated considerable class conflict and political turmoil involving the rapidly growing working and middle classes. The recession at the century's beginning punished workers with inflation, wage erosion, abusive working conditions, and unemployment. Both blue- and white-collar workers responded by rapidly expanding the labor movement. Progressively more combative unions (*sindicatos*) influenced by anarchist and socialist ideas began replacing guilds and mutualist associations. The first true unions (of bakers, shoemakers, plasterers, carpenters, and typographers) formed in 1905, followed quickly by dozens more and by various labor papers and study centers. Marxists founded the first coalition of unions, the General Confederation of Workers (Confederación General de Trabajadores, or CGT), in 1913. When World War I shrank export markets, the sharp recession caused labor turmoil in 1919 that helped unseat the military regime of General Federico Tinoco Granados, who had overthrown President Alfredo González Flores in 1917.

Labor continued to grow and gain political influence after World War I as the CGT organized more trades and industries. A 1921 general strike demanded higher wages and an eight-hour day, to which the government capitulated. Several other strikes and protests followed, the latter eliciting government repression of CGT leaders and violence by workers. In 1923 the CGT moved directly into politics by dissolving itself to form the Reformist Party (Partido Reformista, or PR), led by social Christian Jorge Volio, a former priest. The PR, which forged an alliance between reformist Catholic clergy and workers (first seen in 1889–1893), foretold later cooperation between communist unions and the church. The protections for workers that the PR demanded would become national economic policy within two decades. When the PR began to deemphasize labor issues, the unions broke away and reconstituted the CGT.

Public-sector workers (outside the CGT) in 1925 organized the Civic League (Liga Cívica). The league, influenced by Peruvian Marxist Victor Raúl Haya de la Torre, spawned a broader pro-labor movement that included unionists, Marxists, socialists, and other radicals. When banana and coffee prices collapsed in 1929 as the Great Depression began, United Fruit laid off thousands of workers. In 1931 left and labor elements formed the Costa Rican Communist Party. The Communists organized banana workers, whose miserable working conditions led to a major 1934 strike against United Fruit. The success of the banana strike spread unionization and bred both more violent labor conflict and the communist-dominated Confederation of Costa Rican Workers (Confederación de Trabajadores de Costa Rica, or CTCR).

The misery afflicting Costa Rica's lower classes during the depression eventually reunited social Christians and labor—this time behind Republican Party coffee aristocrat Rafael Angel Calderón Guardia. In 1941 the new president, a social Christian, pushed through the congress a social security program that protected workers, provoking his *cafetalero* allies and many former Republicans to turn against him. To reinforce his shaky government, Calderón Guardia then forged a populist coalition including Catholic archbishop Victor Sanabria and the Communist Party and its unions.

Politically buttressed against the upper class, Calderón and the Communists in 1943 enacted a labor code that formally recognized workers' right to strike. The Communist Party, which changed its name to the Popular Vanguard Party in 1943, played a key role in the election and government of Calderón's vice president and successor, Teodoro Picado Michalski (1944–1948). As middle- and upper-class opposition to the Picado government escalated, the PVP and unions employed intimidation and violence to protect their newfound influence and policy gains.[34]

Class and political tensions and repression thus soared in the middle and late 1940s. These set the stage for the 1948 civil war that would usher in Costa Rica's new economic model and the consolidation of civilian, constitutional democracy.

Politics

In 1906 a new generation of *cafetalero* political leaders, known since as *el Olimpo* (roughly, the Olympians), began. During the late nineteenth century, two political parties of liberal inclination had emerged among the *cafetalero* elite, the ruling National Union Party (Partido Unión Nacional, or PUN) and the Republican Party. PUN presidential candidate Cleto González Víquez failed to win the needed absolute majority of electors in the first round of the 1905 election, but the regime imposed him in the runoff: It declared a state of siege, imprisoned and deported opposition candidates, disqualified most pro-opposition electors, and arrested and intimidated others.

> This was undoubtedly the great contradiction of the liberals, who on the one hand defined themselves as followers of democracy and defenders of the purity and freedom of suffrage, but on the other had not the least scruple about violating the law and not respecting the vote if the results were adverse. On the long road to political democracy, the country was still far from creating a regime that would respect the will of the people expressed at the polls.[35]

Despite the bad example of his own election, González Víquez later distinguished himself in the 1909 election by breaking with tradition and tolerating vigorous opposition and a free campaign. Republican opposition candidate Ricardo Jiménez Oreamuno won the election. Jiménez then made another critical contribution to democratization: He pushed through a 1913 constitutional amendment that established direct presidential elections. This deepened Costa Rican democracy by somewhat reducing elite dominance of elections and paved the way for expanding literacy to increase the citizen population. González Víquez would later serve another term as president (1928–1932) and Jiménez Oreamuno two more (1924–1928, 1932–1936).

Turmoil soon returned despite this positive interlude. In the 1913 presidential election, the two leading vote-getters withdrew from the race, so the congress named Alfredo González Flores president in 1914. When the economic crisis gen-

TABLE 3.3   Key Costa Rican Electoral Developments, 1906–1946

	Constitutional Provision or Law
1913	Direct election of president and legislature (ends indirect election by electors).
	Presidential election by absolute majority; legislative election by proportional representation.
	Elimination of property and education qualifications for voting.
1925	Only parties or political groups may postulate candidates for public office (no independent candidates).
	Grand Electoral Council (Gran Consejo Electoral, or GCE) established to conduct elections.
	Secret ballot established in principle.
1927	Government printing of ballots replaces party-printed ballots.
	Citizen photographic identification cards.
1936	Secret ballot mandatory.
	Election of president by relative majority (minimum of 40 percent); runoff election between top two candidates in case of no first round victor.
1946	New electoral code replaces GCE with stronger National Electoral Tribunal (Tribunal Nacional Electoral, or TNE).
	National Electoral Registry established to reduce voting fraud with photo identity cards

sour ces: Bernhard Thibaut, "Costa Rica," in Dieter Nohlen, ed., *Enciclopedia electoral latinoamericano y del Caribe* (San José, Costa Rica: Instituto Interamericano de Derechos Humanos, 1993), pp. 185–187; Fabrice Edouard Lehoucq, "The Origins of Democracy in Costa Rica in Comparative Perspective," Ph.D. dissertation, Duke University, 1992; and Fabrice Edouard Lehoucq, "Institutional Change and Political Conflict: Evaluating Alternative Explanations of Electoral Reform in Costa Rica," *Electoral Studies* 13, 4 (December 1994).

erated by World War I led to economic reforms and new taxes, frustrated *cafetaleros* instigated a 1917 coup by General Federico Tinoco Granados and his brother. Two years of repressive military rule failed to resolve economic problems and brought widespread popular unrest, At this juncture exiled elites toppled the Tinocos in 1919. Ordinary Costa Ricans had once again forcibly expressed a desire for civilian, constitutional rule.

During the next three decades, Costa Rican politics experienced major political changes driven by socioeconomic forces. As noted above, in 1923 populist, social Christian social worker Jorge Volio Jiménez mobilized the unions of the CGT into the Reformist Party. Volio lost to Ricardo Jiménez Oreamuno, and the union movement temporarily retreated from electoral politics to organizing and ideological ferment. During Jiménez Oreamuno's second presidency (1924–1928), important electoral reforms were passed (Table 3.3), including the establishment of a Grand Electoral Council (Gran Consejo Electoral, or GCE) to oversee elections and the institution of photographic voter identity documents and ballot secrecy. Despite such institutional reforms of elections and despite increasing voter

TABLE 3.4　Evolution of the Costa Rican Electorate and Turnout, Selected Presidential Elections, 1919–1998

	National Population	Registered	Percent Registered	Votes Cast	Turnout % Registered	% Population
1919	453,127	84,987	18.8	48,167	56.7	10.6
1928	484,370	116,933	24.1	71,786	61.4	17.8
1936	570,023	—[a]	—[a]	89,325	—[a]	15.7
1944	685,302	—[a]	—[a]	136,806	—[a]	20.0
1953	868,741	293,678	33.8	197,489	67.2	22.7
1962	1,224,687	483,980	39.5	391,406	80.9	30.2
1970	1,606,476	675,285	39.8	562,766	83.3	33.2
1978	2,098,531	1,058,455	50.4	860,206	84.2	41.0
1986	2,666,000	1,486,474	55.1	1,216,600	81.8	45.6
1990	3,035,000[b]	1,692,050	55.8[b]	1,384,326	81.8	45.6[b]
1994[c]	3,347,000	1,881,348	56.2[d]	1,525,979	81.1	45.6[b]
1998[c]	3,672,000	2,045,980	55.7	1,456,738	71.2	39.7

[a]No data available.

[b]1990 percent registered and turnout as percent of population calculated using IADB population estimates.

[c]1994 and 1998 data based on Supreme Electoral Tribune (TSE) report of election data; percentages of population calculated using IADB population estimates.

[d]Estimate based on Rovira Mas's turnout figures.

sources: Dieter Nohlen, ed., *Enciclopedia electoral latinoamericano y del Caribe* (San José, Costa Rica: Instituto Interamericano de Derechos Humanos, 1993), p. 188; Jorge Rovira Mas, "Costa Rica: 6 de febrero de 1994," *Boletín Electoral Latinoamericano* (January-June 1994), p. 51; Inter-American Development Bank (IADB), *Latin America After a Decade of Reforms: Economic and Social Progress in Latin America, 1997 Report* (Baltimore: Johns Hopkins University Press, 1997), Table A-1; José David Guevara M., "Señalan retos de Rodríguez," *La Nación Digital,* February 3, 1998 <http://www.nacion.co.cr/hn_ee/1998/febrero/03/pais4.html>.

turnout (Table 3.4), repeated electoral fraud and several opposition rebellions kept Costa Rican politics quite tumultuous in the 1920s and 1930s. Again seeking to promote political stability in the mid-1930s, government and opposition deputies in the congress cooperated on further electoral reform (Table 3.3). Again, however, merely changing election laws calmed neither growing class conflict nor the sometimes violent competition among political elites.[36]

The 1940s proved critical in Costa Rican political development. The severe economic difficulties of the 1930s had seriously agitated workers, who had gained considerable power through the success of the communist (PVP)-led CTCR unions. A middle-class, anticommunist political center and center-left began to emerge, though it lagged behind the PVP-CTCR in size and militancy. Calderón Guardia assumed the presidency in 1940 and pursued major reforms to benefit Costa Rican workers. The 1941 social security law incensed both Calderón's predecessor, León Cortés Castro, and much of Costa Rica's elite, who repudiated the president. As noted above, Calderón then turned to his friend Archbishop Sanabria and to the communist PVP and its legislative deputies for help to retain power and to legislate. The Calderonista-PVP coalition soon passed a labor code and other social guarantees (including a minimum wage) that further angered powerful economic interests. In the 1944 election, vice president Teodoro Picado Michalski, Calderón Guardia's designated successor, won by a wide margin in an election that the opposition denounced as heavily fraudulent. Tensions between the regime and its opponents and allies alike intensified during the Picado administration, as PVP and labor union harassment of the opposition escalated.

1946–the Present: Crisis and Consolidation

The intense class and political conflict led to the 1948 civil war, the outcome of which reconfigured the polity and the roles of the state. Assisting in the consolidation of the emergent democratic regime and its activist state were several decades of sustained economic growth and diversification.

Politics

As PVP and union intimidation of government opponents rose in the late 1940s, so, too, did partisan violence and terrorism by the opposition. Government opponents included the anticommunist, middle-sector left (the Center for the Study of National Problems and the Social Democratic Party led by José Figueres Ferrer), moderate conservatives of the PUN led by newspaper publisher Otilio Ulate Blanco, and ultraconservative *cafetalero* interests linked to former president Cortés Castro's Democratic Party (Partido Demócrata). In a futile attempt to ameliorate burgeoning opposition violence, the Picado government and Calderonista and PVP deputies in the congress passed yet another set of electoral reforms in 1946 (Table 3.4). The new law formed an electoral registry to curtail voting fraud and restructured and strengthened the GCE into the National Electoral Tribunal (Tribunal Nacional Electoral, or TNE). The Picado government so desired to limit electoral turmoil that it even ceded control of the new TNE to the opposition for the 1948 election.

Calderón Guardia sought reelection in 1948, but Ulate Blanco of the PUN defeated him easily. Calderonista deputies, however, had captured a majority in the new congress. Unwilling to relinquish the presidency, Calderón and his deputies in the new congress overturned the TNE's certification of Ulate's victory based upon at least some credible evidence of fraud. Social democrat José Figueres, who had been agitating and preparing for a revolt against the Calderón-Picado regime for years, seized upon the annulment of the election as the pretext for rebellion. Figueres and his National Liberation Army fought the regime and union supporters in a bloody, six-week civil war. Backed by anticommunist elements in

TABLE 3.5   Key Costa Rican Electoral Developments, 1947–1979

Constitutional Provision or Law

1949	New constitution (based on 1871 Liberal constitution) adopted; central provisions include:
	Supreme Electoral Tribunal (Tribunal Supremo Electoral, or TSE) replaces TNE; established as "fourth branch of government" to manage electoral rolls, elections, operate civil/electoral registry).
	Universal suffrage (i.e., female suffrage).
	Absolute no reelection of president restored.
	Prohibition of standing armed forces.
1971	Voting mandatory.
	Voting age set at eighteen (previously varied between eighteen and twenty-five, usually twenty-one after 1869).

sources: Bernhard Thibaut, "Costa Rica," in Dieter Nohlen, ed., *Enciclopedia electoral latinoamericano y del Caribe* (San José, Costa Rica: Instituto Interamericano de Derechos Humanos, 1993), pp. 185–187; Fabrice Edouard Lehoucq, "The Origins of Democracy in Costa Rica in Comparative Perspective," Ph.D. dissertation, Duke University, 1992; and Fabrice Edouard Lehoucq, "Institutional Change and Political Conflict: Evaluating Alternative Explanations of Electoral Reform in Costa Rica," *Electoral Studies* 13, 4 (December 1994).

Guatemala and elsewhere in the region and with considerable popular support, the rebels defeated the army and the unions. The vanquished government negotiated its surrender under terms that protected its major figures' safety and property and the social legislation that it had enacted.

The rebel National Liberation junta, led by José Figueres, ruled by decree for eighteen months, having promised to turn over power to 1948 election victor Ulate. A clean election for a constituent assembly was held in which Ulate's PUN slate took three-quarters of the seats. The assembly rejected junta leader Figueres's draft social democratic constitution in favor of revising the 1871 constitution. The 1949 constitution made two critical contributions to democracy: First, the creation of the Supreme Electoral Tribunal (Tribunal Supremo de Elecciones, or TSE) would deepen democracy by ensuring clean elections. Second, the introduction of female suffrage substantially broadened Costa Rican democracy.[37] Election turnout rose from 20.0 percent of the population in 1944 to 30.2 percent by 1962 (Table 3.4).

Other vital provisions of the 1949 constitution (Table 3.5) were absolute prohibitions of reelection of the president and of a standing army. The latter, most observers agree, has virtually eliminated the military as a destabilizing force in Costa Rican politics, a role armed forces exercise throughout the rest of Latin America. Coups and military rule disappeared from Costa Rican politics after 1949 (Table 3.2). The combination of election reform and demilitarization contributed to broadened citizen participation in voter registration and voter turnout in elections after 1949. Turnout rates rose to over 80 percent of registered voters by the 1960s and remained there until 1998 (Table 3.4).

Its backing diminished and having failed to implement many of its revolutionary goals, the National Liberation junta turned over power to Ulate in 1949 as promised. They did so because "during the course of the struggle against Calderón, Figueres and his allies had become committed to substantive and procedural principles of social democracy which have guided their behavior substantially in subsequent years."[38] The transfer of power to Ulate reinforced the integrity of elections in Costa Rica and established the basis of an elite settlement that would consolidate itself within a few years.

Having relinquished power, the former rebel leaders transformed their movement into the National Liberation Party (Partido de Liberación Nacional, or PLN). Though strongly anticommunist, the new party drew its ideology from Figueres's ties to Haya de la Torre's American Popular Revolutionary Alliance (Alianza Popular Revolucionaria Americana, or APRA), from the social democratic ideology of the Center for the Study of National Problems and the Social Democratic Party, and from the reformism of Volio's Reformist Party. The Liberation junta and PLN embraced and retained the social reforms of the Calderón era. Acceptance of state social reformism, however, did not extend to the communist-dominated unions. The Communist Party was outlawed, many unions were dissolved, and both the PLN and the Catholic Church promoted competing labor confederations. Intended to prevent the concentration of union political power that occurred in the early 1940s, this deliberate fragmentation of organized labor was successful and has persisted since.[39]

The PLN's Figueres (Photo 3.2) won the 1953 election, consolidating important changes in national politics. First, the PLN victory definitively included middle-class political forces among Costa Rica's political elite and ended the economic aristocracy's many decades of political hegemony. Second, by turning over power to Unión Nacional opposition candidate Mario Echandi in 1958, the PLN further validated electoral processes. The new election system guided by the Supreme Electoral Tribunal once again proved reliable and fair. This gave the conservative political parties and elite economic interests sufficient confidence to participate in the new democratic regime without fear of the electoral chicanery that plagued Costa Rica through 1948. In the elections of 1966, 1978, and 1990, a unified opposition to the PLN defeated PLN candidates and won the presidency. Indeed, party alternation in power has become a virtual norm of Costa Rican politics. In nine of Costa Rica's eleven elections since 1949, the incumbent party has lost and peacefully transferred power to its victorious opponent.[40]

The consistently transparent fairness of the election system established in 1949 thus became the basis of the third great change in Costa Rican politics after the civil war—the emergence of a democratic elite settlement. In this arrangement a majority of political and economic elites developed confidence in and commitment to a constitutional, democratic political game.[41] This commitment has defined a regime that has now persisted for five decades, making it by far the oldest and most stable of Latin American democracies.[42] The regime embraces Costa

PHOTO 3.2   José Figueres Ferrer, leader of the National Liberation movement and president, 1953–1958 and 1970–1974 (photo by Julio Laínez, courtesy *Tico Times*)

Rica's extensive array of interest groups and accommodates mass participation and even confrontational protests with very little repression.

Economic and Social Forces

Not long after World War II ended, Costa Rica's economic fortunes began to improve. Renewed growth of the industrial world's economies soon increased demand and prices for coffee and bananas. Costa Rica experienced more than three decades of sustained economic growth; GDP per capita almost trebled from 1946 through 1979.[43] With the rise to power of the social democratic PLN, Costa Rica changed its development model. Government assumed a much more active role in promoting economic growth and distributing its benefits. A major development initiative during this era was the Central American Common Market, which promoted economic modernization and diversification.

The revolutionary junta of 1948–1949 nationalized banking and insurance and retained the labor code and social security systems established during the 1940s. The PLN-led state invested in infrastructure and production and promoted an import substitution industrialization model, especially during the era of the CACM. This strategy paid off quickly; GDP per capita rose 27 percent between 1960 and 1970, and 31 percent from 1970 to 1980 (Appendix, Table A.1).[44] Dramatic urbanization and modernization of the capital city (Photo 3.3) ensued

PHOTO 3.3   Capital city of San José, with view of the Central Park (photo by Will Wilson, courtesy the photographer)

between 1960 and the 1990s; the population employed in agriculture declined almost by half and the proportion of GDP generated by manufacturing rose from 14 to 20 percent (Appendix, Table A.1). The new Costa Rican development model also saw the state double its share of overall economic activity (from 5.9 percent to 12 percent) from 1950 to 1970.

During this era the government subsidized health care, basic commodities, services, and housing and generally kept real wages on the rise (Appendix, Table A.3). Costa Rica in the 1970s spent much more heavily on education and social services and less on the military than neighboring Central American nations.[45] These policies redistributed income toward the middle class[46] and gave Costa Rica a solid foundation of increased prosperity. Table A.2 in the Appendix reveals certain other effects of such social policies: Costa Rican literacy, life expectancy, and infant mortality rates became comparable to those of industrial nations.

1980–the Present

In the mid- and late 1970s, falling export prices, rising oil prices, and the decline of the CACM caused another severe recession, which Costa Rica temporarily deferred by heavy international borrowing and deficit spending. In 1980, however, the inevitable happened, and Costa Rica entered a protracted economic crisis marked by currency devaluation. GDP per capita declined sharply during the 1980s, and external debt rose steeply (Appendix, Table A.1). Costa Rica came under considerable external pressure to adopt neoliberal economic policies to curtail public spending and social programs. It complied to some extent, reducing the government share of GDP from 11.2 percent in 1980 to 8.6 percent by 1995. It managed these economic reforms, however, without bringing about a general political crisis of the sort that convulsed Nicaragua, El Salvador, and Guatemala in the 1980s. One source of stability may be seen in Table A.3, which indicates that Costa Rica managed to mollify workers by restoring working-class wages fairly soon after their plunge in 1981 and 1982.

Conclusions

Costa Rican democracy did not, as myth holds, arise from an egalitarian and homogeneous society of small farmers. Nor was the polity stable or free of conflict, military rule, dictatorship, rebellions, or coups d'état during most of its national life before 1948. In fact, from 1821 through 1919 Costa Rican politics much more resembled the politics of neighboring Central American nations than most Ticos care to admit.

Does Costa Rica's great national myth make any valid claims about the nation's democratization? Some elements of the myth have certain merit. For instance, early isolation contributed to civil self-government and limited postindependence fighting. Costa Rica was too resource poor and had too few Indians to permit a militarily enforced coerced labor system. The persistence of many successful family farms and the resultant long-term rural labor shortage meant that large coffee farmers paid high wages for most of the nineteenth century. The heyday of Costa Rican militarism, when it did occur between 1870 and 1919, was more political and bureaucratic than an essential economic tool of the landed oligarchy. The *cafetaleros*, who had dominated the polity without much help from the army before Tomás Guardia, eventually reduced the military's political role as they reestablished their own political dominance.

How, then, did democracy arise? Interelite elections, excluding ordinary citizens, developed (though often deeply flawed) as one important means elites could compete for power. Increasing socioeconomic diversity generated first working-class and then middle-class forces that shouldered their way into the system through decades of increasing organization and mobilization driven by hard times. Political elites repeatedly refined election rules and expanded popular access to the system between 1913 and 1946, even though such measures failed to bring stability.

Calderón Guardia's populist coalition with communist-led labor and the church definitively shattered the hegemony of the *cafetaleros* but was itself destroyed by countervailing middle-sector and upper-class forces in the 1948 civil war. Figueres and the National Liberation movement (1948–1949) and Party (in the 1950s) helped to forge a new and fully liberal democratic regime.[47] It was an inclusive elite settlement that revolved around constitutional democratic rules and truly honest elections as the only means of vying for power. Abolishing the army ensured against military intervention. Ultimately, the stability of the new system rested upon a social democratic development model and widespread popular participation (but with a fragmented and subdued labor sector) to co-opt the mass public.

Notes

1. This chapter draws in part from John A. Booth, "Costa Rica: The Roots of Democratic Stability," in Larry Diamond, Juan J. Linz, and Seymour Martin Lipset, eds., *Democracy in Developing Countries,* vol. 4: *Latin America* (Boulder: Lynne Rienner Publishers–Adamantine Press, 1989), pp. 387–395, and John A. Booth, "Representative Constitutional Democracy in Costa Rica: Adaptation to Crisis in the Turbulent 1980s," in Steve C. Ropp and James A. Morris, eds., *Central America: Crisis and Adaptation* (Albuquerque: University of New Mexico Press, 1984), pp. 158–165.

2. Carolyn Hall, *Costa Rica: Una interpretación geográfica con perspectiva histórica* (San José: Editorial Costa Rica, 1983), pp. 137–138.

3. Ibid., pp. 139–142.

4. Mavis Hiltunen de Biesanz, Richard Biesanz, and Karen Zubris de Biesanz, *Los costarricenses* (San José, Costa Rica: Editorial Universidad Estatal a Distancia, 1979), pp. 46–47.

5. Samuel Stone, *La dinastía de los conquistadores* (San José: Editorial Universidad de Costa Rica–Editorial Universitaria Centroamericana, 1975), p. 55. The general discussion about the origin and characteristics of the Spanish colonists is also drawn from Stone, *La dinastía,* pp. 52–73.

6. Biesanz et al., *Los costarricenses,* p. 45. This and all translations from Spanish-language works (cited from Spanish sources in the notes) are my own.

7. Ibid., pp. 69–74.

8. Only in Guanacaste did extensive haciendas succeed and persist. Unlike the failed cacao plantations of the Atlantic region, in Guanacaste cattle could be raised extensively and with little labor, a successful adaptation; Elizabeth Fonseca, *Costa Rica Colonial: La tierra y el hombre* (San José, Costa Rica: Editorial Universitaria Centroamericana, 1984), pp. 319–320.

9. Biesanz et al., *Los costarricenses,* pp. 57–66; Fonseca, *Costa Rica Colonial*; and Lowell Gudmundson, *Costa Rica Before Coffee: Society and Economy on the Eve of the Export Boom* (Baton Rouge: Louisiana State University Press, 1986).

10. John A. Booth, "Costa Rica," in Gerald Michael Greenfield and Sheldon L. Maram, eds., *Latin American Labor Organizations* (New York: Greenwood Press, 1987), pp. 213–224.

11. Ibid., p. 44; and Biesanz et al., *Los costarricenses,* ch. 2.

12. Carlos Meléndez, "Bosquejo para una historia social costarricense antes de la independencia," in Vladimir de la Cruz, Carlos Meléndez, Yamilet González, Olger Avila, Matilde Cerdas, Astrid Fischel, Clotilde María Obregón, Marco A. Fallas, Eugenio Rodríguez, and Carmen Lila Gómez, *Las instituciones costarricenses del siglo XIX* (San José: Editorial Costa Rica, 1985), pp. 42–43.

13. Oddly and sometimes confusingly for those familiar with Spanish from elsewhere, the Costa Rican adjective for fair skin and hair is *macho,* a synonym for *rubio.* The usage is similar in Nicaragua.

14. In comparison to the authority and development of the colonial governments permitted by the British in North America, the *cabildos* were local in scope and often discontinuous.

15. Stone, *La dinastía*, p. 57.

16. Charles D. Ameringer, *Democracy in Costa Rica* (New York: Praeger, 1982), pp. 11–12.

17. Stone, *La dinastía*, pp. 75–78.

18. See Gudmundson, *Costa Rica Before Coffee*, chs. 2–4, and Mitchell A. Seligson, *Peasants and the Development of Agrarian Capitalism in Costa Rica* (Madison: University of Wisconsin Press, 1980). See also Deborah J. Yashar, *Demanding Democracy: Reform and Reaction in Costa Rica and Guatemala: 1970s–1950s* (Stanford: Stanford University Press, 1997), ch. 2.

19. José Luis Vega Carballo, *Poder político y democracia en Costa Rica* (San José, Costa Rica: Editorial Porvenir, 1982), p. 30; emphasis in the original.

20. Yashar's *Demanding Democracy* (ch. 2) compares the development of the Costa Rican and Guatemalan coffee sectors.

21. Material on organized labor is drawn mainly from Booth, "Costa Rica," pp. 213–224.

22. Underemployment is normally defined as wishing to work full time but finding only part-time employment.

23. Orlando Salazar Mora, *El apogeo de la república liberal en Costa Rica: 1870–1914* (San José: Editorial de la Universidad de Costa Rica, 1990), pp. 275–280.

24. Biesanz et al., *Los costarricenses*, pp. 49–55.

25. This discussion is drawn mainly from the following: Harold H. Bonilla, *Los presidentes*, vol. 1 (San José: Editorial Universidad Nacional a Distancia–Editorial Costa Rica, 1979), pp. 41–87; Biesanz et al., *Los costarricenses*, pp. 55–57; Bernhard Thibaut, "Costa Rica," in Dieter Nohlen, ed., *Enciclopedia electoral latinoamericano y del Caribe* (San José, Costa Rica: Instituto Interamericano de Derechos Humanos, 1993), p. 183.

26. Thibaut, "Costa Rica," p. 185; Stone, *La dinastía*, pp. 215–221; Jorge Enrique Romero Pérez, *Partidos políticos, poder y derecho (Costa Rica)* (San José, Costa Rica: Editores Syntagma, 1979), pp. 64–70.

27. Costa Rica did not formally sever ties with the Central American Federal Republic until 1849, despite the effective separation in 1838 (Thibaut, "Costa Rica," p. 183).

28. Bonilla, *Los presidentes*.

29. Thibaut, "Costa Rica," p. 182.

30. Ibid., p. 88; Matilde Amalia Cerdas A., "Las crisis políticas en Costa Rica: 1821–1870," in de la Cruz et al., *Las instituciones costarricenses del siglo XIX*, pp. 121–122.

31. Quote from Ameringer, *Costa Rican Democracy*, p. 17; for more on Guardia's rule, see Salazar Mora, *El apogeo*, pp. 22–33.

32. Salazar Mora, *El apogeo*, pp. 176–183; Ameringer, *Costa Rican Democracy*, pp. 19–20; Romero Pérez, *Partidos políticos*, pp. 18–23.

33. Ciro F. S. Cardoso and Héctor Pérez Brignoli, *Centro America y la economía occidental (1520–1930)* (San José: Editorial Universidad de Costa Rica, 1977), pp. 265, 284; Victor Bulmer-Thomas, *The Political Economy of Central America Since 1920* (Cambridge: Cambridge University Press, 1987), pp. 312–313.

34. See John A. Peeler, *Latin American Democracies: Colombia, Costa Rica, Venezuela* (Chapel Hill: University of North Carolina Press, 1985), pp. 58–70, on the makeup of the opposition to the Calderón/Picado–Communist–Catholic Church alliance.

35. Salazar Mora, *El apogeo*, p. 222.

36. See Fabrice Lehoucq, "The Origins of Democracy in Costa Rica in Comparative Perspective," Ph.D. dissertation, Duke University, 1992, pp. 63–70.

37. Peeler, *Latin American Democracies*, pp. 74–75.

38. Ibid., p. 74.

39. Booth, "Costa Rica," pp. 221–224.

40. Booth, "Costa Rica: The Roots of Democratic Stability," table 9.2, pp. 396–397, and Nohlen, *Enciclopedia electoral*, pp. 192–205.

41. The PLN and a group of conservative parties had established, without a formal pact, an effective working arrangement among major middle-sector political actors (grouped around the PLN) and the national coffee, commercial, and industrial bourgeoisies (grouped around several more traditional Liberal parties that frequently coalesced to challenge the PLN in elections).

42. Peeler, *Latin American Democracies*, pp. 100–110; Mario Carvajal Herrera, *Actitudes políticas de costarricense* (San José: Editorial Costa Rica, 1978), pp. 137–157.

43. Bulmer-Thomas, *The Political Economy*, pp. 312–313.

44. Bulmer-Thomas's figures for GDP per capita yield even higher growth estimates: 27 percent for 1950–1960, 39 percent for 1960–1970, and 38 percent for 1970–1980 (ibid.).

45. John A. Booth and Thomas W. Walker, *Understanding Central America* (Boulder: Westview Press, 1993), appendix, table 5.

46. Mitchell A. Seligson, Juliana Martínez F., and Juan Diego Trejos S., "Reducción de la pobreza en Costa Rica: el impacto de las políticas públicas," draft report to the Programa de las Naciones Unidad para el Desarrollo (PNUD), San José, Costa Rica, 1995, p. 7.

47. This analysis of Costa Rican democratization largely concurs with that of Yashar in *Demanding Democracy;* she holds that divisions among the *cafetalero* elite in the 1940s permitted the leaders of mobilized civil society a historic opportunity to forge a democratic regime. However, Yashar underestimates Costa Rican civil society (political and labor mobilization) development as early as the late nineteenth century. Early civil society and mass participation arose from a combination of economic forces, modernizing reforms such as education, and such ideological imports as Christian democracy and socialism.

4

THE POLITICAL
FRAMEWORK OF
DEMOCRACY

Observers of Latin America concur that the region's nations share several institutional barriers to democracy: meddling and repressive armed forces, excessively powerful executives, weak legislatures, and weak and dependent courts. All of these tend to contribute to poor election quality, another barrier to democracy. This chapter sketches the basic ground rules and operation of government to determine how Costa Rica handles such problems. It also explores political parties and elections and how they affect the breadth, range, and depth of democracy.

The 1949 Constitution

General Provisions

The constituent assembly elected following the 1948 civil war rewrote Costa Rica's 1871 liberal constitution. The resulting constitution remains in force.

> We, the Representatives of the People of Costa Rica, freely elected Deputies to the National Constituent Assembly, invoking the name of God and reiterating our faith in Democracy, decree and sanction the following Political Constitution of the Republic of Costa Rica.
> Article 1. Costa Rica is a democratic Republic, free and independent.
> Article 2. Sovereignty resides exclusively in the Nation.[1]

These passages clearly delineate the fundamental philosophy of government of Costa Rica. Following a tradition of republicanism begun in the nineteenth century, Costa Rica embraced the idea of government as a *res publica*—a thing of the people. As the preamble notes, freely elected representatives of the citizens drafted the basic rules of national politics. Sovereignty, the right to rule, resides in the nation of citizens, all of whom are "equal before the law."[2]

Costa Rican government is not federal but unitary (dominated by a single, centralized government). The nation's eighty municipal (county) governments have limited powers derived from the constitution. Costa Rica retains a system of archaic provinces, but their only modern public function is as electoral districts for the Legislative Assembly.

The 1949 constitution establishes limited government. To prevent excessive concentration of authority, it divides government into three branches, giving each branch certain checks over the others. Quite unlike most other Latin American nations, Costa Rica's constitution considerably restrains executive power, both through checks by other branches and through specific limitations upon presidential authority. The Legislative Assembly, the judiciary, and the Supreme Electoral Tribunal of Costa Rica each enjoy unusual strength and independence with respect to the executive branch.

Arguably the most outstanding feature of the constitution is its prohibition of a standing army. "The army is proscribed as a permanent institution. For the vigilance and conservation of public order, there will be the necessary police forces."[3] Having no army has several payoffs for democracy: It greatly enhances the authority of civil government by eliminating an institution that in Costa Rica and elsewhere has repeatedly disrupted constitutional rule and undermined democracy.[4] Denied the tempting power of a standing military, public officials and other power contenders must negotiate among themselves on a relatively equal footing. Finally, having no army reduces dramatically the opportunities for Costa Rican rulers to abuse citizens' rights or systematically disregard citizens' wishes.

The constitutional elimination of a standing army has indisputably helped ensure Costa Rica's many decades of unblemished political stability, civilian regimes, and excellent human rights performance—a record unequaled in Latin America. The absence of an army combines with the constitution's extensive protection of citizens' rights to provide a national political climate with few institutional barriers to citizen political participation. By not having an army, therefore, Costa Rica has improved both the breadth and the depth of its democracy. Breadth is greater because virtually everyone may participate freely under democratic rules, encouraging citizen involvement. Democracy is deepened because reducing the repression of civil society permits unfettered expression and pursuit of popular policy preferences.

Personal and Political Rights

The 1949 constitution provides a broad array of political rights and protections.[5] These include prohibitions against slavery, exile, capital punishment, ex post facto laws, special tribunals, compulsion to bear witness against oneself, detention or punishment without due process of law, imprisonment for debts, cruel or unusual punishment, extraction of testimony by violent means, double jeopardy, and monopolies (except those established by law).

The constitution expressly guarantees citizens and residents freedom of movement; privacy of the home, records, and personal papers; and indemnification for property taken by the state. Costa Ricans may freely associate for licit ends, meet peaceably for private or public purposes including to scrutinize the conduct of public officials, petition any public functionary and receive prompt resolution, and obtain freely information from the government (except for state secrets). Costa Ricans have the right to freedom of opinion and spoken and written expression, the right to publish without prior censorship, and the rights to privacy, copyrights and patents, and habeas corpus. The constitution also grants the right of *amparo* (literally, "assistance"), which is a court order "to keep or restore the enjoyment of the other rights consecrated in this constitution."[6]

The Costa Rican constitution's provisions concerning religion, although typical of most Latin American nations, contain interesting inconsistencies. Title VI establishes the Roman Catholic religion as "that of the state, which contributes to its maintenance," yet further says that Ticos enjoy "the free exercise . . . of other cults that are not opposed to universal morality or to good customs."[7] Another provision, however, recalls nineteenth-century anticlericalism: Clergy and laity may not make "any form of political propaganda . . . invoking or employing religious motifs or religious beliefs."[8]

Social Rights and Guarantees

Reflecting the social democratic and social Christian ideologies so influential in Costa Rica during the 1940s, the constitution commits the state to "pursue the greatest well-being of all the inhabitants of the nation, organizing and stimulating production and the most appropriate distribution of wealth."[9] It lists many "unrenounceable" rights and protections for all persons: The family (including mothers, children, the elderly, and the infirm) has the right to special protection by the state, which must establish an autonomous institution (Patronato Nacional de la Infancia, or National Infant Children's Agency) to promote the protection of mothers and minor children. Other family rights and protections include equality of rights among marriage partners and equality of parental obligation toward children born within or outside of marriage.

Labor-related guarantees include the right (and obligation) to work, to a decent minimum wage, to equal pay for equal work, to an eight-hour workday and six-day workweek, to a 50 percent wage bonus for overtime work, to two weeks of paid vacation per year, to organize freely and to strike (for both workers and employers, subject to regulatory legislation and except in public services), to bargain collectively, to indemnification for dismissal without just cause, and to safe and hygienic working conditions.

The government must also promote housing for workers (*vivienda popular*), oversee worker training, provide special protection for working women and children, establish labor courts, protect the unemployed and promote their reemployment, and provide a system of social security—mainly health and medical care—under the Costa Rican Social Security Institute (Caja Costarricense de Seguro Social, or CCSS).

Costa Rica consistently wins the praise of external observers for honoring its constitutional standards of limited government and for respecting its citizens' right to participate in politics. For example, the U.S. Department of State in its glowing 1981 report on Costa Rican human rights practices stated: "Freedom to participate in the political process is provided for in the constitution and respected in practice. Elections are free, competitive and open."[10]

The remainder of this chapter examines the branches of government and how they function, as well as political parties and elections.

The Legislative Branch

"The power to legislate resides in the people, who delegate it, by means of the vote, to the Legislative Assembly."[11] The Costa Rican Legislative Assembly has a single house of fifty-seven members, whose delegates (*diputados*) are elected in proportion to the populations of the nation's seven provinces.[12] Delegates' four-year terms of office coincide with those of the president. *Diputados* may not succeed themselves in office.

The 1949 constitution grants the Legislative Assembly powers that make it one of the stronger legislatures in Latin America: It may legislate, amend the constitution (by a two-thirds vote in each of two successive annual sessions), declare war and peace, ratify treaties, approve the national budget, levy taxes, and suspend certain constitutional rights (by a two-thirds vote).[13] The assembly may also take property for public purposes, authorize public debt, establish a currency system, grant amnesty for certain crimes (by a two-thirds vote), and appoint the magistrates (justices) of the Supreme Court of Justice (Corte Supremo de Justicia, or CSJ).

The Legislative Assembly has considerable authority to write detailed appropriations for specific local projects (*partidas específicas*). It regularly exercises this power by writing into the national budget sums for improvements or construction of plazas, utilities, roads, bridges, and community centers. Such pork barrel funding makes the assembly and its deputies the regular targets of lobbying by citizens and interest groups. Critics contend that the proliferation of narrow local interests within the major parties' legislative benches (for tactical electoral reasons) has combined with the pork barrel function to mire the Legislative Assembly in local budget matters and thus weakened its ability to address important national policy issues.[14]

The Legislative Assembly holds powerful checks upon the executive: It can require information from government ministers, impeach and censure high officials, appoint the powerful national comptroller, and override an executive veto (which requires a two-thirds majority).[15] Members of the assembly enjoy immunity from civil responsibility for declarations made in the legislative body and temporary immunity from civil and lesser criminal charges during their service in the legislature. Such provisions let legislators do their jobs free of untoward pressures from the executive branch and civil society.[16]

To balance legislative authority, the constitution provides certain checks upon the Legislative Assembly:[17] It may not directly authorize scholarships or pensions nor make appropriations that have not arisen following normal budgeting procedures. National ports, docks, and airports must remain under the control of the state, as must water resources, hydrocarbon and radioactive metal deposits, and electrical transmission lines. Legislators may not simultaneously exercise other public functions or hold other posts and may not make contracts with the state. The president may convene special sessions of the Legislative Assembly. Although the power to impeach officials belongs to the assembly, the power to try and to remove them resides with the Supreme Court of Justice.

Laws passed by the assembly must receive the formal sanction of (promulgation by) the executive branch in the form of publication in the official gazette (*Diario Official*). The failure to promulgate a law within ten working days constitutes an executive veto. The executive branch must then return the draft law with stated objections. Should the executive raise constitutional objections to a law passed by the assembly, the Supreme Court of Justice exercises judicial review and may suppress unconstitutional passages.

The Legislative Assembly's leaders are a president and two secretaries, elected annually among the members by simple majority. The powerful assembly president names the members of the body's eight standing commissions (committees) and presides over debate. Annual election of assembly leaders and the possible annual appointment of committee assignments militate against a *diputado*'s spending multiple terms on a particular commission.

The Legislative Assembly has five standing subject area commissions and three standing functional commissions that study proposed legislation and manage the legislature's business.[18] The constitution also authorizes special or ad hoc commissions. The most popular commission assignment is financial affairs (*asuntos hacendarios*), which drafts the national budget. The most powerful is the seven-person special standing commission on drafting and interparliamentary relations, which controls the flow of legislation, rules on motions, and reviews and revises the final text of proposed legislation. The high level of circulation among commissions because of annual reappointment prevents members from acquiring much subject-matter expertise. Staffing for both *diputados* and standing commissions is modest, which also tends to reduce the accumulation of policy expertise. All of these factors combine with the forced turnover of assembly members (no self-succession) to leave the necessarily inexpert legislature at an increasing disadvantage to the executive branch when formulating public policy.

In part because of these limitations, the Costa Rican Legislative Assembly declined sharply in policymaking influence (measured in terms of bills enacted) in comparison to the executive branch between the 1960s and 1980s. In recent decades the assembly has devoted ever more of its time to pork barrel legislation and less to drafting other laws. In sharp contrast, the presidency has issued a growing number of decrees and regulations.[19]

Despite the loss of effective policy influence to the executive, the Legislative Assembly retains great potential power over other branches, in particular through special investigatory commissions.[20] During 1980–1981 a special commission investigated arms trafficking through Costa Rica to leftist rebels in Nicaragua and El Salvador. It found that the administration of President Rodrigo Carazo Odio had helped ship arms and that certain officials had corruptly profited from it. The finding prompted the assembly to pass a new law to regulate commerce in weapons. It also provoked the breakdown of Carazo's legislative coalition, which produced a policy stalemate during the final months of his term. Another legislative commission investigated drug trafficking in Costa Rica in the late 1980s. It found that elements of the judicial police, the Judicial Investigation Organism (Organismo de Investigaciónes Judiciales, or OIJ), had corruptly influenced the sentencing of convicted drug traffickers by some magistrates of the Supreme Court of Justice. The investigation forced three magistrates to resign, generated tightened antinarcotics legislation, and increased assembly oversight of narcotics regulation.[21]

To summarize, through elections Costa Ricans exercise periodic influence over the deputies who make their laws. *Diputados* respond to citizen pressure for pork barrel benefits for their communities. Changing voter preferences have shifted party control of the legislature several times, with at least some effect upon the content of public policy. The PLN held an outright legislative majority during only six of eleven assemblies from 1953 through that elected in 1994 (Table 4.1). In 1998 the PUSC won 27 seats, the PLN 23 seats, and other parties a total of 7 seats. This outcome left the PLN weaker than in the prior assembly and gave the PUSC the most legislative seats. However, as in 1994, it left the president's party without an absolute majority in the assembly, weakening the executive and giving considerable policy influence to a handful of minority parties in the assembly. The law against self-succession assures complete turnover at every election, somewhat democratizing access to the Legislative Assembly.

The Executive Branch

The balance of power between the executive and legislative branches in Costa Rica strongly favored the executive during the period from 1870 through 1948. The 1949 constitution, however, "was designed with one specific purpose: to diminish the powers of the President of the Republic."[22] It succeeded. Despite the framers' imposition of restraints on executive power to a degree unknown elsewhere in Latin America, in recent decades the Costa Rican power pendulum has swung back toward the executive. Indeed, the change has occurred so rapidly that another observer has argued that "Costa Rica changed, in only a decade, from a situation in

TABLE 4.1   Costa Rican Legislative Assembly Elections and Representation, 1953–1998

	Number of Parties Contesting	*Number of Parties Elected*	*Number of Seats to PLN*	*Number of Seats Unity*[a]	*Number of Seats to Others*
1953[b]	4	4	30	–	15
1958[b]	8	5	20	11	14
1962[c]	8	4	29	28	1
1966	5	3	29	26	2
1970	9	4	32	22	3
1974	12	8	27	16	14
1978	15	5	25	27	4
1982	16	5	33	18	6
1986	13	5	29	25[d]	3
1990	14	5	25	29[d]	3
1994	13	6	28	25[d]	4
1998	23	6	23	27[d]	7

[a]Unity (Unidad or Unificación) coalition; did not always fully coalesce.
[b]Assembly had 45 seats until 1962 election, when number rose to 57.
[c]Assembly has 57 seats from 1962 on.
[d]Social Christian Unity Party (Partido Unidad Social Cristiano, or PUSC).

sour ce: Dieter Nohlen, ed., *Enciclopedia electoral latinoamericano y del Caribe* (San José, Costa Rica: Instituto Interamericano de Derechos Humanos, 1993), pp. 192–198; Jorge Rovira Mas, "Costa Rica," *Boletín Electoral Latinoamericano* (January–June, 1994), p. 56; Emilia Mora, "Libertario y PLN con opción otra curul," *La Nación Digital* (February 5, 1998) <http://www.nacion.co.cr/ln_ee/1998/febrero/02/pais1.html>.

which extreme weakness of the executive branch was alleged, to the completely opposite situation of great concentration of that power. . . . Thus it has become a society ruled by a strong presidentialist system."[23] This rapid rise of executive authority has important implications for both the range and depth of democracy.

Costa Rica's president serves a single four-year term and may not be reelected. The president heads the executive branch but shares much authority with cabinet ministers—in administration, making treaties and foreign policy, appointments, budgeting, legislative initiative, and the veto. For instance, in order to veto a law the president must have the assent of a cabinet minister whose responsibilities include the subject matter of the law. The Council of Government (Consejo de Gobierno, or cabinet) enjoys certain important functions independently of the president (to grant clemency, name ambassadors and directors of autonomous agencies, and request the Legislative Assembly to raise military forces or negotiate peace).

The presidency has a few formal powers that may be exercised by the president alone: to name and remove cabinet ministers, to appoint the head and a majority of the directors of autonomous agencies, to serve as the head of state, and to act as the commander in chief of the police and Civil Guard.

Checks upon executive authority by other branches of government include the following: The assembly must pass the budget of the executive branch and may question cabinet ministers and impeach the president. The president must obtain permission from the Legislative Assembly to leave the country. The assembly appoints a national comptroller (*contralor*) to oversee and approve the budget execution of the executive branch, municipalities, and autonomous bureaucracies. The Supreme Court of Justice may exercise judicial review over executive branch decrees, rules, and practices and must judge and may remove executive officials, including the president, if impeached by the assembly.

Despite the many restraints upon Costa Rica's presidency, most observers concur that presidential authority has expanded considerably since the late 1970s.[24] One measure of the absolute increase in Costa Rican executive power may be found in the number of executive rules and decrees issued over recent decades.[25] "The executive branch has a rule-making function that fulfills its responsibility to develop, regulate, and complement legislative action" and also has power to issue decrees and executive orders that expanded markedly in the 1970s.[26] Driven in part by domestic institutional problems, by the economic crisis of the early 1980s, and by the Central American geopolitical crisis of the late 1970s and 1980s, executive decrees and rule making became much more frequent than in the 1960s. From 1960 through 1970, for example, the executive branch issued an average of 239 decrees and regulations per year, but by the period of 1980 through 1990 that number had more than tripled, to 772 per year.[27] Executive power over policy was clearly expanding markedly. Indeed, so greatly has presidential authority increased that some critics view it with alarm:[28]

In 1974 . . . a president of the republic [Daniel Oduber Quirós] discovered that he could utilize legal tools to exercise much greater power, and that power was enlarged in 1978 [during the administration of Rodrigo Carazo Odio] when it began to be wielded with complete disregard of constitutional norms and when the decree was embraced as a medium by which to govern. . . . The controls designed [to restrain the presidency] by the juridical system have proven absolutely inefficacious. . . . The realm of the law has shrunk and that of the executive decree has assumed an exaggerated scope.[29]

As executive power has grown, legislative power has shrunk. As noted above, the Legislative Assembly's legislative production has sharply declined since the 1960s. During the 1960s, average legislative output in laws enacted (199 per year) was similar to the number of executive decrees and regulations; by the 1980s the average number of laws passed fell to only sixty-nine per year. Thus the influence of the executive branch over public policy shifted from rough parity during the 1960s to the executive's issuing eleven times more decrees and regulations than the assembly just two decades later. The executive not only carries out the law, then, but increasingly makes it as the assembly retreats from key policy areas.

The administrative apparatus of the nation consists of centralized ministries that report to the president as well as more than 200 autonomous or decentralized institutions over which the president has little direct control or removal power.[30] These autonomous bureaucracies include the national banks and insurance company, public universities, and various major public utilities (telephones and electricity, water and sewer) and development agencies.

Made autonomous in order to free them from undue political manipulation and to increase their efficiency and technical capacity, the decentralized bureaucracies were originally governed by presidentially appointed directors who were not subject to presidential removal.[31] Many of these agencies enjoyed considerable fiscal autonomy because they operate on constitutionally dedicated revenues or on the revenues from their own services (electricity, telephones). The decentralized bureaucracies have expanded enormously in scope and function. In 1950, for example, all combined had 2,670 employees, but by 1970 there were 29,065—an elevenfold increase.[32] Since the 1970s critics have argued that the autonomous agencies had excessive financial independence (especially to borrow) without adequate legislative or presidential review. The assembly therefore enacted reforms to improve overall interagency planning and coordination and to rein in the autonomous agencies.[33] Their effect, however, was also to increase direct presidential influence over the autonomous bureaucracies.

Overall, the size and functions of the Costa Rican bureaucracy have grown greatly since 1949. In that year Costa Rica had a total of 15,838 public employees, which represented only 6 percent of the nation's economically active population. Six of seven public employees worked in the central ministries, the rest in autonomous bureaucracies. By 1970 there were 50,964 public employees in Costa Rica—almost 10 percent of the economically active population. The number of public employees in the ministries had grown steadily since 1949, but not nearly as fast as that of the autonomous bureaucracies, which now had 37.4 percent of all government employees.[34] This vast expansion of the Costa Rican state and public employment opportunities combined with widespread educational opportunities to provide avenues of social mobility that permitted many Ticos of lower-class origins to reach the middle class.[35]

The framers of the constitution created a weak presidency, but in recent decades presidential power has grown greatly and the executive branch has expanded rapidly in size and scope. Has the simultaneous growth of executive power and weakening of legislative power narrowed the range of Costa Rican democracy? The people's branch of government has less influence over public policy than it once had, and the president and bureaucracy more.

The Judiciary

Independent courts can safeguard democracy by protecting citizens' participatory rights, but Latin American judiciaries are generally not renowned for their independence from executives and legislatures. The 1949 constitution, however, gave the Costa Rican judiciary considerable independence and effective power to restrain the other branches of government.

The constitution substantially reformed and modernized the Costa Rican judiciary and accelerated the growth of the state that had already begun in the 1940s. Compared to its prior powers, the reformed judicial branch gained functional independence from the executive and legislature and financial autonomy through constitutionally dedicated revenues. The expansion of the state and the new social and economic rights of citizens greatly broadened the courts' responsibilities in labor, family, civil service, commercial, and regulatory matters.[36]

In formal terms, the Supreme Court of Justice is the highest court, handling both civil and criminal matters. Justices of the CSJ, appointed by the Legislative Assembly, serve eight-year terms, which are automatically renewed unless the assembly votes (by a two-thirds majority) to deny another term. All other courts are dependencies of the CSJ, which appoints lower court judges. The Supreme Court's powers include judicial review of extant and proposed legislation, hearing appeals from lower courts, and administration of the court system. The CSJ may sit as a plenary body or may divide itself into various smaller appellate panels along functional lines.[37]

Restraints upon the Supreme Court are few. All electoral matters are subject to the sole and final jurisdiction of the Supreme Electoral Tribunal, which wholly insulates elections and their regulation from the courts. The assembly names Supreme Court justices (*magistrados*), fixes the number of justices, and establishes the number, types, and jurisdictions of other courts. CSJ magistrates may not be suspended except for cause, which is done through a secret two-thirds vote of the court itself. Should the Legislative Assembly vote to impeach the president or any member of the assembly, cabinet, or the Supreme Electoral Tribunal, the responsibility for trying the case and for removal resides with the Supreme Court.[38]

The CSJ has largely escaped the corruption and lack of independence of other Latin American high courts. It frequently rules against the government and strongly defends individual rights. Two examples of judicial independence illustrate the CSJ's freedom to challenge other branches of government through judicial review: The court overruled the government's granting of a passport to fugitive financier Robert Vesco in the mid-1970s, despite president José Figueres's heavy-handed personal intervention in favor of Vesco. In the early 1980s, the CSJ also invalidated portions of a press law that restricted the practice of journalism to holders of journalism degrees from the University of Costa Rica. The court ruled that the law violated the 1949 constitution's guarantee of freedom of the press and expression.[39] The ruling permitted a U.S.-trained journalist to work and publish in Costa Rica.

The court system and its responsibilities have expanded rapidly since the late 1940s. Ticos have developed a taste for litigation that may exceed even that of the litigious United States. The volume of cases in Costa Rica's courts, the number of courts, court specialization, and public spending on the judiciary have all grown rapidly.[40] For example, the number of civil and criminal cases handled by the Costa Rican judiciary rose from 68,406 in 1960 to 308,470 in 1990.[41] To handle this growing flood of cases, the Legislative Assembly and CSJ during the 1980s created additional specialized lower courts. To the criminal, civil, and labor law courts extant for decades they added new family law and agrarian law courts. When delays in judicial review on constitutionality became severe in the 1980s, the CSJ added to its own array of appellate panels a new one specializing in constitutional questions.

Political Parties

Political parties, although not formal institutions of government, play critical roles in democracies. Organized to capture and hold ruling power through elections, parties may promote programs shaped by an ideological vision of justice or of a preferred social order. Two important questions about how parties may contribute to democracy are whether they are committed to democratic rules in the national arena and whether they operate democratically internally. Scholars have observed that democracies with two strong but moderate contending parties (as opposed to a fragmented party system or one dominated by radical parties) tend to be fairly stable over the long term.

Costa Rica's constitution guarantees citizens "the right to group themselves into parties [that may] take part in national politics, as long as these commit themselves in their programs to respect the constitutional order."[42] Because representation in the Legislative Assembly and municipal councils is based upon multimember districts (the provinces and *municipios*) and is proportional to each party's share of the vote, some smaller parties and regional parties tend to win office and survive. Indeed, the average number of parties contesting elections to the Legislative Assembly rose from an average of six in the 1950s to roughly fourteen parties in the 1980s and 1990s (see Table 4.1). However, the number of parties elected to the assembly has been more stable; it ranged from three to five in the 1950s and 1960s, peaked at eight in 1974, then stabilized at five or six thereafter.

National Liberation Party

One party has been preeminent in the Costa Rican political scene since the civil war, despite the prevalence of multiple parties. Formed in 1951 by the leaders and followers of the victorious National Liberation movement, the social democratic National Liberation Party has held an absolute majority of seats in six of eleven legislative assemblies elected between 1953 and 1994 (inclusive) (Table 4.1) and won the presidency seven of eleven times (Table 4.2). In 1998 Miguel Angel Rodríguez of the PUSC was elected president, reaffirming the pattern of party alternation in the presidency. The social class base of the PLN is diverse, but the bulk of PLN support comes from middle-class and some working-class elements.

The PLN's original ideology embraced social democratic principles, including solidifying democracy in Costa Rica, giving the state an important role in the national economy, making income distribution more egalitarian, expanding social services, and increasing the size and influence of the middle class. This general

TABLE 4.2 Costa Rican Presidential Elections, 1948–1998

	Number of Presidential Candidates	Victorious Candidate (Party)	Winner's Share of Vote (%)	Winner's Party with Legislative Majority
1948[a]	2	Otilio Ulate Blanco (PUN)	55.3	yes
1953	2	José Figueres Ferrer (PLN)	64.7	yes
1958	3	Mario Echandi Jiménez (PUN)	46.4	no
1962	4	Francisco J. Orlich (PLN)	50.3	yes
1966	2	José J. Trejos Fernández (Unificación)	50.5	no
1970	6	José Figueres Ferrer (PLN)	54.8	yes
1974	8	Daniel Oduber Quirós (PLN)	43.5	no
1978	8	Rodrigo Carazo Odio (Unidad)	50.5	no
1982	6	Luis A. Monge Alvarez (PLN)	58.8	yes
1986	6	Oscar Arias Sánchez (PLN)	52.3	yes
1990	7	Rafael A. Calderón F. (PUSC)	51.4	yes
1994	7	José M. Figueres Olsen (PLN)	49.6	no
1998	12	Miguel A. Rodríguez Echeverría (PUSC)	46.9	no

[a]Term begins in 1949 after National Liberation junta and constituent assembly.

sources: Dieter Nohlen, ed., *Enciclopedia electoral latinoamericano y del Caribe* (San José, Costa Rica: Instituto Interamericano de Derechos Humanos, 1993), pp. 201–204; Jorge Rovira Mas, "Costa Rica," *Boletín Electoral Latinoamericano* (January–June, 1994), p. 51; "Central American Fact Sheet, June 1997," *Mesoamerica,* June 1997, p. 7; Adriana Quirós Robinson and Juan Fernando Lara, "Rodríguez a la cabeza según encuesta de CID-Gallup para Telenoticias," *La Nación Digital,* February 1, 1998, at <http://www.nacion. co.cr>; Tribunal Supremo de Elecciones, "Cómputo de la Elección para Presidente y Vicepresidentes" (February 5, 1998) <http://www.tse.go.cr/Tribunal/presidente.ASP>; Emilia Mora, "Libertario y PLN con opción otra curul," *La Nación Digital* (February 5, 1998) <http://www.nacion.co.cr/ln_ee/1998/febrero/05/pais5.html>; "Rodríguez Presidente," *La Nación Digital* (February 2, 1998) <http://www.nacion.co.cr/ln_ee/1998/ febrero/02/pais1.html>.

philosophy shaped the development of Costa Rican society for thirty years. More recently the PLN has adjusted its national development strategy, forced by the 1980s economic crisis and international pressures to adopt a more limited vision of the state's role in the economy.

> Worried lest the developmental progress of the 1950–1980 period collapse, [the PLN] managed to bring about a restructuring of Costa Rican society, especially its production system, without subjecting it to brusque or accelerated changes, tilting instead toward negotiations with international agencies in order to make the transformations gradual and guided by a spirit more pragmatic than doctrinaire.[43]

These pragmatic adjustments have shifted the PLN's effective ideology from its original social democratic (center-left) orientation toward the ideological center. By the late 1980s, it had adopted a much stronger neoliberal, free market orientation than it originally held, a position quite similar to that of its major opponent, the Social Christian Unity Party (Partido Unidad Social Cristiana, or PUSC). This change probably reflected the rise of financial-sector interests within the party's leadership, at least partly displacing the industrial-sector interests that had prevailed among PLN leaders for decades.[44]

Social Christian Unity Party

Opposition to the PLN for three decades has centered around a coalition of conservative and centrist parties that have assumed the label of Unity (Unidad) or Unification (Unificación). When the Unity coalition has pulled together much of the opposition, it has often defeated the PLN. In 1983 most of the usual Unity coalition partners forged a new party, the Social Christian Unity Party. The PUSC has since emerged as Costa Rica's second great national political force. Culminating its rise, the PUSC defeated the PLN in both presidential and legislative elections in 1990. The PUSC's base includes supporters and activists from various classes, but its leadership comes from both traditional and modern agroexport groups and the commercial bourgeoisie. With Rafael Angel Calderón Fournier as its presidential nominee in 1986 and 1990, the PUSC drew working-class support like that once won for the Republican Party by the nominee's father and Costa Rica's former president, populist Calderón Guardia.[45]

The PUSC has very deep social Christian roots in the Catholic Union Party of the late 1800s, the Reform Party of the 1920s, and Calderón Guardia's movement during the 1940s. Although this tradition "informs the party's rhetoric, its effective ideological foundation is primarily neoliberalism, although moderated by the centrism that underlies Costa Rica's predominant political culture."[46]

Regional Parties and Left Parties

Other important political forces in Costa Rica include three regional parties and parties of the left. In 1974 the regional party Carthaginian Agricultural Union

(Unión Agrícola Cartaginesa, or UAC), representing agrarian interests from the province of Cartago, captured one seat in the Legislative Assembly, a victory it repeated in every subsequent legislative election except 1982. The success of the UAC apparently spawned other regional party imitators, but none has approached its record. The best other regional parties have done was to win a single seat: Alajuelan Democratic Action (Acción Alajuelense Democrática) captured one seat from Alajuela in 1982, and the Valle del General Union (Unión Generaleña), representing the southern Valle del General, won a seat in 1990. Regional and rural interests have also gained ground as the PLN has included more local and regional leaders in its legislative slate to strengthen its electoral base in the provinces.[47]

The most significant leftist movement has been the coalition known as the United People's Party (Partido Pueblo Unido, or PPU), consisting of the old pro-Soviet Popular Vanguard (Communist) Party, the Socialist Party, and the People's Revolutionary Party. Despite their deep involvement in unions and their role in promoting periodic labor unrest, Costa Rica's leftist parties have generally made reformist rather than revolutionary demands. In a 1995 urban survey, for instance, Costa Ricans describing themselves as strongly leftist (only twenty-four of 505 respondents) reported no significant differences from centrist and rightist respondents in their support for democratic norms.[48]

Electoral support for the left has come mainly from the southwestern banana zones around Golfito, from some students and intellectuals, and from San José's working-class neighborhoods. Before 1970 left parties captured only a single seat in the assembly (the 1962 election). Left representation grew to two seats in each of the 1970 and 1974 elections. It peaked as the left parties won four seats among them in both the 1978 and 1982 elections and then declined to two seats in 1986 and one in 1990, then fell to none in 1994.[49]

Costa Rica's left has been very divided. The communist PVP split in 1985 in the wake of the unsuccessful 1984 banana strike. The PPU coalition survived under that name for several elections between 1978 and 1990 but suffered schisms and sharp variations in the number of seats won. Despite its relative freedom to organize and contest elections, the Costa Rican left has suffered from a persistent and vocal anticommunism in the national press. The left's last great blow—perhaps fatal for Legislative Assembly representation—came with its loss of sponsorship and a model when the Soviet Union collapsed at the cold war's end.

In the 1998 election, some leftist elements, critics of the cost and quality of campaigns, and others disgruntled by the ideological convergence of the PLN with the PUSC, recent economic restructuring, and an economic slowdown of 1996–1997 mounted a campaign urging abstention from voting. Among them, the Sovereignty Group (Grupo Soberanía) employed the slogan "You can't trust anyone, so don't vote for anyone." Although their recommendation to abstain from voting or deface ballots in protest aroused sharp criticism, preelection opinion polls reflected popular disillusionment with the major parties and their candidates, and even former president Oscar Arias of the PUSC issued a stinging critique of the campaign and parties just before the vote.[50]

The Party System

On the face of it, the Costa Rican party system seems to be evolving toward greater complexity.[51] The number of parties contesting legislative elections has risen from a mean of around six before 1970 to more than fourteen since 1970 (Table 4.1). Similarly, the number of candidates seeking the presidency has risen steadily—from 2.6 per race prior to 1970 to 7.5 thereafter (Table 4.2). However, closer inspection reveals that the number of parties that actually win assembly seats has risen only slightly—from a mean of 4.0 before 1970 to a mean of 5.5 parties per election from 1970 on (Table 4.1). In presidential elections the combined vote of the PLN and PUSC/Unification has been above 90 percent in eight of eleven elections since the civil war. In the 1986, 1990, and 1994 elections, the combined PLN and PUSC presidential vote total has averaged 98 percent. Ticos angry about the economy, neoliberal reforms, and major party posturing gave the PLN and PUSC a noticeably lower combined vote total in 1998, but it was still about 91 percent.[52] These data, then, do not really suggest an argument for any meaningful increase of diversity of the party system. Only two groups effectively vie for the presidency: the social democratic PLN and the Unity coalition/PUSC. Thus by the 1990s Costa Rica had become virtually bipolar—dominated by alternation in power of the moderate PLN and PUSC.

One reason for the alternation of parties in power is that many voters' tend not to identify consistently with a particular political party and to be strongly oriented toward candidate characteristics (rather than party) in choosing how to vote. Even many party loyalists refuse to express a party preference when polled. More important, some 60 percent of strong party identifiers have been found—their party allegiance notwithstanding—to endorse a change of ruling party every four years.[53]

Despite a growing array of presidential and legislative parties on the ballot over recent decades, Costa Rica's two great centrist forces/parties have alternated in power several times. Although the PLN has succeeded itself in office twice, it has never won three successive presidencies. John Peeler contends that "it is inconceivable that liberal democracy could have been maintained in [Costa Rica] without . . . the regular practice of alternation of parties in the presidency."[54] Costa Ricans by and large endorse party alternation in power, and many contribute to it by deliberately voting for the party that is out of power.

How deep is the commitment of Costa Rica's major political parties to democracy? In their formal ideology, both the PLN and PUSC profess commitment to democracy. But what of their followers and leaders? Carvajal compared party leaders to followers in a 1971 survey and found that elites wanted to change the political system much more than followers, but that only one in seven leaders favored revolutionary change.[55] As to party supporters versus other citizens, a 1995 survey of urban Costa Ricans found no significant difference among Costa Ricans' commitment to democratic norms whether or not they had been active in a campaign, attempted to persuade others how to vote, party oriented in their vote choice, or identified themselves with either the far left or far right of the national political spectrum. Thus Costa Rican partisans and the major parties and their leaders appear committed to democratic rules of the game.

Suffrage and Election Administration

Free and fair elections constitute an essential element of representative democracy because they permit citizens to select their rulers. Honest and open elections allow citizens to evaluate and discuss their rulers, parties, and programs and to endorse incumbents or to organize and vote to replace them. High election quality, therefore, is essential to the breadth and depth of democracy.

Costa Rica repeatedly reformed its election system prior to 1949 (see Chapter 3), but none of the measures adopted brought either clean elections or stability. Nevertheless, certain of these early reforms contained the germ of an idea that finally matured in the 1949 constitution: In order to conduct honest elections, the electoral authority had to be truly free from manipulation by parties and the government. The 1949 constitution again reformed the Costa Rican electoral apparatus—this time seeking to assure that no one could distort the true choice of the electorate. This was accomplished by creating a fully independent electoral authority, the Supreme Electoral Tribunal, with "exclusive responsibility for the organization, direction, and vigilance over acts relative to suffrage [as well as] independence in carrying out its responsibility."[56] The TSE normally consists of three magistrates and six *suplentes* (substitutes) but expands to five magistrates by adding two from among the *suplentes* during election periods. The Supreme Court of Justice appoints TSE magistrates and *suplentes* for staggered six-year terms.

To protect its independence and prevent legislative manipulation, the TSE has constitutional authority to review and approve draft electoral legislation before the Legislative Assembly. The constitution shields both the TSE and the elections from legislative interference. To override the advice of the TSE, the assembly must act by a two-thirds vote of all fifty-seven members. The constitution prohibits the assembly from enacting electoral legislation for six months before or four months after an election.[57]

The TSE operates all national electoral organisms, including the national Civil Registry, which maintains electoral rolls and issues Costa Ricans their mandatory national identity and voter registration cards (*cédulas de identidad*). The constitution empowers the TSE as the sole authority to investigate and rule on charges of political partiality by public employees, to file criminal charges against persons violating electoral laws, to control the police and other security forces during election periods in order "to assure that electoral processes develop in conditions of guarantees and unrestricted liberties,"[58] and to review and validate electoral results.

Under electoral law and by its own regulations, the TSE monitors political campaign compliance with the law and oversees executive branch neutrality in campaigns. It also administers Costa Rica's program of public financing of election campaign costs. So excellent is the TSE's conduct of elections that its structure and practice have provided a model for electoral reform in other nations. Indeed, the Supreme Electoral Tribunal "has all but eradicated the incidence of fraud in Costa Rican elections. Costa Rica's reputation for fairness and honesty in elections is one of the highest in the world."[59]

Voting Requirements

Because voting is considered both a right and a duty, Costa Rican citizens eighteen years or older are required to vote under mild (but seldom imposed) penalties for not voting. The constitution requires the government to inscribe all citizens in the Civil Registry and provide them with a *cédula* with their photograph so that they may vote. Because registration as a voter and a citizen for most legal and business purposes are identical, virtually all Costa Ricans register to vote. Voting must occur at the polling place nearest a citizen's legal residence, a provision that effectively bars absentee voting and causes many Ticos to travel in order to vote. Elections must be conducted under "effective guarantees of liberty, order, purity and impartiality by governing authorities."[60] Minorities are guaranteed representation. Since 1960, when voting became mandatory, turnout in all elections has exceeded 80 percent of registered voters. Over 45 percent of the entire Costa Rican population voted in the 1986, 1990, and 1994 elections (Table 3.4).

Campaigns and Elections

Every fourth year beginning in 1958 Costa Rica has held its national elections on the first Sunday in February.[61] All public officials are elected simultaneously for coterminous four-year periods of office. Costa Rica's election code formally limits campaigns to the six-month period prior to elections. In fact, however, the campaign actually begins informally as early as two years before the election, when possible presidential candidates ("precandidates") within the PLN and PUSC begin jockeying for position. For example, large "private" meetings of partisan groups gather to promote and endorse "precandidates" long before the campaign officially opens.

Candidates

Obtaining a nomination for public office in Costa Rica, especially for the presidency, requires considerable time and energy. Government ministers and other aspiring presidential nominees make major policy speeches and media appearances to test campaign themes and build momentum toward nomination by their party. The PLN nominates its presidential candidate in a closed primary by a direct vote of the party's active members, with the result ratified at the party's national assembly. PLN provincial assemblies nominate candidates for the Legislative Assembly, also ratified by the PLN national assembly. Candidates for municipal councils are chosen by PLN cantonal assemblies. Thus there is considerable democratic rank-and-file participation in the choice of the PLN presidential nominee. Nevertheless, ballot position on the PLN legislative slate (critical to electoral success)[62] is assigned by the PLN national assembly, which tends to be dominated by party insiders.

The PUSC nominates its presidential candidate using a party primary system and a national convention similar to that of the PLN. Other parties' presidential and legislative nominations tend to be less democratic—usually made by insiders in the organizations' executive councils.

Campaign Finance

To reduce the potential for wealth to affect election campaigns, the Costa Rican government subsidizes much of the parties' election costs. The public campaign finance system, however, does not benefit all parties equally. Any party that wins more than 5 percent of the vote in a given election may receive public funds (*la deuda política*) to reimburse campaign costs. In recent years only the PLN and PUSC have met this criterion. Thus the larger parties (based on performance in the previous election) receive most of the public subsidies in advance of the campaign. They therefore avoid having to borrow campaign funds in anticipation of reimbursement at the campaign's end, and they do not have to raise all their funds privately, as small parties do. The government may expend up to 2 percent of the national budget on funding for the campaign, sufficient in recent elections to pour several million dollars into PUSC and PLN campaign coffers.

Beyond public funding, there are no effective limits on "private campaign donations and no ceilings on a party's total campaign spending."[63] All spending on "precampaign candidacies" (seeking the presidential nomination within a party) must be completely privately financed. For the general election campaign, the PLN and PUSC's backing by wealthy economic interests gives them an enormous advantage over smaller parties in obtaining direct private funding.

The campaign finance system obviously strongly and consistently favors the two major parties that can raise private funds easily and (unlike small parties) receive most of their public subsidy during the campaign. It is not surprising that efforts to reform the system by eliminating the larger parties' public funding advantage have failed in an Legislative Assembly dominated by the major parties. Observers and critics have long complained that Costa Rica's mixed public-private campaign finance system has corrupting tendencies upon the parties and their programs. During campaigns both major parties regularly accuse each other of having sold out to economically powerful special interests.

Competing for Office

Costa Rican election campaigns have traditionally involved high levels of "retail" politics in which candidates meet personally with large numbers of citizens at ral-

PHOTO 4.1   Youthful supporters of Rafael Angel Calderón Fournier (photo by Julio Laínez, courtesy *Tico Times*)

lies, meetings, and other public events. The major parties also have promoted extensive direct citizen involvement in campaigns (Photo 4.1). They have organized campaign activities by voting districts, within government offices, and even among university student organizations. They encourage partisans to canvass within their neighborhoods or groups and to display party banners in traditional colors (for instance, green and white for the PLN). Campaigns have slogans, catchy jingles, and songs.

> Political propaganda occupies much of the space and time of the mass media. The parties' slogans are painted in corresponding colors on walls, [roadside] boulders, and posters. The names of some candidates are painted on the highways. . . . Party flags float above homes, trees, and even fences, cars, and bicycles. . . . Paid advertisements with lists of party supporters appear in the newspapers. Drivers honk their horns in patterns that stand for their favorite candidates.[64]

All this makes for colorful and enthusiastic election campaigns in Costa Rica. With such a small populace and compact territory, Costa Rican candidates easily reach out to the public at community events festooned with party banners and the red, white, and blue national colors and enlivened by school bands and local personalities. Candidates strive to visit every community, to be considered one of the common people, and to avoid any appearance of arrogance, the cardinal sin of Costa Rican politics. The acknowledged master of this technique was charismatic PLN founder José Figueres Ferrer. Although a wealthy farmer, educated abroad, highly literate, and a friend of world leaders, "Don Pepe," as he was known, could joke and use idiomatic expressions and a folksy manner in a way that reflected admiration for ordinary Ticos.

Costa Ricans generally campaign with enthusiasm but also with civility. Disturbances and violence are rare. The Supreme Electoral Tribunal investigates and quickly resolves complaints about violations of campaign laws and interparty disputes. During the 1978 campaign, for instance, religious leaders took out newspaper advertisements declaring communism incompatible with Catholicism. A quick complaint to the TSE by the leftist PPU led to the prohibition of propaganda utilizing religious themes (a practiced banned by the constitution).[65]

Since the 1970s, impersonal, "wholesale" techniques of electioneering have replaced much of the person-to-person "retail" campaigning. Candidates depend more upon public opinion polling than upon leadership and party ideology to shape their messages and their media strategies. The major parties employ foreign campaign and media advisers, and Costa Rican campaign managers and pollsters have become more skilled. Television has grown steadily more important as a campaign medium, substantially raising the cost of an effective campaign and leaving poorer parties badly disadvantaged in the competition for votes. The increasing use of television has also reduced the importance of personal appearances and public campaigning for both the PLN and PUSC. Critics have for years lamented the decline of direct contact with citizens during campaigns and characterized the rising cost of campaigns as "shameful."[66]

Presidential campaigns usually focus more on personalities than substantive policy or ideology. Campaigns also emphasize emotionally charged themes, "each candidate trying to convince the electorate that he is the truest democrat, the most authentic Costa Rican, and, except for obvious exceptions, the most sincere anticommunist."[67] Candidates invoke such positive ideas as peace and civic virtue and democracy. They attribute to their opponents a long list of evils: corruption, violence, unconstitutionality, leftist or rightist extremism, and leanings toward planning, socialism, and bureaucracy, to name but a few.

Candidates tend to avoid public mention of their opponents' family, personal, or sexual lives. Such matters and all manner of rumors are nevertheless widely discussed informally by individuals, a process Ticos euphemistically name after the archetypal neighborhood gossip, "Doña Viña." Campaign organizations themselves spread campaign rumors by word of mouth. Despite the rather polite tradition of the formal public campaigns, the 1994 and 1998 presidential campaigns were infamous for their ugliness and acrimony. PLN and PUSC campaign consultants from the United States and Venezuela, both "experts in smear campaigns," coached the highly personal, vitriolic mudslinging in 1994. Accusations of corruption, vote buying, participation in a murder, militarism, and manipulated polls flew between PLN candidate José María Figueres and PUSC nominee Miguel Angel Rodríguez. Similar invective marked the 1998 contest between the PUSC's Miguel Angel Rodríguez Echeverría and the PLN's José Miguel Corrales Bolaños.[68]

Voting

Election day in Costa Rica is a great national celebration or *fiesta cívica* (civic holiday) marked by a carnival atmosphere at polling places. The arrival of a candidate to vote usually provokes a shower of confetti and jubilation from the supporters of that party.

Voting procedures are carefully designed to eliminate fraud and promote the accuracy of the vote count. An unpaid local electoral junta (or board) named by the TSE operates each of the nation's 500 polling places. Voting materials are delivered by the TSE, checked by the junta members, and kept under observation to prevent tampering until election day. A poll watcher from each party may observe the voting and ballot counting at each polling site.

A voter determines where to vote according to published lists of polling places and must present a valid *cédula* there. When confirmed to be on the voter list, each voter receives three ballots signed by members of the electoral junta, one each for the presidential, Legislative Assembly, and municipal council election. In a private booth, the voter dips a thumb in a special purple ink and marks the space on each ballot for the preferred party (Photo 4.2). Folded ballots are deposited in a separate box for each race. Finally, before leaving, the voter dips an index finger in purple ink to demonstrate having voted and to guard against any attempt to vote again. When the polls close, the junta tallies each race, notifies the TSE of the results, then forwards all ballots and materials to the TSE in San José for a definitive and final formal recount.

Ticos are justifiably proud of the excellence and fairness of their electoral apparatus. Indeed, other countries in Central America have implicitly or explicitly recognized the high quality of the Costa Rican election system. Costa Rican advisers have been sought by other countries when setting up new election procedures. Other isthmian nations have adopted key features of the Costa Rican system—a fully independent election authority and details of election apparatus, conduct, and administration—as they moved toward democratic governance. Although elections alone neither constitute nor ensure democracy, as Costa Rica's own history so amply demonstrates, free and fair elections are necessary for democracy at the level of the nation-state.

Conclusions

Costa Rica appears far ahead of most of the rest of Latin America in its consolidation of formal institutions for consistent and reliable democratic rules of the politi-

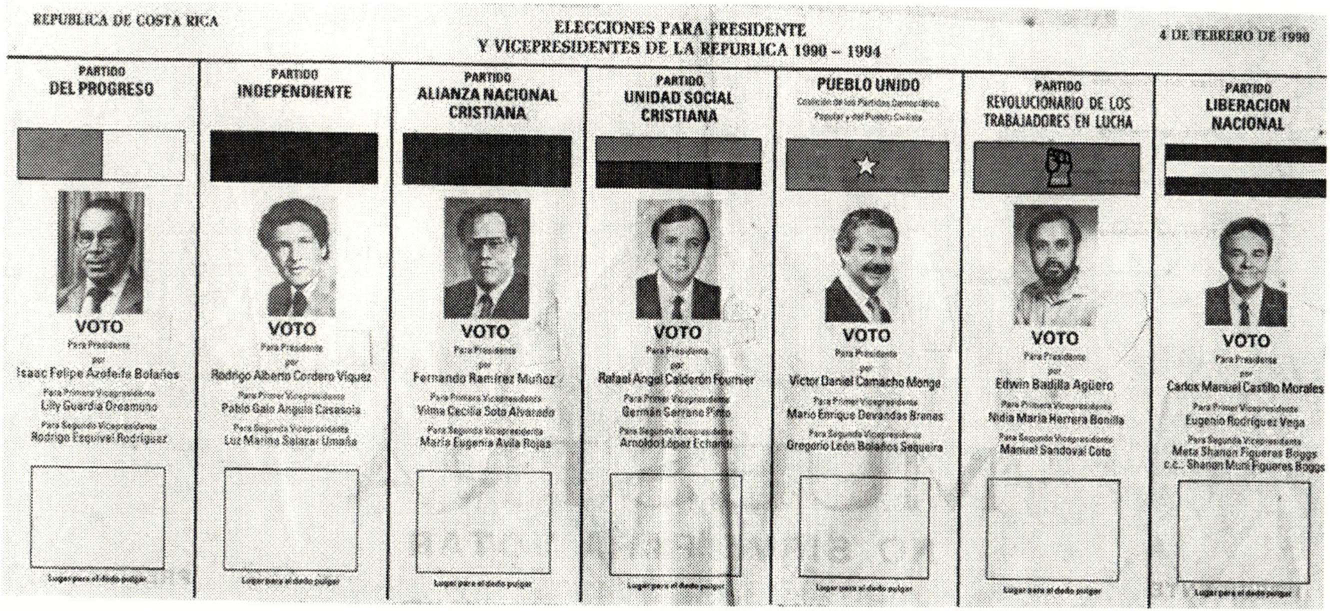

PHOTO 4.2   A presidential election ballot, 1990 (photo courtesy *Tico Times*)

cal game. It has a strong and independent legislature and courts and an executive branch subject to meaningful checks and balances. The independent election system consistently delivers high-quality elections that accurately reflect popular preferences at the polls. Two stable, moderate parties with democratically oriented followers and leaders dominate the multiparty system. The 1949 constitution provides, and government generally respects, extensive political rights that permit and encourage citizens to participate in politics. The absence of a standing army eliminates the menace of militarism to constitutional rule, freedom, and civil society. There are, in short, few formal barriers to broad and deep democracy in Costa Rica.

Within this generally excellent panorama, however, there exist certain troubling features. The power of the executive branch to make policy and to control formerly decentralized bureaucracies has grown markedly in recent decades. The scope and volume of legislative policymaking have eroded as executive power has risen. Critics worry that this shift in Costa Rica's executive-legislative power balance now leaves the presidency subject to too little meaningful legislative or judicial restraint.

The two major political parties have become more alike as the National Liberation Party has drifted toward the ideological center and the left has declined, resulting in less policy choice for voters. Finally, the modernization of political campaigns in Costa Rica has brought poll-driven election tactics and propaganda. The major parties' increasing reliance upon television to reach voters has eroded the traditionally high level of face-to-face campaign activity and driven up campaign costs, making the parties more dependent on private funding. Dissidents encouraged abstention in the 1998 election with some success, as turnout among frustrated voters apparently declined to 71 percent that year from 82 percent in 1994 (Table 3.4). This sharp decline prompted considerable speculation about its meaning for the political system among Tico politicians and pundits.

What is the balance between these positive and negative traits of Costa Rican politics? To some extent the problems cited may well be reducing the depth of democracy. Although these problems are real, Costa Rica is certainly not alone in having them. Indeed, most stable democracies have in recent decades experienced growing concentrations of executive authority, the erosion of personal electoral politics and civil society, and the noxious effects of high costs and television upon electoral politics. On balance, however, Costa Rica's institutional arrangements provide a free and stable electoral regime in which citizens may participate in politics without fear of repression.

Notes

1. *Constitución Política de la República de Costa Rica* (hereafter referred to as "Constitution") (San José, Costa Rica: Imprenta Nacional, 1978), preamble, p. 5.

2. Ibid., title IV, article 32, p. 13.

3. Ibid., title I, article 12, p. 8. Article 12 continues: "Only by continental agreement or for the national defense may military forces be organized; those forces that shall exist shall

always remain subject to civil authority; they shall not deliberate, demonstrate, or make declarations in individual or collective form."

4. Fernando Volio Jiménez, *El militarismo en Costa Rica y otros ensayos* (San José, Costa Rica: Libro Libre, 1985), pp. 13–85; Orlando Salazar Mora, *El apogeo de la República Liberal en Costa Rica, 1870–1914* (San José: Editorial Universidad de Costa Rica, 1990), pp. 271–283.

5. Constitution, title IV, pp. 11–15.

6. Ibid., title IV, article 48, p. 15.

7. Ibid., title VI, article 75, p. 19.

8. Ibid., title IV, article 28, p. 12.

9. Ibid., title V, article 50, p. 16. All other items in this section are drawn from ibid., articles 50–74, pp. 16–19.

10. U.S. Department of State, *Country Reports on Human Rights Practices* (Washington, D.C.: U.S. Government Printing Office, 1981), p. 395.

11. Constitution, title IX, article 105, p. 28.

12. Reapportionment of representation among the provinces occurs after each census.

13. All references to constitutional provisions regarding the Legislative Assembly drawn from Constitution, title IX, pp. 28–38. See also Hugo Alfonso Muñoz, *La Asamblea Legislativa en Costa Rica* (San José: Editorial Costa Rica, 1977), and Carlos José Gutiérrez, *El funcionamiento del sistema jurídico* (San José, Costa Rica: Editorial Juricentro, 1979), pp. 61–107.

14. Mario Echandi, "El poder legislativo en Costa Rica," pp. 43–50, and Rodolfo Cerdas, "El poder legislativo en Costa Rica," pp. 51–62, both in Asociación Nacional de Fomento Económico (ANFE), *El modelo político costarricense* (San José, Costa Rica: ANFE, 1984).

15. Muñoz, *La Asamblea*, pp. 94–112.

16. Ibid., pp. 62–69.

17. Ibid., pp. 104–122.

18. Subject commissions are: governmental and administration, economics, finances, social affairs, and legal affairs. The functional (special permanent) commissions are honors, books and documents, and the powerful drafting and interparliamentary relations (rules); see ibid., pp. 77–85.

19. Carlos José Gutiérrez, "Cambios en el sistema jurídico costarricense," in José Manuel Villasuso, ed., *El nuevo rostro de Costa Rica* (San José, Costa Rica: Centro de Estudios Democráticos de América Latina, 1992), pp. 359–384. Gutiérrez shows that the mean number of laws passed per year by the assembly fell from 199 during the 1960s to only sixtynine during the 1980s, whereas the number of executive decrees nearly tripled during the same period.

20. Muñoz, *La Asamblea*, pp. 82–84.

21. Gutiérrez, *El funcionamiento*, pp. 367–368.

22. Carlos José Gutiérrez Gutiérrez, "Sistema presidencialista y sistema parlamentario," in ANFE, *El modelo político costarricense*, pp. 23–31; quote from p. 27; see also Gutiérrez, *El funcionamiento*, pp. 109–150.

23. Miguel Angel Rodríguez Echeverría, "El poder político y el poder económico," in ANFE, *El modelo político costarricense*, pp. 153–165.

24. Fernando Guier Esquivel, "Sistema presidencialista y sistema parlamentario," pp. 13–22, in ANFE, *El modelo político costarricense,* and Gutiérrez Gutiérrez, "Sistema presidencialista," pp. 23–31.

25. The 1949 constitution recognizes certain legislative and rule-making authority for the executive in article 140, (p. 46), which states that "Decrees, accords, resolutions, and orders of the executive branch in order to be valid require the signatures of the president of the republic and of the minister concerned with the subject [*el Ministro del ramo*]."

26. Gutiérrez, "Cambios en el sistema," p. 369.

27. Ibid., pp. 369–370.

28. Gutiérrez Gutiérrez, "Sistema presidencialista," pp. 28–30; Guier Esquivel, "Sistema presidencialista," pp. 20–22. In *El funcionamiento*, pp. 139–142, Gutiérrez reports ascending decree and rule making by the executive since the early 1950s.

29. Gutiérrez Gutiérrez, "Sistema presidencialista," p. 29.

30. Constitution, title XIV, p. 58.

31. Rodríguez Echeverría, "Poder político," p. 160, notes that in constitutional reforms during the late 1960s the Legislative Assembly sharply curtailed the independence of autonomous bureaucracies from the presidency by giving presidents the authority to appoint four of seven directors to boards upon taking office and to replace the chief administrator.

32. Gutiérrez, *El funcionamiento*, p. 121.

33. Guido Fernández, "Descentralización administrativa o funcional," pp. 123–130; Rafael Calderón Fournier, "Descentralización administrativa o funcional," pp. 107–113; and Rodríguez Echeverría, "Poder político," pp. 153–165, all in ANFE, *El modelo político costarricense*; Wilburg Jiménez Castro, "Cambios ocurridos en las instituciones públicas costarricenses," in Villasuso, *El nuevo rostro*, pp. 385–395.

34. Gutiérrez, *El funcionamiento*, p. 121.

35. Ibid., pp. 118–119.

36. Gutiérrez, "Cambios en el sistema,", pp. 362–383.

37. Constitution, title XI, pp. 48–51.

38. Constitution, title IX, article 121, paragraphs 9 and 10, pp. 33–34.

39. "All may communicate their thoughts by word or in writing and publish them without prior censorship." Constitution, title IV, article 29, p. 12.

40. Gutiérrez, *El funcionamiento*, pp. 150–239.

41. Gutiérrez, "Cambios en el sistema," pp. 377–383. Overall case volume grew markedly over the three decades of this study, but criminal cases expanded fastest, from 50.3 percent of all cases in 1960 to 64.0 percent of all cases in 1990 (pp. 377–378).

42. Constitution, title VIII, article 93, p. 25.

43. Jorge Rovira Mas, "Costa Rica," *Boletín Electoral Latinoamericano* (January-June 1994), p. 50; see also p. 49.

44. Regine Stiechen, "Cambios en la orientación política-ideológica de los partidos políticos en la década de los '80," in Villasuso, *El nuevo rostro*, pp. 265–275.

45. Bernhard Thibaut, "Costa Rica," in Dieter Nohlen, ed., *Enciclopedia electoral latinoamericano y del Caribe* (San José, Costa Rica: Instituto Interamericano de Derechos Humanos, 1993), p. 184; Stiechen, "Cambios," pp. 265–276; Oscar Aguilar B., "Una nueva vía política social-cristiana," pp. 277–286; and Gutiérrez, "Cambios en el sistema," pp. 375–377, all in Villasuso, *El nuevo rostro*.

46. Rovira Mas, "Costa Rica," pp. 51–52. See also Stiechen, "Cambios," pp. 265–275.

47. Cerdas, "El poder legislativo," pp. 54–55.

48. This survey of 505 citizens, financed by the Heinz Foundation and University of Pittsburgh Latin American Center, was conducted under my direction in the urban centers of Costa Rica's *meseta central* in 1995. See Chapter 6, note 2, for methodological details.

49. Rovira Mas, "Costa Rica," p. 56.

50. Guillermo Escofet, "'Don't Vote' Drive Urged," *Tico Times,* January 27, 1998, at <http://www.ticotimes.co.cr>; "Protesta contra el voto" and Rónald Matute, "Oscar Arias censura campaña," both in *La Nación Digital,* January 27, 1998, at <http://www.nacion.co.cr>.

51. Ronald H. McDonald and J. Mark Ruhl, *Party Politics and Elections in Latin America* (Boulder: Westview Press, 1989), pp. 169–182; Stiechen, "Cambios," pp. 265–275.

52. Nohlen, "Costa Rica," pp. 201–205; Rovira Mas, "Costa Rica," p. 51. The 1998 combined PLN-PUSC vote count is based on the results with over 90 percent of precincts counted, from Tribunal Supremo de Elecciones, "Votos para Presidente y Vicepresidentes en todo el País," *Computo de las Elecciones* (February 2, 1998) <http://www.tse.go.cr/graficos/presidente.ASP>.

53. Mario Carvajal Herrera, *Actitudes políticas del costarricense* (San José: Editorial Costa Rica, 1978), pp. 156–157; and Mavis Hiltunen de Biesanz, Richard Biesanz, and Karen Zubris de Biesanz, *Los costarricenses* (San José, Costa Rica: Editorial Universidad Estatal a Distancia, 1979), pp. 587–588.

54. John A. Peeler, *Latin American Democracies: Colombia, Costa Rica, Venezuela* (Chapel Hill: University of North Carolina Press, 1985), p. 113.

55. Carvajal Herrera, *Actitudes políticas,* pp. 147–148.

56. Constitution, title VIII, article 99, p. 25.

57. Ibid., article 97, pp. 24–25.

58. Ibid., article 102, pp. 26–27.

59. Charles D. Ameringer, *Democracy in Costa Rica* (New York: Praeger, 1982), p. 51.

60. Constitution, title VIII, article 95, pp. 22–23.

61. This section draws heavily on Biesanz et al., *Los costarricenses,* pp. 577–588; Carvajal Herrera, *Actitudes políticas,* pp. 85–111; and McDonald and Ruhl, *Party Politics,* pp. 177–182.

62. In multimember electoral districts, ballot position or order is critical to a candidate's chance of election. For instance, if a party gets half the vote in a province with eight *diputados,* the first four candidates on its list are elected and the last four lose out.

63. McDonald and Ruhl, *Party Politics,* p. 178.

64. Biesanz et al., *Los costarricenses,* p. 581.

65. Ibid., p. 583.

66. Daniel Camacho, "Costa Rica: Una transición hacia menos democracia," in Carlos Barba Solano, José Luis Barros Horcasitas, and Javier Hurtado, eds., *Transiciones a la democracia en Europa y América Latina* (Mexico City: Facultad Latinoamericano de Ciencias Sociales, Universidad de Guadalajara, Miguel Angel Porrúa–Librero Editor, 1991), pp. 493–502; and Biesanz et al., *Los costarricenses,* pp. 581–582.

67. Biesanz et al., *Los costarricenses,* p. 583.

68. Quote from *Mesoamerica,* November 1993, p. 9. See also *Mesoamerica,* January 1994, pp. 9–10, and June 1997, pp. 8–9; Matute, "Oscar Arias censura campaña"; and "Papeleta presidencial, elecciones 1998," *La Nación Digital,* January 27, 1998, at <http://www.nacion.co.cr>.

5

SOCIAL STRUCTURE
AND CIVIL SOCIETY

Costa Rica's great national myth holds in part that its democracy has roots in a social structure with minimal class divisions and a homogeneous population and culture. As the Biesanzes have noted, this argument sometimes assumes amusing dimensions: "Despite the great value that Costa Ricans place upon democracy, equality, and tolerance, their society manifests inequalities of many types. Although many Ticos begin any commentary about social stratification by denying that there are classes in their country, they [then] immediately insist that all Costa Ricans are of the middle class."[1]

Costa Rica is considerably less homogeneous and egalitarian than its myth suggests. This has had important implications for the nation's organizational life, especially during the severe recession of the 1980s. This chapter explores Costa Rica's social and economic divisions and some of the nation's main institutions, interest sectors, and groups.

Social Structure and Cleavages

Driven by powerful modernizing forces, Costa Rican social structure has changed at an ever accelerating pace since independence (Chapter 3). With the advent of coffee exporting in the mid-nineteenth century, the predominantly rural, agrarian society began to evolve quickly. The population boomed from only 60,000 in 1821 to an estimated 3.7 million projected for 1998.[2] Coffee's expansion spread people throughout most of the cultivable national territory by the mid-twentieth century. Coffee also spurred railroad construction, which led to the banana industry, new racial and ethnic groups, and new economic classes and organizations. Cities grew rapidly. Public education expanded and eventually became virtually universal. Middle-class political forces captured the state in the 1948 civil war and for several decades employed their power to promote economic development and redistribute wealth and income to the middle classes. Employment in industry and in the service sector burgeoned.

Social Classes

These social forces have driven powerful alterations in the class structure. In the early nineteenth century, most Costa Ricans were peasants, and there were also a small, urban, middle sector of artisans and government and commercial employees and a tiny aristocracy of larger landowners descended from the conquerors. A century and a half later, the Biesanzes described Costa Rica's 1970s class structure in the following useful terms:

- An upper class (2 percent of the population) made up half of aristocratic families and half of the nouveaux riches, who together earned about 20 percent of national income from larger landholdings, industries, and commercial firms.
- An upper middle class (5 percent of the populace) of prosperous businesspeople, professionals, and agriculturalists who earned another 10 percent of national income.
- A lower middle class (15 percent of the people) of small business owners, public and private white-collar employees, lower-status professionals such as teachers, and prosperous small farmers (earning perhaps 18 percent of national income).
- A working class of better-paid factory workers, lower-level white-collar and blue-collar public employees, service workers, manual laborers, and peasant smallholders (50 percent of the population), earning some 45 percent of income.
- A lower class of landless and land-poor peasants, domestic servants, unskilled urban laborers, and urban informal workers (roughly one-fourth of the populace), earning only 7 percent of national income.[3]

This description of the class structure remained largely valid in the 1990s, although the economic crisis of the 1980s and resultant public policy changes may have begun to alter the class system somewhat.

Income Distribution

Another way to examine Costa Rica's economic divisions is in terms of income distribution. Table 5.1 presents data on the total share of national income earned by different strata of Tico households from 1961 through 1992. The households

TABLE 5.1   Estimated Income Distribution Among Costa Rican Households,
1961–1992

	1961	1971	1983	1986	1988	1992
Poorest 10%	2.8	2.1	1.6	1.3	1.6	1.6
Poorest 20%	6.2	5.4	4.7	4.3	4.8	4.9
Next 20%	7.6	9.3	9.4	9.5	9.9	9.4
Next 20%	9.5	13.7	14.0	14.4	14.8	14.5
Next 20%	17.0	21.0	20.6	21.9	22.1	22.1
Richest 20%	59.7	50.6	51.3	50.1	48.4	49.1
Richest 10%	45.5	34.4	36.1	33.7	31.7	32.2
Gini coefficient[a]	.50	.43	.45	.44	.42	.43
Median monthly income, constant 1992 *colones*	48,989	52,455	59,572	67,125	61,024	69,554
GDP per capita, constant 1990 U.S. dollars	1,081	1,474	1,706	1,775	1,807	1,943

[a]The Gini coefficient measures inequality in distribution, ranging from greatest possible inequality at 1.0 to perfect equality at 0.0.

sour ces: Mitchell A. Seligson, Juliana Martínez F., and Juan Diego Trejos S., "Reducción de la pobreza en Costa Rica: El impacto de las políticas públicas," draft manuscript, United Nations Development Program, San José, Costa Rica, November 11, 1995. GDP per capita estimated from Inter-American Development Bank (IADB), *Economic and Social Progress in Latin America: Agricultural Development, 1986* (Washington, D.C.: IADB, 1986), table 3, and IADB, *Economic and Social Progress in Latin America: Overcoming Volatility, 1995 Report* (Baltimore: Johns Hopkins University Press, 1985.

are separated into fifths (quintiles) from richest to poorest, plus an extra category of the poorest and richest 10 percent of households.

The data reveal, first, that income distribution in Costa Rica is very unequal. The wealthiest 10 percent of Costa Ricans earned about one-third of all income in 1992. Meanwhile, the poorest quintile earned less than 5 percent of all income. Second, despite Costa Rica's social democratic policies and development efforts, the poorest fifth of Tico families actually lost income share (from 6.2 percent in 1961 to 4.9 percent in 1992). Third, the wealthiest quintile of Tico households also lost income share—though from a much more comfortable position—from 59.7 percent in 1961 down to 49.1 percent by 1992.

Finally, and in sharp contrast to the rich and poor, Costa Rica's middle three income quintiles (roughly the Biesanzes' working and lower middle classes) did well during these three decades. Their combined share of national income rose from 34.1 percent in 1961 to 46.0 percent in 1992. Median family income in constant terms (Table 5.1) rose roughly 44 percent from 1961 through 1992. Thus middle-income Costa Ricans prospered relatively and absolutely, and did so by capturing income share from both the nation's wealthiest and poorest families.[4] Even though not all Ticos are "middle class," then, the income and standard of living of these middle strata markedly improved after the 1960s.

Although Costa Rica's middle sectors did well, the plight of the nation's very poorest citizens worsened relatively and absolutely from the early 1960s through the late 1980s. One measure suggests that the average real disposable income of the poorest fifth of Costa Rican families fell at least 5 percent between 1961 and 1986.[5]

The overall impact of the economic crisis of the 1980s upon this social structure has not fully played out, but by the mid-1990s some effects had become apparent. In the short term, there was some pain for everyone. The crisis hurt wealthier Costa Ricans as their businesses deteriorated and incomes shrank. Many middle-, working-class, and poor Ticos lost their jobs. The incomes of all classes eroded simultaneously, and the ranks of the poor grew rapidly. Real wages in both the public and private sectors dropped as much as 40 percent, and open unemployment rose from below 6 to over 9 percent between 1979 and 1993.[6]

The hardship continued for several years. Table 5.1 reveals that the median income of Costa Rican households fell more than 9 percent between 1986 and 1988. The most dramatic evidence of this general decline in incomes in the 1980s was a veritable explosion of the informal economic sector. The newly unemployed and newly poor scrambled to sustain themselves in any way possible—as ambulatory vendors, unregulated taxi drivers, and the like.

Conservative elements among the upper and upper middle classes seized the opportunity presented by the 1980s crisis to press the state for neoliberal economic reforms. They sought to lower their taxes and increase their income and wealth by privatizing state enterprises and trimming public employment, regulation, and public services. Costa Rica enacted many such policies during the late 1980s and early 1990s (Chapter 8).[7] Less affluent Ticos also mobilized politically to defend themselves as their incomes fell and service costs rose. Government redressed some grievances of the poor and the middle classes by raising wages (Appendix, Table A.3) and providing public assistance with housing and welfare.[8]

These class-based struggles raise a critical question: What actually happened to the relative distribution of income during the 1980s? Did the economic crunch and the resultant new policies shift income back toward the rich? Toward the middle class? Toward the poor? One might suspect that the upper class, with its superior resources with which to influence public policy, would have bested the less-advantaged groups in this struggle.

Table 5.1 shows no dramatic, short-run redistribution of income away from the middle classes. The recession's general impact on incomes was fairly evenly distributed in the early years. There did occur, however, some subtle deviations from this pattern that portended greater change in the future: The poorest 20 percent of Ticos lost income share between 1983 and 1986 but more than recovered the lost ground by 1988. The income share of the richest 20 percent of Costa Ricans continued its long erosion through 1988 but recovered somewhat by 1992. In contrast, the second poorest and middle quintiles of families each lost some income between 1988 and 1992. Their combined income share fell from 25.7 to 24.9 percent. This reversed a three-decade trend of increasing income for the middle sectors. These income shifts reflect the first measurable income redistributive effects of neoliberal policies and could foretell future growth of income inequality. Over the long term, cuts in national spending and investment in education and health will erode the well-being of poorer Ticos. The Figueres Olsen administration (1994–1998) continued to cut government jobs and curtail public services.[9]

These incipient trends notwithstanding, Costa Rican income distribution remained remarkably stable during the turbulent 1980s given the severity of the recession. All classes lost real income, and all classes recovered significantly by the early 1990s. Despite the nation's constitutional social guarantees, social welfare programs, and redistributive policies, the poorest Costa Ricans became relatively poorer from the 1960s through the early 1990s. Prior to the late 1980s, the real and rather consistent winners were the working and middle classes, whose real incomes and income shares rose markedly. One may reasonably surmise that such improving circumstances for the middle majority of the population would contribute greatly to political stability. One may find in the real and relative income declines of the late 1980s and early 1990s cause for the political mobilization observed among both rich and poor.

Minorities

Compared to much of Latin America, Costa Rica is relatively racially and culturally homogeneous because its original indigenous and black populations were largely assimilated into the predominantly mestizo, culturally Hispanic population. However, the myth of racial and ethnic homogeneity often leads Costa Ricans to overlook their minorities and the discrimination against them. (Photo 5.1 illustrates Costa Rica's diversity.)

Blacks.   About 3 percent of Costa Ricans are blacks of Jamaican origin, most Protestants and many of them English speaking. Most are descendants of railroad and banana workers brought in during the nineteenth century, and most live in the Atlantic lowlands. African Costa Ricans today make up about one-third of the population of the Atlantic zone.

Costa Ricans of African origin have historically experienced pronounced racial discrimination. After United Fruit moved its operations to the Pacific coast in the 1930s, taking with it most of the Atlantic region's employment, blacks were prohibited from migrating to follow the jobs. Although the revolutionary junta of 1948–1949 lifted the ban on blacks' mobility and placed an antidiscrimination clause in the 1949 constitution, African Ticos—still concentrated heavily in the Atlantic zone—have suffered economically ever since the banana company pull-

PHOTO 5.1   Costa Rican faces (photo by K. Lambert, courtesy *Tico Times*)

out. Poverty is widespread, as is racism. Many still speak English and resent the Hispanicization of education. Limón, the major city of the Atlantic zone, experienced major outbreaks of rioting over hard times in 1979 and again in 1996.[10]

Indigenous People.   Costa Rica has a small contingent of indigenous people, perhaps 1 percent of the national population, concentrated mainly in "indigenous reserves" in the southern parts of the country. Divided among several distinct language and ethnic groups, Indians suffer from very low public-service levels and much poverty and disease. More than twenty reserves legally incorporate over 6 percent of the national territory, but their populations have use of only an estimated 60 percent of that. Historically, the government, private sector, and other Costa Ricans have exploited the Indians and their lands. Persistent difficulties have included encroachment upon their (nominally) legally protected reserves by the ever spreading mestizo populace, illegal logging, and mineral concessions by the government.

The Legislative Assembly formed the National Commission for Indian Affairs (Comisión Nacional de Asuntos Indígenas, or CONAI) in 1973 to protect Indian

interests. Despite CONAI, Indians continue to complain of abuse and discrimination. They have mobilized politically and protested their plight since the 1970s,
with the rate of protest increasing into the 1990s. One powerful irritant and
source of recent mobilization was that the law treated Indians as foreigners in
Costa Rica rather than as citizens. They finally received full political rights by a
constitutional amendment in the early 1990s.[11]

Other Minorities.   Other minorities include small populations of foreign origin.
Among the older groups are Italians, French, Germans, and Chinese. Germans
became important participants in the coffee industry. Many German-origin Ticos
were interned in the United States during World War II for security reasons.
Italian, French, and German Costa Ricans have significantly integrated themselves
into the population and national cultural, political, and economic life.

A small Jewish community developed prior to World War II. Many early Jewish
immigrants began life in Costa Rica as itinerant peddlers and eventually established commercial enterprises in the larger cities. Despite a period of official anti-
Semitism during the government of León Cortés and despite widespread cultural
anti-Semitism, Jews have achieved business, professional, and political influence.

The Chinese first came to Costa Rica as contract workers for railroad construction. Chinese Costa Ricans, also targets of discrimination, have found their own
entrepreneurial niche. They reside especially in smaller towns and act as commercial intermediaries or operate small hotels, stores, and restaurants.

Foreigners.   Since the mid-twentieth century, an important immigrant commu-
nity has been foreign retirees (*pensionados*), especially from the United States.
Beneficial tax laws, the excellent climate, and the modest cost of living in Costa
Rica have attracted tens of thousands of foreigners, many from the United States.
Because these expatriates normally retain their citizenship of origin, the *pension-
ado* community remains on the margin of national politics. However, a weekly
English-language newspaper, the *Tico Times*, serves this community and from
time to time breaks a story that affects domestic politics.

The largest foreign populations in Costa Rica are other Latin Americans.
Nicaraguans have long crossed into Costa Rica as migrant laborers for the northern provinces' coffee harvests or simply to live and work in Costa Rica's better
economy. During Nicaragua's civil wars and revolution of the late 1970s and
1980s, hundreds of thousands of Nicaraguans came as political and economic
refugees. During the 1980s Costa Rica detained thousands of Nicaraguans in
crowded camps under extremely trying conditions. Refugee camp residents complained of being taken advantage of by local farmers as nearly captive labor for
the coffee harvest (mainly by farmers who refused to pay promised wages to
Nicaraguans fearful of complaining to authorities).

Opponents of the Nicaraguan dictator Anastasio Somoza Debayle in 1978 and
1979 located their revolutionary shadow government in San José and openly re-

cruited and trained guerrilla forces on Costa Rican soil. When the Sandinista revolutionaries won in Nicaragua in July 1979, conservative and Somocista exiles flooded into Costa Rica. Aided by the United States and other rightist forces, Nicaraguan counterrevolutionary (*contra*) elements fought for eleven years to oust the Sandinistas.[12] The resultant anticommunist political violence and terrorism within Costa Rica by both exiles and Ticos significantly threatened the nation's stability (Chapter 6). This violence led president Oscar Arias Sánchez (1986–1990) aggressively to promote the regional Central American peace accord of August 1987 in hopes of stabilizing regional politics and thus diminishing political turbulence in Costa Rica. Despite the end of the Sandinista revolution in Nicaragua in 1990, many Nicaraguans remained and new illegal immigrants traveled to Costa Rica seeking work. The Nicaraguan government and immigrants in Costa Rica alike have protested mistreatment by Costa Rican officials.[13]

Religion

Roman Catholicism. The Costa Rican Catholic Church played a limited political role during much of the nineteenth century because of its weak institutional presence.[14] Later, under the leadership of the dynamic archbishop Bernardo Thiel, the church hierarchy sought to influence the 1889 election and formed the short-lived Catholic Union (Unión Católica) political party. Motivated both by rising Liberal anticlericalism in Costa Rica and by new social Christian theological currents within Catholicism, the clergy and Catholic Union challenged the *cafetaleros'* traditional dominance of the government. The Liberals quickly suppressed this first burst of Catholic political activism. The government eventually reached an understanding with the church hierarchy by which the latter quietly supported the regime.

From time to time, however, resurgent social Christianity—typically pushed by a few influentials within the hierarchy or clergy—would pull the church back into politics to promote social reform. Former priest Jorge Volio and leftist unions founded the Reformist Party in 1923, but the party disbanded after failing to win the presidency. Archbishop Victor Sanabria Martínez allied with President Calderón Guardia and the communist labor unions in 1943 to rescue Calderón's social and labor legislation. Father Benjamín Núñez formed Catholic labor unions during the 1940s, fought with the National Liberation movement in 1948, and became labor minister in the 1948–1949 revolutionary government.

Influenced by the reformism of the Second Vatican Council and the Medellín Latin American Bishops Conference of 1968, bishop of Alajuela Román Arrieta became another progressive voice. In the 1970s he endorsed a government agrarian reform scheme, which aroused fierce criticism from conservatives and large-holding agricultural interests. Liberation theology influenced elements founded the Central American Theological Institute (Instituto Teológico de America Central, or ITAC), which briefly merged with the archdiocese's traditionally conservative Central Seminary. There also appeared a left-leaning weekly newspaper, *Pueblo,* in 1972, and some religious elements embraced pastoral strategies of political mobilization in their ministry to the poor.

Much more typical of Costa Rican Catholicism since the civil war has been the church hierarchy's fairly consistent conservatism: support of the government and its development model, constant anticommunism, anti-Protestantism, and encouragement of *solidarismo* (an antiunion, probusiness substitute for organized labor). Under the conservative tutelage of Archbishop Carlos Humberto Rodríguez Quirós, most social activism was squashed. John Paul II has reinforced these conservative tendencies of the Costa Rican hierarchy, producing what Miguel Picado has characterized as "Costa Rican Catholic neoconservatism." According to Picado, "What is novel . . . is that church organs . . . and the orientation imposed upon religious information by the major media of mass communication offer a sampler of the propositions of the social doctrine of the church that reinforce neoliberal ideas and the institutions that best represent the interests of neoconservative sectors."[15]

Protestantism.[16]   During the nineteenth century, the government tolerated early Protestantism because of Roman Catholic institutional weakness, Liberal anticlericalism, and because Protestant sects largely confined their efforts to groups considered outsiders (Jamaicans in the Atlantic zone, foreigners in the capital city). But in the late nineteenth century, evangelical Protestant sects entered Costa Rica intent upon "saving" Catholic Ticos. Thus ensued several decades of interdenominational conflict: The *evangélicos* labored to convert the Catholics that some missionaries considered heathen. Catholic clergy responded with strident anti-Protestant propaganda. After the Second Vatican Council, however, Catholic institutional hostility toward the *evangélicos* diminished notably and interdenominational relations improved.

At first Protestantism spread very slowly, but more missionaries arrived, mainly from the United States, and Costa Rica became a center for training evangelical missionaries. In the 1960s Protestant Ticos still were less than 2 percent of the population, but by the 1990s that figure had risen fivefold. Protestant missionaries followed proselytizing tactics that proved very successful. They tended to form small congregations in poor and marginal communities. External financial support, especially from U.S. churches, enabled Protestant pastors to work with and serve their congregations much more easily than the understaffed Catholic clergy.

Among the Protestants, the number of Pentecostal missions and churches began to increase sharply in the 1970s. The Pentecostals seemed to gain adherents in direct proportion to the deterioration of the economy in the 1970s and again in the 1980s and thus enjoyed explosive growth among the poor in many areas. Critics accuse the Pentecostals and other fundamentalist Protestants of having a profoundly conservative political effect by diverting their poor congregants from mobilizing politically to struggle with the real social problems that confront them.[17] Whatever its political implications, Protestantism had gained a strong beachhead in Costa Rica by the 1990s.

Communications Media

In the nineteenth century, both the Liberals and the Catholic Church used the press to persuade and educate.[18] This eventually helped "generate a society in which negotiation and consensus gained an advantage over repression."[19] As an instrument of powerful politicoeconomic and social forces, the press developed with relatively little censorship or state interference. This freedom permitted the print media, and later radio and television, to make important contributions to political discourse, discussion, and democratization.

A gradually shifting array of daily and weekly newspapers, most with a partisan slant, has been published in San José for over a century. Radio, especially news programming, became a powerful medium during the 1950s. Radio was particularly influential in rural Costa Rica, much less penetrated than the cities by the capital's newspapers. Television developed rapidly during the 1970s and 1980s, supplanting newspapers as the principal source of news for a majority of the population by the end of the 1980s. Cable television systems developed and expanded rapidly in the 1990s. During the Oduber and Carazo administrations (1974–1982), the government established publicly funded cultural and educational television, Radio Nacional, and then the state-supported National System of Radio and Television (Sistema Nacional de Radio y Televisión, or SINART).

Costa Rica has also become a center for book publishing. The government partly subsidizes some publishing through the Ministry of Culture, Youth, and Sport (Editorial Costa Rica) and through the presses of several public universities (e.g., Editorial Universidad de Costa Rica, Editorial Universidad Estatal a Distancia). Several think tanks and intergovernmental entities operate editorial houses as well.[20] There are several smaller, private presses of various ideological perspectives, and individuals, unions, interest groups, and political parties also publish many books. Much of this flood of book publication draws upon a boom of Costa Rican scholarship driven by the rapid growth of higher education, numerous *licenciatura* (roughly equivalent to a master's degree) theses, and the proliferation of research scholars and university faculty with foreign doctorates.

The mass media mostly function without censorship. Indeed, a tradition of investigative journalism has developed, periodically embarrassing the government of the moment. The constitution's article 29 guarantees freedom of expression and press without prior censorship but also establishes civil responsibility for any harm that might be committed in their exercise.[21] In 1989 the Supreme Court of Justice ruled that citizens affected by inaccurate or contentious published information had a "right to rectification or reply" in the offending medium.[22] General press freedom notwithstanding, official censorship of pornographic and violent materials in the press, movies, and broadcast media prevailed for many decades.

The censorship of prurient materials, once common, largely broke down by the 1980s.

A press law dating from the early twentieth century has aroused debate, legislative scrutiny, and legal challenge over the decades but has also withstood most efforts to revise or eliminate it. There have been certain encroachments upon press freedom by the courts and the executive branch in recent years. A court in 1994 sentenced *La Nación* columnist Bosco Valverde to a fine and suspended one-year prison term for "offending the honor and decorum of a public official"—specifically, several judges. Also in 1994 the Supreme Court of Justice issued guidelines restricting the press from naming persons or companies under investigation by the police. Stung by an arms purchase scandal and other problems, President Figueres Olsen issued a 1996 decree permitting the government not to disclose information concerning security-related "state secrets," and he has withheld information from the press on a variety of issues.[23]

The government partially regulates access to the practice of journalism through the state-sanctioned College of Journalists (Colegio de Periodistas), one of many quasi-statal professional associations. Only Costa Ricans may own mass communications media, but this law has been evaded on occasion when convenient for political reasons.[24] Debate and discussion in the printed press are vigorous, and Costa Ricans enjoy basically unrestricted access to publications from a wide array of ideological perspectives.

Despite the virtual absence of formal censorship and the general accessibility of diverse ideological materials in print, the media have pronounced and fairly systematic biases. Ownership is highly concentrated, politically conservative, and tied to major business sectors. Major mass media (television, most radio, and major newspapers) tend to be overtly anticommunist and in recent decades fairly critical of the prevailing social democratic development model.

During the 1980s Costa Rica's media generally embraced neoliberal proposals to reduce the state's economic role. Major newspapers' editorials have generally denounced Catholic Church social activism.[25] Criticism of Nicaragua's Sandinista government was consistently strident during the 1980s. *La Nación*—the daily with the largest circulation—cooperated with the CIA in the publication of a Nicaraguan exile newspaper called *Nicaragua Hoy* (Nicaragua today). According to Martha Honey, this insert in *La Nación* was linked to Costa Rican–based anti-Sandinista groups and had CIA financing. Honey also reports that numerous print and broadcast journalists were on the CIA payroll or received payments from a Nicaraguan *contra* organization to promote anti-Sandinista news items during this period. Other journalists were fired or reassigned for insufficient cooperation with the anti-Sandinista line of their media. During the 1980s Costa Rica also permitted various *contra* radio stations to broadcast into Nicaragua, including one operated by the U.S.-funded Voice of America.[26]

Despite the biases of media owners, Costa Ricans still employ the newspapers to communicate an enormous range of political views to each other. Paid newspaper advertisements known as *campos pagados* constitute a major form of social and political discourse in Costa Rica. Ticos regularly congratulate, console, or castigate each other about all manner of social events and public issues. Individuals and interest groups also employ *campos pagados* to argue with the government, the media, and each other or to announce political preferences. During election campaigns the newspapers bulge with these spaces in which groups and individuals endorse particular candidates.

Education

At independence Costa Rica had only a handful of schools and very few literate citizens.[27] But education quickly became a central value of Liberals, and national elites embraced it as a key to modernization and development. The first higher education institution was the Universidad de Santo Tomás, founded in 1821 to provide secondary and some professional education.

An 1825 law charged municipalities with forming primary schools. The constitution of 1844 mentioned education as a right of citizens and the responsibility of the national government. The 1847 constitution more firmly committed the state to education and provided for equal instruction for both sexes.[28] The government established its first national education ministry (Public Instruction) in 1847.

During the 1850s and 1860s, the government took further steps forward in education. Public school construction expanded. Catholic religious orders also began to establish parochial schools. In 1869 alone, for instance, three public and private high schools were founded. Most important, the 1869 constitution established the full constitutional character of education that prevails largely unchanged today: "The primary education of both sexes shall be obligatory, free and supported by the Nation. Its immediate supervision corresponds to the Municipalities, and its supreme inspection to the Government."[29] Subsequent laws created an overall organizational plan for public education and built many more schools. An 1881 decree established full national authority to regulate all aspects of education, including parochial schools.

A national economic and fiscal crisis in the early 1880s forced Costa Rica to review its commitment to education. The near collapse of the public budget at first shut down many schools. The national government in 1888 even closed the Universidad de Santo Tomás, perennially strapped for funding and students.[30]

Costa Rica, however, refused to retreat from its commitment to basic education and fought back with major reforms. The government of President Mauro Fernandéz reformed the entire school curriculum and reorganized the whole education system. The government sharply increased spending on public schools beginning in 1886: Education budgets rose from an average of only 6 percent of the national budget for 1869–1885 to around 18 percent for 1886–1900.[31] Local school boards were established for every municipality, which helped democratize and deepen local citizens' commitment to education. (The Liberal government's reformers also temporarily expelled the Jesuits from the country and closed several parochial schools to curb church influence on education.)

From then on Costa Rica's public education system gradually expanded its services throughout the national territory and to more grade levels. This eventually gave Costa Rica one of Latin America's highest literacy levels. Visitors trekking in rural Costa Rica were often astonished to find rural primary schools and their intrepid teachers in places of great isolation and privation. From 1900 to 1950, public education absorbed around 16 percent of the national budget and reached nearly 30 percent by the 1970s.

Arguably the most important effects of this love affair with education have been socialization of citizens, democratization, and social mobility. The rapid spread of literacy brought many Ticos into the electorate prior to 1913, when literacy was dropped as a requisite for voting.[32] The schools inculcated several generations with the norms of consensus, conflict avoidance, and patriotism and with the patriotic myths of homogeneity and equality. For much of the twentieth century, the education system enabled innumerable Ticos from working-class backgrounds to move up the social and economic ladder, especially into expanding public and private employment.

Education became a virtual civil religion, embraced by rulers and citizens alike. "The preoccupation with education and the response of different governments to the demand for more education, above all between 1948 and 1980, produced a real expansion of the opportunities of access to education for Costa Ricans and also a hope of social mobility."[33] As more Ticos took advantage of education and the doors it opened, they demanded more education and it became more accessible. Some 98 percent of primary-age children and perhaps one-third of secondary-age children attended school in 1980—both large increases over 1950.[34]

Higher education was the last frontier, expanding dramatically beginning in the 1970s. Founded in 1940 after the country had gone fifty years without a university, the Universidad de Costa Rica would serve as the only national source of higher education other than a seminary for almost three decades. But in the 1970s the government founded several new universities to broaden access and supply a burgeoning demand. By the late 1980s, Costa Rica had four public universities, and five private universities had also appeared. In 1989 there were almost 69,000 university students in tiny Costa Rica, with one-sixth of them enrolled in the private institutions. Overall, university enrollment had risen fivefold since 1970.[35]

Such great national investments in education and the national myths about its value have created powerful vested interests and expectations. Citizens demand education services from the government. Rural communities want neighborhood schools even though tiny rural schools may deliver inferior education. A growing proportion of the national education budget has been dedicated to national-level administration. Unions such as the National Association of Teachers (Asociación Nacional de Educadores, or ANDE) and the National High School Teachers Association (Asociación de Profesores de Segunda Enseñanza, or APSE) represent most of the public school faculty. Teachers have struck several times to defend their wages and benefits.

Virtually free access to public higher education has placed a great and growing burden on the state and created a vast and easily mobilized constituency of university students and faculty. Universities have mobilized faculty and students into massive demonstrations to defend the higher education budget from government pressures to economize and raise tuition and fees.

The economic crisis of the 1980s shocked Costa Rica's education system in several ways. First, education spending fell drastically from a peak of 29.1 percent of the national budget in 1982 to 19.1 percent.[36] Funding cuts contributed to the deterioration of school facilities, the doubling up of schedules, reduction of the length of the school day and year, more unqualified teachers, and increased failure and dropout rates. Such calamitous material and instructional changes aggravated an already notable tendency toward stratification of education quality. There had long been a pronounced quality gap between the public schools and the private and parochial schools used by more prosperous Ticos. The fiscal crisis widened this breach so much that critics worried that it might soon sharpen class inequalities of all sorts.[37]

The financially strapped governments of the 1980s–1990s found themselves unable to rebuild education budgets as governments had a century before after similar difficulties. Under intense neoliberal pressures from international lending and development agencies, the government had to curtail—not increase—public spending by cutting services and promoting privatization. Indeed, there is evidence that the World Bank and other lenders considered Costa Rica's educational development *excessive* for a Third World nation and that it might have to "give up some of what it had achieved."[38]

The choices facing the deteriorated education system seemed so serious in the early 1990s that some observers believed that the nation's democracy and distributive justice hung in the balance. Jorge Rovira feared that both the deterioration of public schools and the proliferation of private universities would deepen and entrench inequalities in the society rather than reduce them as the education system had done for so long.[39] For Yolanda Rojas, the grave challenges of public education required Costa Rica to "consider the rights of all Costa Ricans without distinction of any sort so that we may deepen our democracy rather than destroy it."[40]

Organizations and Political Mobilization

High levels of formal organization characterize Costa Rica. The country has long provided its citizens with a human rights climate that facilitates and welcomes association and organization. Ticos tend to belong to groups of many sorts (see also Chapter 6) and through them to mobilize and press demands upon the government.

Following a corporatist tendency common in Latin America, Costa Rica's government helps establish and legitimize some organizations and even gives them certain public functions. Unlike some of its Central American neighbors, the Costa Rican government tends to respond favorably to and accept as legitimate a wide array of groups, even those outside this favored corporatist interest arena. A 1973 nationwide survey of organizations and their projects in over 100 communities found that a large majority had received some form of outside assistance, usually from the national or municipal governments.[41]

The government has long encouraged the growth of organizations. It began by establishing guilds of artisans in the 1830s and has subsequently promoted organizations ranging from professional associations to cooperatives; health, nutrition, and community improvement groups; and even labor unions. There is also a rich historical record of independently formed civil society. Professionals guilds and mutual aid societies appeared in the 1850s, early community improvement groups in the 1880s, and modern labor unions in the early twentieth century. Costa Rica thus has an abundant associational life.[42]

In the twentieth century, the state has chartered professional colleges (*colegios*, analogous to bar associations in the United States) for attorneys, physicians, journalists, architects, engineers, pharmacists, and others. The professional colleges have a quasi-statal character: They are government-chartered monopolies, and some them even regulate and license practitioners. Despite this public function, the *colegios* also actively represent and promote the interests of their members before the state. The professional colleges constitute important representatives of middle-sector interests.

Outside the corporatist interest sector exist manifold other interest and pressure groups. Business organizations function more purely as pressure groups than the professional colleges, and they lack regulatory authority. Considerably compensating for this absence of formal authority, however, is their resource wealth. They enjoy all the tools of effective pressure groups that their members' wealth and organization can purchase, including access to policymakers, the capacity to use the press to shape public opinion, and resources for litigation. Among many others, such business organizations as the National Association for the Promotion of Enterprise (Asociación Nacional de Fomento de la Empresa, or ANFE), Costa Rican Association of Business Managers (Asociación Costarricense de Gerentes de Empresa, or ACOGE), the Chamber of Commerce, Chamber of Industry, and the National Union of Chambers of Commerce represent general or particular business-sector interests. Business groups tend to lobby for lower taxes, less government regulation, and the privatization of public enterprises. Some business groups promote ideological education along conservative lines through sponsored newspaper columns. Because they can mold public opinion through the media, contribute heavily to political candidates and parties, and skillfully lobby the executive and legislature, they have considerable political influence. Their members have also often served in government posts.

During the early 1980s, when economic crisis provoked extensive popular protests and the Sandinista revolution in Nicaragua seemed most threatening, business groups spearheaded by the Chamber of Commerce made boldly forceful demands upon the administration of Luis Alberto Monge. Indeed, in July 1984 they seemed almost to threaten a legal and institutional challenge to the regime should President Monge not quickly restrain the unions and popular unrest, drop proposed consumer protections, and assume a more belligerent posture toward Nicaragua.[43] Although these business interests had key links to Monge's administration, the government countered them with other mobilized groups, avoided an institutional crisis, and directed foreign policy toward a less confrontational line (Chapter 9).

Organized labor is an important part of civil society, although in the late twentieth century it has badly divided and declined. Overall, only about 19 percent of the workforce was organized in unions in the late 1970s, a period when membership was probably near its peak.[44] Government policies had fragmented and hobbled—but did not suppress—the labor movement after the 1948 defeat of the Calderón-communist governing coalition. After a period of resurgence in membership during the 1970s, several things undermined the organized workforce and political decline of labor: further fragmentation of various confederations, increasing ideological and employer antagonism, the decline of the Communist Party and its external sponsors, and tactical blunders by particular unions. Many private-sector unions vanished during the 1980s, leaving the movement heavily concentrated in the public sector. Some powerful unions remain independent of any central labor organization, especially those of teachers, telephone and electrical workers, and public health workers, bank employees, and public works employees. These public employees unions, like professional colleges, have strongly represented middle-class interests.[45]

The solidarity association (*asociación solidarista*) is another type of labor organization in Costa Rica. This sector is the most dynamic on the labor scene, much to the chagrin of other labor organizers who deeply resent both the success and goals of *solidarismo*. Solidarity associations involve modest profit-sharing contributions to employees by the owners of a business. Private-sector workers use the associations as self-help entities that can provide loans, support for medical care, and even separation pay, which labor law does not guarantee to private-sector workers. Business interests have promoted the solidarity movement as a conservative alternative to labor unions. They appear to have undercut class-conscious worker mobilization, reduced conflictive labor relations, and raised productivity.[46]

There are myriad community-level groups in Costa Rica, some promoted by the government and others that have arisen spontaneously. Since the late 1960s, the National Community Development Directorate (Dirección Nacional de Desarrollo de la Comunidad, or DINADECO) has promoted the formation of local community development associations. Properly constituted by citizens of a town or neighborhood, these groups receive *personería jurídica* (a formal, legal status) from the government, which permits them to receive and spend legislatively appropriated funds for local improvement projects.

Community development associations bring neighbors together to help with local civic projects, collaborate with government agencies, and pressure local and national public officials to fund their projects. Health-related agencies have also encouraged local groups to foment such projects as infant nutrition and health clinics. Schools have parent organizations to promote cooperation with and improvement of local schools. Demands from such groups contribute heavily to escalating pork barrel spending by the Legislative Assembly.

Costa Rica has many local organizations not sponsored by the government. These civil society groups have sprung up spontaneously in response to the problems of rapid urbanization and economic hard times. In urban areas organizations of housing squatters have invaded land to build homes and then pressed the government for services, utilities, and land titles. Advising and organizing such squatter groups are nongovernmental organizations such as the Democratic Front for Housing (Frente Democrática de Vivienda, or FDV) and the National Patriotic Committee (Comité Patriótico Nacional, or COPAN).

Rural areas, too, have experienced widespread organization and mobilization independent of government. Rural economic deterioration during the 1980s brought a boom in peasant organizations and mobilizations—some spontaneous, some promoted by national union confederations (Photo 5.2). The Union of Small and Medium Farmers (Unión de Pequeños y Medianos Agricultores, or UPA-Nacional) organized peasants nationwide to demand land reform and other public assistance. Over half of the 142 agrarian groups registered with the labor ministry in 1990 were independent.[47]

There are sorts of organizations in Costa Rica too numerous to list. Their interests range from ideological issues to sports, environmental protection to social and cultural activities. Chapter 6 provides examples of the activities of and participation driven by such organizations. When civil society interests require action from the government, Costa Rican organizations usually first contact proper authorities through normal channels and enlist influential citizens to endorse their cause. Should such efforts fail, some groups escalate to confrontational tactics such as demonstrations, strikes, boycotts, or acts of civil disobedience. Often true to its national myth of consensus, the government usually responds to confrontation with study and compromise rather than repression.

Conclusions

Costa Ricans are divided into socioeconomic classes with sharp inequalities of income, wealth, and educational access. The rise to power of the National Liberation Party after the 1948 civil war gave middle-class interests unprecedented political clout for several decades. Guided by a social democratic development program and an activist state, they used it to redistribute income toward middle-income groups and away from the wealthy—and even to some extent away from the poor. Powerful economic and institutional interests such as the wealthy, business associations, the Catholic Church, and the media have resented and resisted this program.

The economic crisis of the 1980s provided conservatives an opportunity and powerful external allies with which to challenge and undermine the social demo-

PHOTO 5.2   Peasants' and farmers' organizations rally, 1995 (photo by Julio Laínez, courtesy *Tico Times*)

cratic development model. They have largely succeeded in promoting a new neoliberal development model, especially in the policy arena (Chapter 8). The economic traumas of the 1980s hurt most Ticos, and many of them mobilized to protect their interests. This increased political mobilization swelled Costa Rica's already large civil society and generated more conflict among social classes than the nation was accustomed to.

Income distribution and services had clearly shifted away from the middle sectors by the early 1990s, and severe poverty afflicted more Ticos than in several prior decades. A 1994 study used dramatic terms to describe the growing inequality and consequent political mobilization: "The existent differentiation between distinguished residential areas and popular slums is so sharp that it testifies to the disintegration of the social fabric."[48]

Costa Rica's myths of classlessness and homogeneity thus break down before careful scrutiny. Class, race, institutional position, and interests divide Ticos in diverse ways. Some of these differences frequently set them at odds with one another or with the government. The Biesanzes, however, point out that the myth of tolerance "benefits all groups, given that it constitutes a challenge for the 'white' majority to try to live in accord with its established values and to attempt to resolve the problems of minorities."[49] The shared ideals of consensus, peaceful problem solving, and equality of opportunity—no matter how far they are from actual truth—thus encourage Costa Ricans, rulers and ruled alike, to treat each other with a restraint and respect often absent in several neighboring countries.

This shared culture has helped keep Costa Rica considerably more peaceable than its neighbors, but it has not prevented inequality, social mobilization, conflict, and political turmoil. The following chapters examine political participation and political culture in more detail. They seek to understand how Costa Ricans engage each other and the state in the political arena, as well as the attitudes and values they bring to the process.

Notes

1. Mavis Hiltunen de Biesanz, Richard Biesanz, and Karen Zubris de Biesanz, *Los costarricenses* (San José, Costa Rica: Editorial Universidad Estatal a Distancia, 1979), pp. 281–282.

2. Estimate based on Inter-American Development Bank (IADB), *Latin America After a Decade of Reform: Economic and Social Progress in Latin America, 1997 Report* (Baltimore: Johns Hopkins University Press, 1997), tables A-1, A-2.

3. Based on Biesanz et al., *Los costarricenses*, pp. 244–251. Income shares for each group are very rough estimates; the Biesanzes did not estimate shares for all classes.

4. The Gini coefficients in Table 5.1 confirm declining income inequality, but the benefits clearly failed to reach the poor.

5. Estimate derived from income distribution and median income data in Table 5.1.

6. Carlos Castro Valverde, "Sector público y ajuste estructural en Costa Rica (1983–1992)," in Trevor Burns, ed., *La transformación neoliberal del sector público: Ajuste estructural y sector público en Centroamérica y el Caribe* (Managua: Coordinador Regional de Investigaciones Económicas y Sociales, 1995), pp. 74, 104–105.

7. Castro Valverde (ibid., pp. 63–67) shows that taxes were shifted to the poor and that government sharply reduced spending and investment in education and health.

8. Ibid., pp. 66–67. See also Jorge Rovira Mas, *Costa Rica en los años '80* (San José, Costa Rica: Editorial Porvenir, 1989), pp. 108–135.

9. Larry Rohter, "Costa Rica Chafes at New Austerity," *New York Times*, September 30, 1996, p. A7.

10. Biesanz et al., *Los costarricenses*, pp. 273–277; Carlos Meléndez and Quince Duncan, *El Negro en Costa Rica* (San José: Editorial Costa Rica, 1972); John A. Booth, Alvaro Hernández C., and Miguel Mondol V., *Tipología de comunidades,* vol. 2: *Estudio para una tipología de comunidades* (San José, Costa Rica: Direccion Nacional de Desarrollo de la Comunidad–Acción Internacional Técnica, 1973); Rohter, "Costa Rica Chafes," p. A7; "The Black Community in Costa Rica," *Mesoamerica*, March 1994, pp. 11–13.

11. Marcos Guevara Berger and Rubén Chacón Castro, *Territorios indios en Costa Rica: Orígenes, situación actual y perspectivas* (San José, Costa Rica: García Hermanos, 1992); Biesanz et al., *Los costarricenses*, pp. 270–273; *Mesoamerica*, December 1993, p. 10.

12. Biesanz et al., *Los costarricenses*, pp. 277–280; Martha Honey, *Hostile Acts: U.S. Policy in Costa Rica in the 1980s* (Gainesville: University of Florida Press, 1994).

13. *Mesoamerica*, February 1995, p. 4.

14. Costa Rica became a diocese in 1850, having been previously under the Managua diocese. This section draws heavily on Philip Williams, *The Catholic Church and Politics in Nicaragua and Costa Rica* (Pittsburgh: University of Pittsburgh Press, 1989), chs. 5–7; and Biesanz et al., *Los costarricenses*, ch. 9.

15. Miguel Picado, "Cambios dentro del catolicismo costarricense en los últimos años," in Juan Manuel Villasuso, ed., *El nuevo rostro de Costa Rica* (Heredia, Costa Rica: Centro de Estudios Democráticos de América Latina, 1992), p. 46.

16. This section is drawn from Biesanz et al., *Los costarricenses*, pp. 499–506; Picado, "Cambios dentro del catolicismo," pp. 50–51; Jaime Valverde, *Las sectas en Costa Rica: Pentecostalismo y conflicto social* (San José, Costa Rica: Editorial Departamento Ecuménico de Investigaciones–Centro de Coordinación de Evangelización y Realidad Social–Consejo Superior Universitario Centroamericano, 1990).

17. Valverde, *Las sectas en Costa Rica*, pp. 74–80.

18. This section is based on María Pérez Y., "Costa Rica: Las comunicaciones al ritmo del mundo," pp. 209–250, and Eduardo Ulibarri, "Los medios de comunicación: Diversidad con desafíos," pp. 251–262, both in Villasuso, *El nuevo rostro*.

19. Pérez Y., "Costa Rica: Las comunicaciones," p. 213.

20. For instance, there are the social democratic movement's Latin American Center for Democratic Studies (Centro de Estudios Democráticos de América Latina, or CEDAL), the Latin American Social Science Faculty (Facultad Latinoamericano de Ciéncias Sociales, or FLACSO), and the Superior University Council of Central America (Consejo Superior Universitario de Centro America, or CSUCA), whose publishing house is known as the Editorial Universitaria Centroamericana (EDUCA).

21. This law functions similarly to the civil law tradition of libel in Britain and the United States, by which one may recover damages for injury caused by the irresponsible publication of falsehoods.

22. Ulibarri, "Los medios," pp. 260–261.

23. *Mesoamerica*, August 1994, pp. 9–10; June 1996, p. 10; and "Press Freedom in the Americas: Breaking the Chains of Censorship," April 1996, pp. 7–8.

24. For instance, a U.S.-financed Voice of America transmitter started in 1985, and Radio Impacto, a CIA operation set up in 1982, broadcast anti-Sandinista propaganda into Nicaragua. See Honey, *Hostile Acts*, pp. 258–259.

25. Picado, "Cambios dentro del catolicismo," p. 46.

26. Honey, *Hostile Acts*, pp. 255–261.

27. This section is based on Astrid Fischel, *Consenso y represión: Una interpretación socio-política de la educación costarricense* (San José: Editorial Costa Rica, 1987); Yolanda M. Rojas, "Transformaciones recientes en la educación costarricense," pp. 97–122, and Jorge Rovira M., "Las universidades en los años ochenta," pp. 123–140, both in Villasuso, *El nuevo rostro*; and Biesanz et al., *Los costarricenses*, ch. 8.

28. Constitution of 1847, in Fischel, *Consenso y represión*, p. 63.

29. Article 6, constitution of 1869, from Fischel, *Consenso y represión*, pp. 64–65.

30. Costa Rica had no university per se until 1940, when the Universidad de Costa Rica opened. Certain schools, such as the law school, remained open as separate entities.

31. Fischel, *Consenso y represión*, tables 1 and 2.

32. Bernhard Thibaut, "Costa Rica," in Dieter Nohlen, ed., *Enciclopedia electoral latinoamericana y del Caribe* (San José, Costa Rica: Instituto Interamericano de Derechos Humanos, 1993), p. 185.

33. Rojas, "Transformaciones recientes," p. 101.

34. Ibid., p. 166.

35. Rovira M., "Las universidades," pp. 124–127.

36. Rojas, "Transformaciones recientes," p. 107.

37. My conversations with faculty revealed that universities were also hard hit, eroding programs, research efforts, salaries, and faculty quality.

38. Rojas, "Transformaciones recientes," p. 100.

39. Rovira M., "Las universidades," pp. 133–137.

40. Rojas, "Transformaciones recientes," p. 122.

41. Booth et al., *Tipología de comunidades*.

42. Oscar Arias Sánchez has studied interest groups and *colegios* in his *Grupos de presión en Costa Rica* (San José: Editorial Costa Rica, 1971) and political elites in his *Quién gobierna en Costa Rica?* (San José, Costa Rica: Editorial Universitaria Centroamericana, 1976).

43. Carlos Sojo, *Costa Rica: Política exterior y sandinismo* (San José, Costa Rica: Facultad Latinoamericano de Ciencias Sociales, 1991), pp. 119–123.

44. John A. Booth, "Costa Rican Labor Unions," in Gerald W. Greenfield and Sheldon L. Maram, eds., *Latin American Labor Unions* (New York: Greenwood Press, 1987); Manuel Rojas B., "Un sindicalismo del sector público," in Villasuso, *El nuevo rostro*, pp. 181–189; Elisa Donato M. and Manuel Rojas B., *Sindicatos, política y economía: 1972–1986* (San José, Costa Rica: Ediciones Alma Mater, 1987).

45. Four major confederations divided the rest of the unionized workforce in the late 1970s. About half the organized workforce was linked to the communist-dominated General Confederation of Workers (Confederación General de Trabajadores, or CGT) and other leftist unions combined into the Unitary Confederation of Workers (Confederación Unitaria de Trabajadores, or CUT) in 1981. A series of unsuccessful banana strikes during the 1980s split the CGT and caused a loss of members and affiliates. Other union associations were linked to the Social Christian movement or were part of two social democratic coalitions, the Costa Rican Confederation of Democratic Workers (Confederación Costarricense de Trabajadores Democráticos, or CCTD) and the Authentic Confederation of Democratic Workers (Confederación Auténtica de Trabajadores Democráticos, or CATD). The CUT split in the mid-1980s, giving rise to the Confederation of Workers of Costa Rica (Confederación de Trabajadores de Costa Rica, or CCTR). The National Workers Confederation (Confederación Nacional de Trabajadores, or CNT) broke away from the CCTD also during the mid-1980s. In 1986 another effort was made to form a general federation of independent union confederations, giving rise to the Permanent Council of Workers (Consejo Permanente de los Trabajadores, or CPT). See Rojas, "Un sindicalismo del sector público," pp. 187–188.

46. Gustavo Blanco and Orlando Navarro, *El solidarismo: Pensamiento y dinámica social de un movimiento obrero patronal* (San José: Editorial Costa Rica, 1984); Oscar Bejarano, "El solidarismo costarricense," in Villasuso, *El nuevo rostro*, pp. 203–298; Centro de Estudios Democráticos de América Latina (CEDAL) and Asociación de Servicios de Promoción Laboral (ASEPROLA), *El problema solidarista y la respuesta sindical en Centroamérica* (Heredia, Costa Rica: CEDAL-ASEPROLA, 1989).

47. Jorge Mora A., "Los movimientos sociales agrarios en la Costa Rica de la década de los ochenta," in Villasuso, *El nuevo rostro*, p. 155.

48. Programa de las Naciones Unidad para el Desarrollo (PNUD), *Estado de la nación en desarrollo humano sostenible 1994* (San José, Costa Rica: Programa de las Naciones Unidas para el Desarrollo–La Defensoría de los Habitantes de la República–Consejo Nacional de Rectores, 1994), p. 12.

49. Biesanz et al., *Los costarricenses*, p. 282.

6

POLITICAL PARTICIPATION

Classical democratic theory views citizen political participation as the essence of democracy. Formal democratic rules of the game specify the rights and protections of citizens that enable them to take part in ruling their community. The very structure of representative democracy, however, necessarily reduces citizen involvement in making and executing decisions even though citizens elect their leaders. Although participation is thus limited in a representative democracy like Costa Rica, the amount and nature of actual citizen activity nevertheless remains a critical aspect of democracy and its quality.

Democracy's success may also stem from civil society, from citizens' involvement in organizations. Belonging to groups may nurture both political participation and commitment to democracy. Moreover, the representation of citizens' interests through organizations may shape public policy, and vigorous civil society may improve government performance.[1]

This chapter explores the structure, level, and determinants of citizen participation in Costa Rica and the impact of civil society upon both participation and democratic norms.

Exploring Participation

One way to study political participation is through the use of survey research, specifically, by asking a representative sample of citizens whether they vote, contact public officials, and so on. Its political freedom has made Costa Rica a prime site for public opinion surveys, so considerable data exist on the types, levels, and

TABLE 6.1   Political Participation Levels, 1973 and 1995 (percent involved)

Type of Participation	1973[a]	1995[b]
Voted last election	83.8	87.6[c]
Attend at least one organization's meetings[d]	66.1	–[e]
Worked with neighbors on community project	55.9	42.0
Attend school group meetings[d]	26.8	36.3
Attend communal organization meetings[d]	20.8	36.2
Contact one or more public officials	30.6	35.3
Ever member of a political party	21.5	–[e]
Ever tried to convince someone how to vote	–[e]	28.1
Ever worked for a candidate or party	–[e]	25.8
Contact municipal council member	10.6	18.9
Contact legislative assembly deputy	10.3	10.8
Attend cooperative meetings[d]	10.5	8.5
Contact president	3.4	8.3
Attend union meetings[d]	5.3	8.1
Attend civic association meetings[d]	4.0	5.1

[a]1973 sample is a national sample of 1446 Costa Rican family heads.
[b]1995 sample is an urban, *meseta central* sample of 701 citizens.
[c]Datum based on 660 respondents 18 or older at time of 1994 election.
[d]Attend at least "from time to time."
[e]No comparable item available.
sour ces: 1973 and 1995 surveys.

structure of political participation there. This section relies primarily upon two surveys: a national sample of 1,446 Costa Rican heads of family conducted in 1973 and an urban sample of 701 Costa Rican citizens conducted in 1995.[2] These surveys had important differences: The first was a national sample, the second urban only; the first was a survey of family heads, the second a cross-section of urban citizens. Finally, the 1973 and 1995 surveys do not contain precisely identical items on political participation, although many of them are quite similar.[3] These differences require us to make comparative inferences with caution, but they nevertheless provide much information about Costa Ricans' political behavior and attitudes.

The 1973 National Survey

Early students of participation once believed that most citizens of most societies were not very politically active, especially in the Third World. Comparative research that defined participation broadly proved such impressions to be incorrect.[4] The 1973 national sample survey revealed that Costa Ricans participated in many political activities and at rates comparable to the rest of Latin America and to the industrial democracies.[5]

Levels.   What were the nature and levels of citizen activity in Costa Rica in 1973? Table 6.1 demonstrates that voting was the most common activity, with almost 84 percent involved. Nearly two-thirds of respondents belonged to at least one organization. Almost 56 percent of Costa Rican heads of families reported working on at least one community improvement project, and more than one in five said they occasionally attended community organization meetings. More than one-fifth of the respondents were political party members. About three in ten had contacted at least one public official, about one in ten had contacted a municipal council member, and another tenth a legislative deputy. Clearly, overall political participation was diverse and widespread despite the rarity of some activities.

Structure.   What patterns did Costa Ricans' participation reveal? As in other nations, a study of the relationships or correlations among types of citizen action revealed clusters (modes) of related activities. A statistical technique known as factor analysis applied to seventeen different participation variables revealed several modes. For example, various activities in organizations were much more strongly linked to each other than to other citizen actions, thus forming a group activism mode. Five other distinct modes also emerged: voting (Photo 6.1), contacting public officials, partisan activism (Photo 6.2), discussing politics, and communal activism.[6] For further analysis, indicators were constructed based upon the variables defining each mode.

The modes of participation in Costa Rica were generally similar to those found in other democracies.[7] To some extent, of course, participation modes in particular nations depend upon the peculiarities of individual political systems. For instance, some authoritarian regimes suppress elections and parties. In contrast, group activism and contacting public officials have been detected even in very repressive regimes.

Communal activism entails citizens' collective self-help efforts on behalf of their communities. By the time of the 1973 survey, Costa Rica had encouraged citizen involvement in community improvement efforts for over ten years. The National Community Development Directorate had organized hundreds of community development associations, and the Catholic Church had for decades promoted its own community improvement groups. It is little wonder, then, that communal activism appeared as a distinctive political behavior.

In comparative terms, four modes of participation found in Costa Rica—voting, party activism, group activism, and contacting public officials—had been identified elsewhere. Levels of participation appeared comparatively ordinary except for two things: First, Ticos voted more than citizens of most other nations (probably because voting was mandatory). Second, party activism (attending party meetings and rallies) was exceptionally high in Costa Rica.[8]

Concentration.   How concentrated or dispersed was political participation among Costa Ricans in the 1970s? Did a few citizens perform the bulk of the ac-

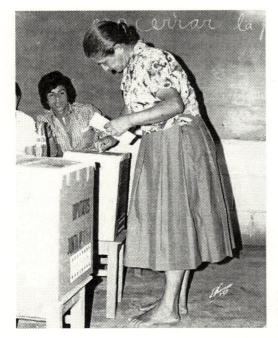

PHOTO 6.1   Political participation: voting (photo by Julio Laínez, courtesy *Tico Times*)

PHOTO 6.2   Political participation: a Monge campaign rally, 1982 (photo by Julio Laínez, courtesy *Tico Times*)

tivity, leaving most people largely inactive, or was participation broadly distributed?

The 1973 study found that one person in seven reported no political participation at all. The most activism reported by any individual was twenty-one separate activities. The most frequently reported number was two (16 percent), and the mean was 3.6. Put another way, about three in ten Costa Ricans reported engaging in only one activity or fewer. Another three in ten reported two or three activities, and the remaining 40 percent claimed four or more political activities. This and other evidence revealed some concentration of participation among an activist segment of the population. However, there was certainly no tendency for a handful of Costa Rican activists to dominate—half the respondents had engaged in two to five activities.[9]

Another way to evaluate the concentration of citizen activity was to examine whether modes of participation were statistically associated with one another. The indicators (indexes) for each mode in the 1973 survey were modestly intercorrelated (see Appendix, Table A.8). Organizational activism associated most strongly with each of the other modes, and voting the least. This evidence also confirmed a certain dispersion of participation among Costa Ricans rather than extreme concentration among a few activists. The correlation of organizational activism—a measure of civil society—with other forms of participation supports the claim that group membership leads citizens to engage the government.

Correlates of Participation.   Because not all citizens participate at equal rates, it is useful to know what shapes or "correlates with" political activity. Prior research has identified several key factors including education, income, occupational status, sex, age, the size and location of one's community, and certain attitudes and information.[10]

Community Context.   With one exception, Costa Ricans in 1973 tended to be more active the more prosperous were their communities.[11] The clear and strong exception to this pattern involved communal self-help activism, which was considerably more common in poorer communities. Participation in most activities (except in organizations and communal projects) was lower in isolated rural communities lying outside the *meseta central.* Communal participation was the opposite—high in peripheral areas. Although the effect of community size on other types of participation was negligible, it sharply increased communal activism in smaller communities and lowered it in larger ones. It is clear that the lack of services and resources that characterized small, rural towns motivated Costa Ricans to work together to improve their communities.

Socioeconomic Factors.   The 1973 survey revealed a strong tendency for Costa Ricans with higher incomes, more education, and higher occupational status to be more active in most modes of participation.[12] This pattern had one important exception, however: communal activism. Participation in communal self-help projects was found to correlate with such socioeconomic status (SES) factors in essentially the opposite way to other participation modes: Communalism was higher among Costa Ricans with lower incomes, less education, and lower occupational status.

The explanation for this difference is that in Costa Rica, as in most societies, higher income, education, and occupational status all convey upon their beneficiaries critical resources for participation—such as higher levels of information and communications skills. They also tend strongly to give their beneficiaries higher stakes in society—for example, property, economic, and social advantages—that need promotion and defense. In contrast, citizens of lower SES could be expected to face many pressing needs but have fewer resources with which to pursue them. They would be less likely to engage the government than higher SES Ticos but more likely to work with their neighbors to improve their lives and communities.

Sex, Age, and Religion.   There was a clear tendency for Costa Rican female heads of household to participate less than males in all six modes of participation. This pattern was strongest for communal activism and for group membership. Three factors probably account for lower participation by women: First, traditional social roles would tend to let men dominate the political and communal arenas. Second, men would probably have had greater resources than women (higher SES, for instance), better enabling them to participate. Third, other factors equal, females heading households would likely have less opportunity than men with spouses to participate outside the household because of childcare obligations.

The 1973 study found that rates of all modes of participation generally increased the older citizens became, up through age fifty-five, then declined fairly sharply thereafter.[13] The reasons for this life-cycle-related rise and decline in participation are complex, with several factors involved. Very young citizens are less likely than others to be married and have families and more likely to be mobile, factors that reduce the motivation for participation. In contrast, the older citizens become through the late middle years, the more likely they are to have higher incomes, more property, and greater family and communal commitments that may draw them into politics. As citizens become elderly, their incomes and health tend to decline, reducing their resources for participation.

The 1973 survey found religious identification to have a modest effect upon political participation. Catholics (90 percent of the sample) had slightly higher participation rates on all six participation modes than others (the bulk of whom were Protestants of one sort or another).

The 1995 Urban Survey

Levels.   What were the nature and levels of citizen activity in urban Costa Rica in 1995? How much did they resemble those found in 1973? Table 6.1 presents the levels of various citizen political activities from the 1995 survey; some items may be directly compared to levels reported in 1973. Voting was the most common activity, reported by 88 percent. (There is a very small amount of overreporting of voting among our respondents, a common phenomenon in most participation surveys.[14]) Forty-two percent of Costa Rican urban citizens reported working on at least one community improvement project, and more than one-third said they attended community organization meetings at least from time to time.[15] Although the 1995 survey did not ask for political party membership, it did ask about campaign activity. Over 28 percent had tried to convince someone else how to vote, and almost 26 percent had worked for a political party. More than one-third of the respondents had contacted at least one public official, one in five had contacted a municipal council member, and one in ten a legislative deputy. One person in twelve reported having contacted the president or having attended cooperative meetings and union meetings.

Clearly, and as was true for the 1973 national head of household sample overall, political participation was rather widespread in urban Costa Rica in 1995. This was true despite many activities being undertaken by small fractions of the urban population. Comparatively speaking, Table 6.1 reveals that urban Costa Ricans in 1995 reported considerably less communal activism than did the 1973 national sample. This makes sense, given the strong negative relationship found between various indicators of urbanism and communalism in 1973. Self-help activity was much more common in small, rural, poor communities isolated from the national capital. Conversely, on most other comparable items, the 1995 urban sample reported somewhat higher levels of participation than the 1973 national sample. Again, this is not surprising, given that urbanites on average had higher levels of resources than rural dwellers, who were included in the earlier sample. Moreover, the accessibility of public officials and organizations is greater for urban dwellers than for rural ones.

Structure.   What patterns did urban Costa Ricans' citizen activism reveal in 1995? Were there similar modes to those found in 1973? Factor analysis of fifteen participation variables revealed five modes, some of them quite similar to those found in 1973: Group activism, voting, contacting public officials, and communal activism were virtually identical to the 1973 modes. A campaign activism mode appeared, including working for a candidate or party, which likely tapped into the mode labeled "party activism" in 1973. There were no political communication items in the 1995 survey. For further analysis, indicators were constructed for each of the five 1995 modes.[16]

The modes of participation in Costa Rica in both 1973 and 1995 were quite similar to those found in other democracies. Of particular interest here is to compare Costa Rica's modes of participation to those of the rest of urban Central America in the early 1990s. Surveys employing identical participation items were conducted in urban areas of the five other nations of the isthmus in 1991 and 1992. A factor analysis of participation variables for the pooled 4,200 respondents of all six Central American urban samples produced a highly similar result to that reported here for Costa Rica.[17] Five modes emerged: voting, contacting public officials, campaigning, group activism, and communalism.[18] Even though in such countries as Guatemala, El Salvador, and Nicaragua formal democratization is recent and many types of citizen participation have only lately become safe to engage in, the general modal patterns of urban citizen action observed there differ little from Costa Rica's.

If the structure of participation is similar across Central America's now formally democratic regimes in the early 1990s, what about levels of participation? One suspects that levels of activity in the different modes might vary quite a bit according to the histories of repression in each nation. A study of the effect of repression upon the political participation of urban Central Americans found that high levels of political repression strongly predicted low levels of citizen activism.[19]

The data in Table 6.2 generally corroborate this finding. Overall participation rates in the more repressive regimes (Guatemala, El Salvador, and Nicaragua) were substantially lower than in the less repressive nations (Panama, Honduras, and Costa Rica). Least repressive Costa Rica led the isthmus in voting and communal activism, tied for first in contacting, and was in a virtual dead heat with Honduras for first in overall participation. Yet although Costa Rica is the least repressive, Ticos came in second in campaign activity and fourth overall in group activism. The low level of group activism stems partly from Costa Rica's very low level of labor organization (see Chapter 5). Nevertheless, overall Costa Rica has a rather politically active urban citizenry.

Concentration.   How concentrated was political participation among urban Costa Ricans in the 1990s? Were a few citizens responsible for most of the activity, or did a broad array become involved?

An overall participation indicator for the 1995 survey revealed that fewer than one person in fifty reported no political participation at all.[20] Thus far fewer urbanites in 1995 were completely inactive than the one in seven family heads reported in the 1973 national sample. As in the 1973 national sample, the highest score reported was twenty-one. The most frequently reported score for the 1995 urban sample was four, and the mean was 5.6—much higher than for the 1973 national survey. About 36 percent of 1995 urban Ticos had taken part in six to ten activities, double the rate for the 1973 sample. Thus 1995 urbanites sample had more widely distributed participation than found the nationwide sample in 1973.

A second way to evaluate the concentration of citizen activity is to examine how much the individual modes of participation are related to or associated with each other. The indicators (indexes) for each mode in the 1995 survey were only modestly intercorrelated (see Appendix, Table A.9). Communalism had the strongest overlap with other modes, especially contacting public officials. This makes considerable sense given what we know about Costa Rica's Legislative Assembly, which generously dispenses financing to community projects around

TABLE 6.2 Urban Costa Rican Participation Compared to Other Central America Countries

Variable	Costa Rica	Guatemala	Honduras	El Salvador	Nicaragua	Panama	Region
Voting[a]	1.91	1.51	1.86	1.39	1.62	1.72	1.67
Campaigning[b]	.87	.25	1.08	.18	.47	.84	.62
Contacting public officials[c]	.56	.41	.77	.32	.17	.56	.46
Communal self-help activism[d]	1.80	1.09	.87	1.05	1.56	1.28	1.27
Group activism[e]	.47	.66	1.05	.33	.43	.84	.63
Overall participation[f]	5.62	4.01	5.65	3.22	4.32	5.22	4.70

not e: Differences of means between countries on all participation and democratic norms items significant at the .0001 level or greater.

[a]Registered to vote plus voted in last election; yes = 1, no = 0 for each; range = 0–2.

[b]Attempted to persuade others how to vote or worked on campaign in last or prior election; 1 = yes, 0 = no for each; range = 0–3.

[c]Ever contacted president, legislative deputy, city council member, or national government agency; yes = 1, no = 0; range = 0–4.

[d]Involvement in five community self-help activities; 1 = yes, 0 = no for each; range = 0–5.

[e]Sometimes attend union, civic association, cooperative, or professional association meetings; yes = 1, no = 0 for each; range = 0–4.

[f]Sum of scores on contacting, communal, campaigning, voting, and group activity; range = 0–18.

sour ce: John A. Booth and Patricia Bayer Richard, "Repression, Participation, and Democratic Norms in Urban Central America," *American Journal of Political Science* 40 (November 1996); 1215, table 1.

the nation. Group activism overlapped somewhat with contacting and with communalism but not with voting or campaigning. Campaign activism associated most with contacting and communal activism. Voting had only tenuous links to other modes, but this was likely because it varied so little—almost everyone was registered to vote and more than 80 percent voted.

Overall, then, there was only modest concentration of participation among urban Costa Ricans in the 1990s. Almost all urbanites engaged in at least some political activities, and many took part in quite a few. The pattern appears to indicate somewhat less concentration of participation than among the 1973 national sample. Urban Costa Ricans, therefore, seem to be fairly actively engaged in the polity.

Correlates of Participation.   What factors shaped the political activism of urban Costa Ricans?

Socioeconomic Factors.[21]   The 1995 survey revealed a fairly strong tendency for Costa Ricans with higher incomes and more education to be more active in most modes of participation. As the breakdowns of participation levels by levels of income and education in Table 6.3 demonstrate, higher educational attainment corresponded with significantly higher average participation levels on all participation modes except voting. Higher family income generally contributed to higher citizen activism, except for voting and contacting.[22]

With one exception, these patterns resembled those found in 1973. Unlike the earlier sample, communal activism in the 1995 urban study correlated positively with SES factors. Among these urban residents, communalism was more common, not less, among those with more income and education. The explanation for this difference most likely derives from the exclusively urban 1995 sample. There is no rural population of much poorer, much less educated, and much more community involved citizens. I suspect that had we also conducted a rural survey in 1995, the results on communalism would have shown the poorer, less-educated rural Ticos to be more active in communal affairs than their urban counterparts.

Sex, Age, and Religion.   In the 1995 urban sample, there were no significant differences in the levels of political participation between men and women (Table 6.3). Women were slightly less active overall, but the difference was statistically meaningless. This finding is in sharp contrast to the 1973 result, which consistently showed female heads of household to participate less than males. Urban women's participation may have caught up with men's in Costa Rica by the mid-1990s. It is also possible that were the data available, one might detect greater male-female differences in the countryside where male-dominant roles and male resource advantages would likely have persisted more than in rural areas. There may also be a difference related to the survey strategy. The 1973 sample included family heads, whereas the 1995 sample is a cross-section of all urban women. The 1995 female sample thus included many women with fewer childcare responsibilities than the 1973 female family heads.

TABLE 6.3 Demographic Factors and Participation in Costa Rica, 1995

Variable	Voting	Campaigning	Contacting	Communal Activism	Group Activism	Overall Participation
Education						
Up to 6 years	1.71	1.05	.28	1.54	.42	5.01
7–11 years	1.68	1.14	.40	1.81	.79	5.79
12 years or more	1.81	1.38	.46	2.00	2.32	7.94
Significance[a]	NS	*	*	*	***	***
Family income[b]						
Lowest	1.71	1.21	.42	1.61	.49	5.43
Medium low	1.70	1.30	.34	1.81	1.21	6.33
Medium high	1.81	.94	.35	1.79	1.71	6.60
Highest	1.79	1.43	.48	2.29	1.84	7.81
Significance[a]	NS	*	NS	**	***	***
Sex						
Male	1.73	1.26	.40	1.89	1.33	6.55
Female	1.75	1.15	.37	1.72	1.09	6.05
Significance[a]	NS	NS	NS	NS	NS	NS
Age						
18–25	1.33	1.32	.24	1.13	.96	4.98
26–35	1.82	1.22	.40	1.17	1.35	6.50
36–45	1.83	1.14	.44	2.29	1.52	7.17
46–55	1.97	1.33	.46	2.06	1.41	7.23
56 or older	1.78	.92	.37	1.74	.42	5.23
Significance[a]	***	NS	NS	***	***	***
Religion						
Catholic	1.75	1.19	.35	1.79	1.12	6.16
Protestant	1.64	1.11	.48	1.79	1.18	6.20
None or other	1.81	1.40	.56	1.92	2.08	7.77
Significance[a]	NS	NS	*	NS	**	*

[a]Significance of difference of means (analysis of variance): * = .05, ** = .01, *** = .001, NS = not significant.

[b]Family income categories are: lowest = up to 50,000 *colones* per month; medium low = 50,001–110,000; medium high = 110,001–170,000; and highest = over 170,000 *colones* per month.

sour ce: 1995 survey.

Table 6.3 also presents participation means by age levels. As in 1973, Costa Ricans in 1995 tended to become more active up through age fifty-five, after which participation declined. The expected life-cycle pattern generally held for voting, communalism, and group activity but not for campaigning and contacting. Campaigning appeared to vary randomly across the age cohorts of urban Ticos.

The 1995 survey found religious identification to affect only some modes of political participation. Further, it found that the direction of association between religious identification and contacting, group activism, and overall participation to have reversed from the 1973 findings. Catholics (80 percent of the respondents) were modestly less politically active than Protestants. The remainder of respondents (including other religions and those professing none) made up the most active cohort. (In 1973 Catholics had slightly higher participation rates on all six participation modes than other religious identifiers.) The 1995 differences were significant only for contacting, group activism, and overall participation, but the patterns were fairly consistent. This finding suggests that religious minorities in Costa Rica were organized and more active contacters than Catholics—perhaps in defense of their interests in this legally and predominantly Catholic society.

Attitudes.   Among the variables in the 1995 urban study that were not available in 1973 were several items that explore Ticos' beliefs and opinions. Students of political participation elsewhere have noted several attitudes that appear to influence citizens' propensity to engage in politics. Among the attitudes found to shape participation in Central America are the following:[23] Interpersonal trust involves a belief that others can be trusted in general and will not be prone to take advantage of one. Life satisfaction taps the sense of being satisfied with one's situation and resources. Anticommunism measures antagonism toward communists and communist regimes. Support for democratic norms is measured by a scale that taps tolerance for democratic liberties.[24] Left-right ideological orientation is a measure in which respondents classify themselves as left oriented or right oriented along an intensity scale. Finally, respondents were asked to choose whether the nation needed radical change, reform, or no change at all.

Breakdowns of how these attitudes affected participation may be found in the Appendix in Table A.7. The data reveal generally inconclusive relationships and very few strong or systematic patterns, with a few exceptions: Those who are more trusting engage significantly more in contacting officials and communal and group activities. The stronger citizens' democratic norms, the more active they are in groups. Those who prefer radical changes in the political system campaign more and participate more in groups than those preferring moderate or no change.

In an attempt to summarize findings on attitudes, the attitudinal variables and major demographic variables were introduced into a multiple regression analysis of each participation index from the 1995 sample. Multiple regression permits an examination of the independent contribution of each attitude to participation levels, holding other variable effects constant. The result, simply stated, is that none of the attitudes contributed significantly to the variation of any of the participation variables when demographic effects were filtered out. In fact, age and education were the only significant factors in shaping participation.

Unconventional Participation

The forms of citizen action discussed so far all involve legal, generally accepted types of activity that occur within normal channels. They do not involve protesting or demonstrating against government policy, civil disobedience, or committing acts of political violence. Although Ticos view themselves as politically orderly, especially in comparison to their neighbors in the isthmus, their nation has been no stranger to protest, confrontation, and even violence and terrorism. The tumultuous 1940s, culminating in the 1948 civil war, underscores this point, but confrontational and sometimes violent participation remains part of Costa Rican politics.

Such confrontational political activities often invoke strong disapproval or may violate the law. Survey research thus works poorly for studying such participation because most respondents are reluctant to discuss it with an unknown interviewer, making it impossible to report precisely on levels and types of unconventional political activity. Various other sources, however, offer interesting insights into unconventional activism.

Agrarian Movements and Protests.   Costa Rica has a tradition of agrarian protest and conflict as its small producers and rural wage workers have contended with changing economic times and problems. In recent decades various forces have altered the agricultural economy: the exhaustion of the agrarian frontier, expanding production of such land-hungry agroexport products as cattle, the promotion of nontraditional agricultural exports, the decline of traditional exports such as bananas, and the increasing efficiency of modern production methods that reduce rural wage labor.

Intensified by the economic crisis of the early 1980s, these changes profoundly affected key segments of Costa Rican agriculture. Agriculture, though remaining important, declined in contribution to GDP from around 19 percent in 1970 to less than 16 percent in 1995.[25] The percentage of workers engaged in agriculture has fallen by almost half since 1960 (Appendix, Table A.1). Recent international economic pressures have led the government to reduce programs that once helped small farmers.[26]

Landless and land-poor Costa Rican peasants, displaced by rural population growth or market forces, have at various times protested and invaded property, seeking land to cultivate. On occasion acting alone but often within organized movements, peasants have illegally occupied and cultivated parcels of land belonging to the state or private individuals.[27] When pressured to vacate the invaded property, peasants have typically responded with organization, petitions to government, protests, lawsuits, and sometimes violent resistance. Government agrarian reform agencies such as the Institute of Land and Colonization (Instituto de Tierras y Colonización, or ITCO), later replaced by the Institute of Agrarian Development (Instituto de Desarrollo Agrario, or IDA), have often defused such conflicts by purchasing the land and deeding it to the occupiers or by finding alternative land for colonization. In the 1980s, however, "there occurred a marked deterioration in the conditions of production and survival of the majority of producers. At the same time, the institutional capabilities to respond and channel the demands—made by thousands of families who had lost the means, land, or work to obtain the income necessary to subsist—were sorely limited."[28]

Responding to intensifying agrarian problems during the 1980s, some 20,000 small producers joined the UPA Nacional and other farm organizations. UPA Nacional organized farmers' protests nationwide to pressure the government for land and accelerated agrarian reform. During the 1980s the number of farmers' unions jumped dramatically. Some 126 new agrarian groups registered with the Labor Ministry from 1983 to 1990, a ninefold increase in only eight years. Of the 142 peasant organizations registered in 1990, 57 percent were independent, 30 percent were affiliated with social Christian and social democratic unions, and 6 percent with the (by then declining) communist unions.[29]

Although strikes are nominally economic rather than political, in Costa Rica they have important political dimensions because the Labor Ministry must approve them and the state often becomes involved in negotiating settlements. Costa Rica's banana workers' union, founded in the 1930s, has periodically struck for better working conditions and higher wages and has regularly mobilized protests. In 1984, for instance, stung by the news that the Compañía Bananera de Costa Rica would switch more than 2,800 acres of banana cultivation to oil palm, a much less labor-intensive crop, members of the Golfito Workers Union (Unión de Trabajadores de Golfito, or UTG) illegally occupied the plantation in question. Upon learning soon afterward that the company would abandon an even larger banana plantation, the UTG mounted a sixty-two-day strike—the nation's longest ever. These efforts failed catastrophically when the company used the labor unrest to justify completely ceasing production in the region.

Urban Protests. Costa Rica's urban population has grown rapidly, from about one-third of the national population in 1960 to approximately half by the mid-1990s (Appendix, Table A.2). Urban growth accelerated notably during the 1980s and 1990s, especially in metropolitan San José and other meseta central cities.[30] Urban growth and the economic crisis of the 1980s shaped urban political protest and conflict—especially struggles for housing and urban services and the efforts of the burgeoning informal economic sector to defend itself from regulation.

The Center for Studies of Social Action (Centro de Estudios para la Acción Social, or CEPAS) reviewed newspaper reports of urban movements from 1950 through the mid-1980s and found that in the 1950s urban Costa Ricans took to the streets mainly to protest the state's plans to centralize and improve electric and water utilities and raise their rates.[31] During the 1960s urban movements arose around the struggle for housing, a predominant theme ever since (Photo 6.3). Significant numbers of urban squatters began to invade and build rudimentary houses on private and public property—even road and bridge rights of way. Squatters organized politically to resist removal and to press for services and land titles. In the 1970s public protests, some including violence, manifested public anger about telephone service costs and the quality and cost of public transportation.

PHOTO 6.3   Unconventional participation: a COPAN housing protest (photo by María E. Esquivel, courtesy *Tico Times*)

During the 1980s 47 percent of Costa Rica's urban movements involved housing conflicts (land titling for squatters, housing construction, and slum removal), 19 percent protested the cost or quality of public mass transport, and smaller percentages protested water quality and rates, electrical rates, and the regulation of informal-sector businesses (itinerant vendors). These vendors were people trying desperately to survive by selling small quantities of anything from earrings to oranges, toothpaste to T-shirts. They increasingly clogged the sidewalks and streets, including those outside established shops and stores. These businesses pressed the cities and national government to regulate and remove the informal vendors, who loudly and occasionally violently protested police efforts to dislodge them.

In tactical terms, of 167 urban movements in Costa Rica between 1980 and 1986, 28 percent were protest demonstrations, 22 percent blocked streets and highways, and 20 percent involved invasions of land or forced removals from invaded land. Another 30 percent took forms ranging from the occupation of public buildings and offices to public denunciations to hunger strikes. In the struggle for housing, "the invasion of land was the most efficacious form of protest and that most employed to secure one's own shelter."[32]

Several multicommunity housing movements took part in organizing housing struggles and protests, including COPAN, the Democratic Front for Housing

(Frente Democrática de Vivienda, or FDV), the Costa Rican Front for Housing (Frente Costarricense de Vivienda, or FCV), and the National Association for Housing (Asociación Nacional de Vivienda, or ANAVI). These organizations enjoyed so much success in so many neighborhoods that they became political resources for electoral politicians. "A good share of these movements provoked land invasions and created new squatter settlements of diverse sizes or enlarged existing ones."[33] Some of these settlements were extensive: Los Guidos in San Miguel de Desamparados had 17,000 inhabitants, and Chacarita in Puntarenas had 16,848 inhabitants, half the city's population. The housing organizations have often won policy concessions from the government. There is evidence, however, that political parties have co-opted some groups and the participation of their members rather than the groups' having developed into a powerful independent political force.[34]

Political Violence.   In comparison to other Central American nations, Costa Rica has had little political violence. That is not to affirm, however, that there has been none. During the 1940s considerable violent and confrontational mobilization both in favor of and against the government of Calderón Guardia and his communist allies culminated in the 1948 civil war (see Chapter 3). Since then three main types of political violence have occurred: riots, violent labor and land conflicts, and armed extremist movements.

Rioting occurs sporadically in Costa Rica as groups of demonstrators confront police. One particularly violent outbreak of rioting took place in the Atlantic coast port of Limón in August 1979. In that incident Limón residents, many of them black, clashed repeatedly with police after a demonstration over problems afflicting the local economy, unemployment, and inferior services got out of hand.

More recent examples of riots reveal the continued vitality of confrontation as a mode of participation. One involved residents of a housing project in Pavas, a San José suburb. In 1993 the Housing Ministry attempted to relocate some squatters onto land designated for a school without notifying the residents. Community members protested and set up a roadblock. "Civil guards sent in to remove the blockade threw tear gas bombs and the situation escalated to a full-scale riot."[35] In another case residents of the Colorado district of Guanacaste had lobbied the Legislative Assembly to grant them the status of a *cantón* (county). When the assembly voted down the initiative, "Colorado residents took to the streets to protest.... [They] set up a roadblock, which denied access to the ferry that is the major link over the Tempisque River."[36] This action cut off the passage of supplies to and from a major salt-processing plant and a cement factory. In resulting negotiations with the government, the community won at least part of its demands—limited fiscal and administrative autonomy from the existing county government.

Labor unions and peasant groups sometimes clash violently with the Civil Guard. For example, during a May 1993 banana workers' strike against the Geest

PHOTO 6.4   Unconventional participation: street vendors chain themselves together to protest efforts to regulate them, 1991 (photo courtesy *Tico Times*)

Caribbean company, workers blockaded the entrance to a plantation in Sarapiquí. When the Rural Guard attempted to clear the barrier, workers threw stones, injuring sixteen officers. Police gunfire wounded eighteen workers.[37] Such violent conflicts between workers and civil authorities, though not the predominant mode of government-union interaction, have nonetheless occurred frequently in Costa Rica.[38]

There appears to be a sense among Costa Rican activists that a violent confrontation with public authorities, especially if it is well covered by the press, may elicit conciliatory policy from the government. It is a typical pattern for a confrontation that turns violent to cause public authorities to call for calm, meet with the movement's leaders to negotiate an end to the confrontation, study the problem at issue, and make policy concessions. Ticos know of their government's long historical record of responding quickly—and often favorably—to the occupation of buildings, blocking of roads, or invasion of land. This reiterated and well-publicized pattern clearly encourages protesters to escalate their tactics when organizing, lobbying, or peaceful protests fail to gain their objectives (Photo 6.4).[39]

Armed Extremist Groups.   Since its civil war, Costa Rica has experienced other sporadic violence, including occasional terrorism by armed domestic groups of the right and left. Revolutionary groups from Panama, Nicaragua, and other Central American countries have also operated in Costa Rica. These foreign actors have so influenced Costa Rican radicals that it has been difficult to determine whether those responsible for violent acts are domestic or external.

Nicaraguan insurgents have been particularly active in Costa Rica. In the late 1970s, the FSLN sought to overthrow the government of Anastasio Somoza Debayle. During the presidency of Rodrigo Carazo Odio, the FSLN operated relatively openly in Costa Rica, with guerrilla camps in the north, open recruiting in the streets, and the Nicaraguan revolutionary government in exile installed in San José. As Costa Ricans' enthusiasm for the Nicaraguan revolution quickly waned after the FSLN's victory in 1979, Nicaraguan exile counterrevolutionary (*contra*) forces soon also operated openly in Costa Rica. During this turbulent period from the late 1970s through much of the 1980s, foreign groups and their antagonists committed many violent and terrorist acts.[40] President Monge (1982–1986) was especially tolerant of *contra* presence and activity, cooperation that the United States compensated through massive foreign assistance.[41] His successor, Oscar Arias Sánchez, however, was much less tolerant of the *contras* and led wider Central American efforts to bring peace to the region. These actions substantially curtailed foreign political violence within Costa Rica by 1990.

Costa Rican native armed groups have also created problems. Rightist elements have been organized, armed, and active for decades. Best known among them has been the harshly anticommunist Free Costa Rica Movement (Movimiento Costa Rica Libre, or MCRL), founded in 1961 and affiliated with the World Anti-Communist League based in Taiwan.[42] The MCRL pledged to defend Costa Rica from communism, by force if need be. In the 1960s and 1970s, much of its public activity involved publishing newspaper advertisements denouncing alleged cases of communist influence. However, during the Sandinista insurgency and revolution in Nicaragua (1978–1990) the MCRL became increasingly violent. It cooperated with other anticommunist elements, the Sandinistas' enemies (the *contras*), and their CIA and Argentine military backers and engaged in various acts of political violence. The MCRL was involved in a Nicaraguan *contra* assault on the radio station News of the Continent (Radio Noticias del Continente) in 1980 and in the violent disruption of a demonstration against terrorism and a mob attack on the Nicaraguan embassy in 1981. MCRL members participated in an attack on the Nicaraguan embassy in 1985, and former members took part in a 1985 bombing of a power facility that exported electricity to Nicaragua.[43]

During the 1980s numerous other armed groups arose under the guise of "auxiliary" police forces. In 1981 Costa Rica established the Organization for National Emergencies (Organización para Emergencias Nacionales, or OPEN), similar in conception to the U.S. National Guard. The government also authorized other private security forces to bolster relatively scarce police resources at a time of considerable regional turmoil.

At least six paramilitary groups, ranging in size from a few dozen to about 1,000 members, became active. . . . They carried out military training exercises on private farms, and four of the groups became integrated into the National Reserve (originally called OPEN) where they received military instruction with U.S. weapons donated to

Costa Rica's Civil Guard. . . . All worked closely with the contras, were backed by large landowners and big businessmen, and were protected by the Ministry of Security.[44]

Paramilitary ranks rose into the thousands by the early 1990s. In addition to assisting the Nicaraguan *contras,* OPEN and other paramilitary groups spied on and intimidated suspected leftists and helped landowners evict or intimidate rural squatters.[45]

Many Ticos and outside observers became alarmed by the development of this rightist paramilitary infrastructure. Although this process was deeply entangled in the U.S. effort to help Nicaraguan counterrevolutionary forces topple the Sandinista revolution, thousands of Costa Ricans had joined groups that resembled in organization and ideology—if not in the extremes of terrorist behavior— the anticommunist death squads in El Salvador and Guatemala. Of course during the 1980s many Costa Ricans feared that revolutionary communism, spreading from the revolution in Nicaragua and insurgencies in El Salvador and Guatemala, might sweep over their country, and paramilitary group members no doubt viewed themselves as defending their nation from imminent communist expansion. Nevertheless, many others believed such paramilitary forces gravely threatened the country's democratic stability.

Despite the massive buildup on the right during the 1980s, there was little domestic revolutionary activity on the left. The Marxist parties and labor and peasant movements generally pursued a reformist agenda. Very few leftist organizations have employed political terror in service to a revolutionary agenda. The most notorious exception was the Marxist-Leninist revolutionary La Familia (the Family), which on March 16, 1981, bombed a U.S. embassy vehicle ferrying marine guards (three were injured). On the same day, the group attacked the consulate of Honduras.[46] The police soon captured several of La Familia's members in a spectacular chase and shoot-out. In June 1981 leftist terrorists killed four members of the security forces. In July a police officer shot to death in police custody a female suspect in the attack on the U.S. Marines.[47] Domestic leftist terror, however, subsided by the mid-1980s.

On balance, Costa Rica had a turbulent decade in the 1980s, as severe domestic economic problems motivated many citizens to mobilize and protest and as the geopolitical storms raging elsewhere in Central America spawned domestic violence. As the international environment cooled both in Mesoamerica and in the larger world after 1989–1990, political violence in Costa Rica diminished sharply. Bombings and assassinations subsided as foreign revolutionaries and counterrevolutionaries largely went home or quit the revolution business. What remained was Costa Ricans' own domestic political grievances, sometimes sufficient to mobilize violence—typically protester clashes with the police. Extreme right threats to the regime and citizenry ebbed with declining regional geopolitical turmoil.

Civil Society

Robert Putnam and others, following the argument of Alexis de Tocqueville, believe that civil society—citizen involvement in formal organizations—contributes importantly to the success of democracy.[48] In a study of Italy, Putnam contends that citizens' engagement in groups of many kinds enhances governmental performance. He argues that membership in groups creates "social capital," networks, norms, and social trust that help citizens cooperate for their mutual benefit. This concept may be usefully expanded to include "political capital," civic norms that support democratic governance (support for democratic liberties, opposition to military rule) and conventional political participation. Such attitudes would predispose citizens to support democratic government.[49]

Evidence above and in earlier chapters reveals that Costa Ricans do engage their government in many different ways: lobbying for appropriations for community improvements, contacting public officials, voting, trying to persuade others how to vote. It is also quite clear that they expect government to respond to these demands, whether expressed by conventional or unconventional means. Leslie Anderson argues, for example, that

> peasants have some familiarity with democratic political conditions in Costa Rica and know more or less what kinds of political action hold some possibility of success. They know that public opinion places some restraints on the behavior of the democratic state. . . . They know from national history and campaign rhetoric that the government feels some obligation to all citizens and will invest some of its resources in social development.[50]

But elsewhere she contends that peasants who organize confront such problems as agrarian agencies and police so manipulative and antagonistic toward peasant activism that they "raise great questions about the nature and depth of the Costa Rican democracy."[51]

How can we measure whether civil society creates social and political capital? To what extent does involvement in groups in Costa Rica build resources of trust, political knowledge, participation, and democratic norms to take advantage of the Costa Rican government's "obligation to all citizens"?

One way to answer these questions is to examine how participation in organizations affects various elements of social and political capital. Table 6.4 breaks down six social and political capital variables by levels of two types of civil society behavior: group activism and communal activism. The social and political capital variables are citizens' degree of interpersonal trust, political knowledge, support for democratic norms, and participation (voting, campaigning, and contacting public officials).

The findings in Table 6.4 support the civil society argument in Costa Rica. The impact of higher levels of group activism upon all six social and political capital variables was positive and significant: the greater the group activism, the higher

TABLE 6.4   Mean Levels of Political Capital by Levels of Civil Society, Urban Costa Rica

	Group Activism				Communal Activism			
	Low (424)	Medium (81)	High (149)	Significance[a]	Low (208)	Medium (232)	High (215)	Significance[a]
Interpersonal trust	.72	.90	1.07	****	.73	.86	.88	NS
Political knowledge	.70	1.08	1.09	****	.74	.81	.95	*
Democratic norms	6.55	6.84	7.36	****	6.67	6.86	6.78	NS
Voting	1.71	1.67	1.86	*	1.68	1.75	1.79	NS
Campaigning	1.08	1.25	1.48	**	.95	1.05	1.59	****
Contacting public officials	.30	.54	.56	****	.18	.30	.67	****

[a]Significance of difference of means (analysis of variance): * = .05, ** = .01, *** = .001, **** = .0001, NS = not significant.
sour ce: 1995 survey.

the levels of trust, political knowledge, democratic norms, and all three types of participation. The impact of participating in communal-level civil society was less clear. Political knowledge, campaigning, and contacting public officials all increased significantly among those most communally active. Communalism's effect on voting, democratic norms, and trust was not significant.

Because some of both the civil society and political capital variables are affected by demographics such as sex, education, and standard of living, these apparent links require a closer look. A multiple regression analysis was performed for each social and political capital variable, including both the civil society measures and demographics, in order to determine the truly independent effects of group and communal activism. The analysis substantially refocuses the evidence revealed in Table 6.4. When the effects of demographic variables are held constant, most of the previously detected effects of group membership on political capital vanish. They stem actually from sex and education. Females had lower knowledge scores and democratic norms. Respondents with higher education had higher levels of trust, political knowledge, and democratic norms. However, there were two exceptions to this pattern: First, campaigning was clearly independently increased by higher communalism. Second, contacting public officials rose with higher group activism and increased markedly with greater communal activism.

Thus in the urban milieu of the mid-1990s, much of the apparent social and political capital of interpersonal trust, political knowledge, and democratic norms derived from education and sex rather than from civil society. Civil society activities did lead urban Ticos to work for political campaigns and to contact public officials. This squares with other recent findings that organized urban dwellers in Costa Rica, especially in poorer neighborhoods, are likely to engage in partisan activity and that politicos seek contacts with their organizations. These groups "created a new political arena in the country and were the active social base of deputies, ministers, and even presidents."[52]

Summary and Conclusions

Costa Ricans have actively participated in politics in recent decades at levels comparable to industrialized countries. Some modes of their participation are both enduring and comparable to those found elsewhere in Central America—voting, campaigning, organizational and communal activity, and contacting officials.

The government welcomes and rewards participation of many sorts. It encourages conventional political activity and often responds favorably to citizen pressure through the national budget, legislation, and administrative action. The state also rewards and thus encourages much unconventional activity—even some violent confrontations with authorities.

One leaves this review of participation and policy response in Costa with a sense that there exists something of an open dialogue between the citizenry and the government: Expecting attention, citizens mobilize and petition the state. The state dedicates personnel, programs, and resources to attend to citizen demands, thus reinforcing the propensity of Costa Ricans to bring pressure upon their government. This dialogue takes place through the formal channels of representative government (citizens petitioning municipal councils and Legislative Assembly deputies), through the efforts of political parties to mobilize and co-opt other interests and organizations in their struggle to capture power, and through an almost ritualized direct communication between mobilized citizen protesters and public officials.

Events of 1998 require me to close this chapter with a note of caution about participation through voting and the parties. Several groups urged Ticos to abstain from the 1998 election to protest economic difficulties, the PUSC-PLN joint domination of the polity, and the poverty of meaningful options offered voters. This campaign apparently succeeded. Turnout in 1998 declined by almost a seventh below its usual average of 82 percent for 1962 through 1994 (see Table 3.4). Another form of abstention, the casting of blank and null (defaced or improperly marked) ballots, jumped by two thirds in 1998 (see Chapter 4). Such a sharp deviation from well-established participation patterns strongly suggests that Costa Rica's well-ingrained institutional participation channels can be disrupted. It remains to be determined whether this remarkable 1998 voter protest and withdrawal constitute merely a salutary wake-up call to the regime and parties from disgruntled citizens and groups, or whether it marks a true erosion of Costa Rican democracy.

Notes

1. Robert D. Putnam, *Making Democracy Work: Civic Traditions in Modern Italy* (Princeton: Princeton University Press, 1993); and Robert D. Putnam, "Bowling Alone: America's Declining Social Capital," *Journal of Democracy* 6 (January 1995): 65–78.

2. The 1973 survey involved a stratified probability sample of 1,446 Costa Rican family heads conducted under my direction by DINADECO, at that time an agency of the Ministry of Government. Funding for the study was provided by the U.S. Agency for International Development and DINADECO. The 1995 survey of 701 Costa Ricans was conducted under my direction, with funding from the Latin American Center of the University of Pittsburgh. Fieldwork was supervised by Cynthia Chalker of the University of Pittsburgh. The questionnaire was designed and the field research conducted as a part of a cooperative six-nation study of Central American urban dwellers) in collaboration with Chalker and Mitchell Seligson of the University of Pittsburgh and with the active participation of his students Andrew Stein, Annabelle Conroy, Orlando Pérez, and Ricardo Córdova. Guatemalan fieldwork was funded by a grant from the North-South Center of the University of Miami and conducted by the Asociación de Investigación y Estudios Sociales (ASIES) of Guatemala City. Funding for these surveys came from a variety of sources, including the North-South Center, the University of Pittsburgh, and the University of North Texas. The 1973 Costa Rica survey, the 1995 Costa Rica survey, and the five other Central American surveys all were drawn from sampling units stratified by predominant economic class, with sample size proportionate to estimated population. Cluster sampling and age quotas were used in all the 1995 urban surveys. The 1973 survey em-

ployed random sampling of dwelling units. Unless otherwise specified, all references to the surveys in tables are drawn from these sources.

3. I participated directly in the design of the questionnaire and samples in both Costa Rican surveys.

4. The low participation thesis was advanced most forcefully by Lester Milbrath in *Political Participation* (Chicago: Rand McNally, 1965). The major studies debunking this myth were Sidney Verba and Norman H. Nie, *Participation in America: Political Democracy and Social Equality* (New York: Harper and Row, 1972), and Sidney Verba, Norman H. Nie, and Jae-on Kim, *The Modes of Democratic Participation: A Cross-National Comparison* (Beverly Hills: Sage, 1971). On Latin America, see John A. Booth, "Political Participation in Latin America: Levels, Structure, Context, Concentration, and Rationality," *Latin American Research Review* 14 (Fall 1979): 29–60.

5. John A. Booth, "A Replication: Modes of Political Participation in Costa Rica," *Western Political Quarterly* 29 (December 1976): 627–633; Mitchell A. Seligson and John A. Booth, "Peasants as Activists: A Re-evaluation of Political Participation in the Countryside," *Comparative Political Studies* 12 (April 1979): 29–59.

6. John A. Booth, "Democracy and Citizen Action in Costa Rica: The Modes and Correlates of Popular Participation in Politics," Ph.D. dissertation, University of Texas at Austin, 1975, pp. 114–136.

7. Booth, "Political Participation in Latin America"; Verba and Nie, *Participation in America*; Verba, Nie, and Kim, *The Modes of Democratic Participation*.

8. Booth, "Democracy and Citizen Action," pp. 139–140.

9. Ibid., pp. 101–114.

10. Verba and Nie, *Participation in America*, chs. 8–13; Jack H. Nagel, *Participation* (Englewood Cliffs, N.J.: Prentice-Hall, 1987), chs. 4–5; M. Margaret Conway, *Political Participation in the United States* (Washington, D.C.: Congressional Quarterly Press, 1991), ch. 2; Steven J. Rosenstone and John Mark Hansen, *Mobilization, Participation, and Democracy in America* (New York: Macmillan, 1993), chs. 4–5; John A. Booth and Patricia Bayer Richard, "Repression, Participation, and Democratic Norms in Urban Central America," *American Journal of Political Science* 40 (November 1996): 1205–1232.

11. Booth, "Democracy and Citizen Action," chs. 4–5.

12. This pattern is consistent with most other comparative research on participation cited above. Data reported in this section drawn from ibid., ch. 6.

13. Verba and Nie, *Participation in America*, pp. 145–148, found a somewhat similar pattern in the United States. See also Conway, *Political Participation*, pp. 17–21.

14. Seligson et al. estimated the overreporting of voting in this urban Costa Rican sample to be no more than 2 percent—within the error margin of the survey; see Mitchell A. Seligson, Annabelle Conroy, Ricardo Córdova Macías, Orlando J. Pérez, and Andrew J. Stein, "Who Votes in Central America? A Comparative Analysis," in Mitchell A. Seligson and John A. Booth, eds., *Elections and Democracy in Central America, Revisited* (Chapel Hill: University of North Carolina Press, 1995), pp. 154–158.

15. In a 1992 study of poor urban neighborhoods in San José, 40 percent of respondents reported belonging to a political party and 12.5 to a community organization. Alejandro Portes and José Itzigsohn, "The Party or the Grassroots: A Comparative Analysis of Urban Political Participation in the Caribbean Basin," *International Journal of Urban and Regional Research* 18 (September 1994): 497.

16. Index construction was generally quite simple. In almost every case, all items related to a mode as defined by the factor analysis results were standardized and summed. Higher values of the indexes correspond to higher levels of participation.

17. In this chapter and elsewhere in the book, the samples from each country, in reality varying somewhat in number, have been weighted to roughly 700 respondents per nation. This eliminates possible distortions due to sample size of comparisons between nations.

18. See Booth and Richard, "Repression, Participation, and Democratic Norms," tables 1, 4, and 5.

19. Ibid., tables 4 and 5.

20. The overall index was created by summing the separate indexes for the five modes of participation.

21. Because the 1995 sample is only urban, there little variation in community context to analyze.

22. Voting likely failed to show significant differences in means against either education or income levels because it varies so little. More than 80 percent of Costa Ricans vote; almost all register.

23. Booth and Richard, "Repression, Participation, and Democratic Norms," table 3.

24. Two major approaches to measuring democratic political culture have emerged, one associated with the civic culture/polyarchy concept and the other with political tolerance. The former measures democratic culture in terms of the general willingness to extend political participation rights to others. The latter measures democratic norms in terms of willingness to grant political rights to disliked groups. Our measures of support for democratic liberties included fourteen items tapping respondents' attitudes toward political participation rights in general and for regime critics. We constructed an overall democratic norms measure that is the arithmetic mean of respondents' scores for all fourteen items. See Booth and Richard, "Repression, Participation, and Democratic Norms."

25. Estimate from Inter-American Development Bank (IADB), *Economic and Social Progress in Latin America: Overcoming Volatility, 1995 Report* (Baltimore: Johns Hopkins University Press, 1995), tables B1 and B8.

26. Lucía Chinchilla, "Cambios en la agricultura costarricense en los últimos años," pp. 457–470, and Jorge Mora A., "Los movimientos sociales agrarios en la Costa Rica de la década de los ochenta," pp. 143–160, both in Juan Manuel Villasuso, ed., *El nuevo rostro de Costa Rica* (San José: Centro de Estudios Democráticos de América Latina, 1992).

27. Mitchell A. Seligson, *Peasants of Costa Rica and the Development of Agrarian Capitalism* (Madison: University of Wisconsin Press, 1980); Jorge Mora A., *Movimientos campesinos en Costa Rica* (San José, Costa Rica: Facultad Latinoamericano de Ciencias Sociales, 1992); and Leslie Anderson, "Mixed Blessings: Disruption and Organization Among Peasant Unions in Costa Rica," *Latin American Research Review* 26, 1 (1991): 111–143; Leslie Anderson, *The Political Ecology of the Modern Peasant* (Baltimore: Johns Hopkins University Press, 1994); and Jorge Rovira Mas, *Costa Rica en los años '80* (San José, Costa Rica: Editorial Porvenir, 1989), pp. 114–120.

28. Mora, "Los movimientos sociales agrarios," p. 153.

29. Mora, *Movimientos campesinos*, p. 49. See also Anderson, "Mixed Blessings," and Leslie Anderson, "Alternative Action in Costa Rica: Peasants as Positive Participants," *Journal of Latin American Studies* 22 (February 1990): 89–113.

30. Jorge Vargas C., "Los movimientos urbanos en Costa Rica durante los ochenta," in Villasuso, *El nuevo rostro*, p. 165; and Rovira Mas, *Costa Rica en los años '80*, pp. 108–114.

31. Cited in Vargas C., "Los movimientos urbanos," pp. 176–177.

32. Ibid., p. 176.

33. Ibid., p. 178.

34. Portes and Itzigsohn, "The Party or the Grassroots," pp. 491–508.

35. "Costa Rica," *Mesoamerica*, November 1993, p. 10.

36. Ibid., May 1996, p. 9.

37. Ibid., June 1994, p. 11.

38. "Behind the Myth of Rural Equity," *Latin American Weekly Report*, September 30, 1983, pp. 10–11; "Paramilitary Row in Rural Evictions," *Latin American Weekly Report*, June 13, 1991, p. 9.

39. Anderson, "Alternative Action"; Anderson, "Mixed Blessings," p. 143.

40. One series of domestic and foreign incidents involved the radio station Radio Noticias del Continente in 1980–1981. The station broadcast from Costa Rica news on human rights violations by Latin American military governments. It was attacked on at least two occasions, once with incendiaries by a light plane and another time on the ground by former Nicaraguan national guard elements and others, who were captured by the police. The Carazo government eventually closed the station. Anticommunist supporters of the captured Nicaraguans later hijacked a Costa Rican aircraft and forced the Costa Rican government to release the Nicaraguan prisoners. See *Latin American Weekly Report*, November 14, 1980, p. 12; January 2, 1981, p. 12; February 20, 1981, p. 11; November 11, 1981, p. 11; and Martha Honey, *Hostile Acts: U.S. Policy in Costa Rica in the 1980s* (Gainesville: University Press of Florida, 1994), pp. 245–246, 296, 377.

41. Honey, *Hostile Acts*, chs. 8–10; John A. Booth, "Central America and the United States: Cycles of Containment and Response," in John D. Martz, ed., *United States Policy in Latin America: A Decade of Crisis and Challenge* (Lincoln: University of Nebraska Press, 1995), pp. 191–192, 201–202.

42. Honey, *Hostile Acts*, pp. 203, 245, 313–317.

43. Ibid.

44. Ibid., p. 333; see also pp. 334–337.

45. "Paramilitary Row," p. 9.

46. A few days later, 15,000 Costa Ricans responded with a multiparty march in San José to protest terrorism, but the demonstration itself was disrupted by MCRL rightists complaining about Costa Rican relations with Cuba.

47. *Latin American Weekly Report*, March 27, 1981, p. 11; April 3, 1981, p. 11; May 15, 1991, p. 8; June 26, 1981, p. 12; July 10, 1981, p. 11.

48. Putnam, *Making Democracy Work*; Putnam, "Bowling Alone," pp. 65–78.

49. See John A. Booth and Patricia Bayer Richard, "Civil Society, Political Capital, and Democratization in Central America," *Journal of Politics* 60, 3 (1998).

50. Anderson, *The Political Ecology of the Modern Peasant*, p. 31.

51. Quote from Anderson, "Mixed Blessings," p. 143; see also Anderson, "Alternative Action."

52. Vargas C., "Los movimientos urbanos," p. 177. See also Portes and Itzigsohn, "The Party or the Grassroots," pp. 504–506.

7

POLITICAL CULTURE

Political theorists and scientists argue that the political culture of mass publics is critical to democracy.[1] A society whose citizens are antagonistic to participation or democratic norms will have poorer prospects for democracy than one whose citizens embrace them. Elites, of course, play a key role in establishing and maintaining systems of government, one arguably more important than the values of mass publics.[2] Elite commitment to democracy appears essential to a democratic regime's establishment and survival, but the mass public's values—though perhaps less significant than elites'—help undergird democracy and constrain elite behavior.[3]

Latin American Political Culture and Costa Rica

A persistent image of Latin America is that its political culture embraces neither democratic norms nor democracy itself. Guillermo O'Donnell predicted that a coalition of middle- and upper-class authoritarians would indefinitely block Latin American democracy through bureaucratic authoritarianism.[4] Glen Dealy has argued that when Latin Americans speak of democracy, they refer not to political pluralism and competing interests but to "political monism or *monistic* democracy: that is, the centralization and control of potentially competing interests . . . an attempt to eliminate competition among groups."[5] Howard J. Wiarda has described Latin America as "Catholic, corporate, stratified, authoritarian, hierarchical, patrimonialist, and semifeudal to its core" and concluded "that democracy United States–style is probably ill suited to the nations of Iberia and Latin America."[6] From this perspective democratic Costa Rica has long seemed anomalous.

Some students of democratization advance reasons for pessimism about Latin America, and again Costa Rica appears anomalous. Ronald Inglehart contends that nations reach democracy through centuries of sociocultural change. Western democratic regimes, he argues, developed only after the advent of Protestantism led to increased economic prosperity, followed by greater interpersonal trust and then by democratic norms among mass publics.[7] However, other scholars have found conflicting evidence—high levels of support for democracy in Mexico, Nicaragua, and Costa Rica, all three predominantly Catholic, poor, and with low interpersonal trust among their citizens.[8]

These theories raise intriguing questions: What are the general outlines of Costa Rican political culture? To what extent do masses and elites commit themselves to political democracy? How do Ticos' democratic norms compare with those of their Central American neighbors? How widespread is the commitment to democracy?

Overview

Costa Rican political culture contains certain contradictory strains captured in part by one observer's comment that "Costa Rica's democratic reformism and respect for human rights have been tempered by other crosscurrents—traditional religious values, anticommunism, and racism—which have worked to create a largely conservative society."[9] Martha Honey believes that such contradictions arose from historical forces. Because of the country's comparatively "uneventful" history, "Costa Rica has developed a national character which is a curious blend of smug self-contentment, social enlightenment, humanistic values, anticommunism, and pro-Americanism. . . . In both their personal and political behavior, Costa Ricans are nonconfrontational. They prefer accommodation to conflict . . . [and] tend to rely on the pervasive, paternalistic welfare state."[10]

In their overview, the Biesanzes describe Ticos as having "faith in the system, general acceptance of it as legitimate. . . . They prefer to let scandals die and are not easily aroused to passionate defense of a position or cause; they prefer peace and compromise and leave most problems to the government."[11] They report that women have less interest in politics and less power than men, that the young are less engaged in politics, and that Ticos are quite proud of their political system and elections.[12]

Mass Political Culture

These expert impressions suggest some important themes running through Costa Rican culture. The 1995 survey of urban Costa Ricans provides data that even permit comparisons among Ticos and other Central Americans. The following discussion examines political culture by exploring three themes: general political culture, attitudes toward government, and democratic and authoritarian attitudes.

General Political Culture

Table 7.1 presents breakdowns of several basic political culture items for the 1995 urban sample. First, Costa Ricans manifested low levels of interpersonal trust:

TABLE 7.1   General Political Culture of Costa Rican Citizens, 1995 Urban Sample

	Percent	(N)
Life satisfaction index		
Very low	5.0	(34)
Medium low	11.6	(82)
Medium high	29.0	(203)
Very high	54.5	(382)
Interpersonal trust index		
Very low	43.6	(286)
Medium low	35.6	(234)
Medium high	15.7	(103)
Very high	5.1	(33)
Religious fundamentalism index		
Low	4.3	(30)
Medium	18.0	(123)
High	77.5	(533)
Anticommunism index		
Low	7.2	(49)
Medium	41.3	(278)
High	51.4	(347)
Left-right orientation[a]		
Extreme left	2.1	(14)
Moderate left	8.4	(54)
Center	37.2	(241)
Moderate right	34.3	(222)
Far right	18.0	(117)

n o t e: Indexes of interpersonal trust, religious fundamentalism, life satisfaction, and anticommunism each constructed from multiple related items; grouped as indicated for presentation.

[a]Left-right orientation was a ten-point scale on which respondents positioned themselves; grouped in two-point increments for presentation.

more than 79 percent fell in the low end of the trust scale. This raises an important problem, given Inglehart's theory that interpersonal trust is essential for the formation of democratic values.

Urban Costa Ricans reported high levels of religious fundamentalism, an irony in a society that many observers characterize as only weakly influenced by the Catholic Church. Eighty percent of our sample reported being Catholic (three-quarters of them actively practicing their faith), 13.1 percent were Protestants, and 4.6 percent reported having no religion.[13]

How satisfied were Costa Rican respondents with their lives in general? Life satisfaction has some bearing on citizens' penchant for political participation in Central America, with the less satisfied more active in politics and more committed to democratic norms.[14] Table 7.1 reveals a fair level of contentment among urban Ticos in 1995. Despite the political turmoil reported in Chapter 6, at least in 1995 most urban citizens seemed more content than dissatisfied with their lives. Only 15.6 percent reported low or medium low life satisfaction, but 54.5 percent had very high life satisfaction.

As predicted, urban Costa Ricans are intolerant of communism. Table 7.1 reveals that only about one of fourteen Ticos manifested low levels of anticommunism, whereas over half scored high on the measure. This is consistent with the nation's lengthy history of intense anticommunism in the press and official culture and dates in significant measure from communist participation in the Calderón Guardia regime and the 1948 civil war. When respondents chose their "least liked group" in society, 34.4 percent volunteered "communists," second only to homosexuals at 44.4 percent. Ironically, Costa Rican communists have enjoyed considerable political freedom and relatively free access to public office since soon after the civil war.

Given such anticommunism, one would expect Costa Ricans to identify more with the center and right of the ideological spectrum. Indeed, Ticos tended to be conservative. Although those who placed themselves in the political center were the most common (37.2 percent), over half saw themselves on the right, five times more than on the left.

Citizens' Attitudes Toward Government

What of Costa Ricans' attitudes toward the government and perception of how it treats them? Do citizens support the constitutional regime? Do they perceive themselves as free to participate in the public arena, able to affect public policy, and well treated by public officials?

Table 7.2 contains data that help answer these questions, beginning with diffuse support, which taps how respondents' evaluate national institutions—the political system in general, the Legislative Assembly, courts, government, and so on. The diffuse support index combines several of these items plus one measuring general pride in the Costa Rican political system. Costa Ricans clearly felt positive about their system: Some 81.1 percent were in the positive end of the scale and 39.4 at the very highest levels. The regime—as distinct from the specific government of the moment—enjoyed a large reservoir of diffuse support from its urban citizens.

One way to determine why such a large percentage of Costa Ricans feel such pride in their regime is to explore how they perceive their treatment by the government, how much freedom they have to participate, and how much influence they have on public policy. Almost twice as many respondents (49.0 percent) reported that "offices of the government" had treated them well or very well as reported bad or very bad treatment (26.7 percent). The middle-range response, translated into English in the table as "average," is the Spanish word "*regular.*" A more accurate translation from Costa Rican Spanish would be "okay but not that

TABLE 7.2   Attitudes Toward Government, 1995 Urban Sample

	Percent	*(N)*
Diffuse support index		
Very low	4.5	(31)
Medium low	14.4	(99)
Medium high	41.7	(285)
Very high	39.4	(270)
Perceived treatment by government offices[a]		
Very badly	10.3	(63)
Badly	16.4	(76)
Average ("*regular*")	28.1	(171)
Well	42.1	(256)
Very well	6.9	(42)
Perceived freedom to participate index		
Much fear	6.2	(41)
A little fear	16.7	(109)
Complete freedom	77.1	(500)
Perceived institutional respect for human rights index[b]		
Poor	27.4	(160)
Medium	26.7	(156)
Good	45.8	(267)
Political efficacy		
Low	23.7	(164)
Medium	52.2	(362)
High	24.1	(167)

n o t e: Indexes of diffuse support, freedom to participate, and political efficacy each constructed from multiple items; grouped as indicated for presentation.

[a]"How have you been treated by government offices?"

[b]Index composed of sum of opinions (yes = 1, no = 2) as to whether the Costa Rican police and judges "respect life."

great," connoting that the 28.1 percent of respondents in that range found their treatment only marginally acceptable. Few bureaucratic encounters (in Costa Rica or anywhere) are sources of joy for citizens, so to find that roughly half of Ticos evaluate their contacts with government offices favorably suggests a reasonable level of success by the government among this urban population. I surmise that citizens of rural areas, typically less well served by government, would likely express less satisfaction.

Do Costa Ricans believe that they may participate in politics without fear of intimidation? This perception is important to democracy because it would indicate citizens' perception of the risks of political involvement. The 1995 urban survey asked urban Costa Ricans whether they felt any "fear" or felt "completely free" to take part in politics and their communities (vote, participate in community issues, seek office, and participate in demonstrations). Table 7.2 presents the perceived freedom to participate index, constructed from these four items. It reveals that the vast bulk of Costa Ricans—77.1 percent—perceived themselves to be completely free to participate. Only 6.2 percent expressed "much fear" about participation.

Another measure of citizens' perception of political freedom involves their perception of the government's respect for human rights. The media have for decades inundated Costa Ricans with information about the violently repressive behavior of neighboring governments. During the late 1970s and 1980s, tens of thousands of refugees came to Costa Rica fleeing political repression elsewhere in the isthmus. How did Ticos view their own regime's respect for human rights, in particular the respect for life of their courts and police? Table 7.2 reveals that 45.8 percent of those responding to the 1995 survey perceived Costa Rican institutions' respect for human rights to be good (i.e., that both police and judges respect human life). However, despite the nation's generally positive evaluations from human rights agencies, citizens' view of institutional human rights performance contained important reservations. Over a quarter of the respondents believed that the respect for human life was only medium, and another quarter viewed it as poor.[15] Such reservations about institutional human rights performance, one may surmise, might well temper Costa Ricans' pride in their system and willingness to engage in certain types of participation.

A final question about citizen attitudes toward government involves the question of perceived efficacy, whether participation has any impact. Citizens who believe that their efforts to alter policy have some likelihood of success appear more likely to participate and to evaluate government positively. The 1995 survey included two items concerning whether "it is worth the trouble" to vote and to participate. Combined they provide an index of political efficacy, displayed in Table 7.2. Although only one person in four expressed a high level of efficacy, another half of the sample fell in the medium range. Urban Ticos, then, perceived themselves to be at least somewhat politically efficacious and a quarter strongly so. This perception by the mass public fits the images of participation from Chapter 6, in which citizens vote, campaign, and contact public officials.

In order to evaluate the overall contribution of these perceptions of government to Ticos' diffuse support for the political system, a multiple regression analysis was performed.[16] Only three variables had any impact on diffuse support: perceived respect for human rights (the strongest effect), perceived freedom to participate, and age. Thus evaluations of government mattered significantly in determining Costa Ricans' pride in their system. Citizens who viewed the regime as respectful of human rights, who believed themselves free to participate, and who were older had more pride in the regime.

Democratic Versus Authoritarian Values

Having learned that Costa Ricans take great pride in their system and tend to be ideologically conservative and anticommunist, one should also inquire about their commitment to democracy. How many Ticos hold democratic values, and how strongly? Is the mass public inclined more toward democracy or authoritarianism? How do Costa Ricans compare with their Central American neighbors in their commitment to democracy?

For the purposes of this discussion, I assume that democracy and authoritarianism constitute antithetical political systems. They lie on opposing ends of a continuum in which participation and authority over decisions are either concentrated and limited to a few citizens (authoritarianism) or widely dispersed among the citizenry (democracy). In this simple scheme, support for democratic principles and methods would constitute the negation or repudiation of authoritarian principles and methods and vice versa. The 1995 urban sample contained various items that tapped into such beliefs about Costa Ricans' preferences for democratic or authoritarian approaches to government. These items concerned fundamental *principles* about citizens' rights to take part and the *methodology* of participation.[17]

Democratic Principles. Table 7.3 demonstrates that respondents strongly favored general participation rights (73.7 percent in the most positive group). They also strongly opposed suppressing civil liberties (56.5 percent in the most positive group). In contrast, extending rights to regime critics, a tougher test of democratic principles, elicited less enthusiasm than the first two (only 38.8 percent fell in the most positive group). Nevertheless, even in this case of rights for regime critics 61.4 percent of Ticos placed themselves in the prodemocracy end of the scale. Only from 6.6 to 38.6 percent gave the authoritarian response to any of these items. That over one-third of Costa Ricans would deny participation rights to regime critics suggests a significant authoritarian undercurrent. Costa Rica's "authoritarians," however, might rejoin that given Costa Rica's history, such regime critics as communists might undermine existing democratic liberties if given the right to hold office or speak on television. Thus they might justify their reticence to extend participation rights to regime critics as a desire to preserve existing democracy.

Democratic Methodology. Do Costa Ricans also support democratic forms, methods of governance consonant with the participation rights they largely espouse? This seems a particularly important question given skepticism about extending participation rights to regime critics on the part of some. Table 7.3 details the answers of the 1995 urban respondents to questions about certain political methods.

One question examines the preference for strong leadership, a commonplace among Latin Americans and widely viewed as authoritarian. When asked whether Costa Rica needs "a strong hand to govern it," seven in ten responded affirmatively. Because respect for strong leadership is a widespread Latin American cultural value, however, this alone may not connote an authoritarianism. Other items help clarify the picture. Asked whether circumstances might ever justify a coup d'état, 30.6 percent responded affirmatively, an authoritarian reply. But when only three in ten

TABLE 7.3   Democratic and Authoritarian Values, 1995 Urban Sample

	Percent	(N)
Democratic principles		
Index of support for general participation rights		
Low (1–3)	2.4	(17)
Medium low (4–5)	4.2	(29)
Medium high (6–7)	19.8	(139)
High (8–10)	73.7	(517)
Index of support for regime critics' participation rights		
Low (1–3)	16.4	(115)
Medium low (4–5)	22.2	(156)
Medium high (6–7)	22.6	(158)
High (8–10)	38.8	(272)
Index of opposition to the suppression of democratic liberties		
Low (1–3)	7.2	(50)
Medium low (4–5)	13.0	(90)
Medium high (6–7)	23.4	(163)
High (8–10)	56.5	(393)
Democratic methodology		
"Does Costa Rica need a strong hand to govern it?"		
No	29.7	(206)
Yes	70.3	(488)
"Can a coup d'état ever be justified?"		
No	69.4	(477)
Yes	30.6	(210)
Index of support for civil disobedience		
Low (1–3)	84.0	(589)
Medium low (4–5)	11.7	(82)
Medium high (6–7)	2.8	(19)
High (8–10)	1.6	(11)
"Do you prefer dictatorship or democracy?"		
Democracy	92.3	(637)
Both the same	3.8	(26)
Dictatorship	3.8	(26)
"Which would you prefer: radical change of the political system, reforms, or no change at all?"		
No change	20.2	(139)
Reforms	77.4	(534)
Radical change	2.4	(17)

note: Indexes of support for general participation rights, regime critics' rights, opposition to suppression of democratic liberties, and civil disobedience each constructed from multiple items; responses scales 1–10 with 1 = low, 10 = high; grouped here as indicated for presentation.

would justify a coup, far fewer than the seven in ten favoring strong leadership, it suggests that strong leadership preference is a poor measure of authoritarianism.

The remaining three items, however, provide a strong counterpoint to these possibly authoritarian leanings. When asked whether the system should be changed radically, reformed, or not changed, 77.4 percent of Costa Ricans preferred gradual reforms, and only 2.2 percent wanted radical changes. When asked whether they preferred dictatorship or democracy, 92.3 percent preferred a democratic regime. And when asked a series of items about the acceptability of civil disobedience (here combined into an index), 95.7 percent opposed such confrontational techniques.

How do Costa Ricans compare to other Central Americans in their commitment to democracy? Are the urban citizens of the region's premier democracy the most committed to democratic norms of all Central Americans? Intriguingly, Ticos did not have the strongest commitment to democratic liberties among Central Americans. Table 7.4 presents the breakdown by country of three key measures of democracy and the index of support for civil disobedience among the urban dwellers of six Central American nations. On these 1–10 scales (1 being the lowest support for democracy and 10 the highest), Costa Ricans ranked first in the region on opposition to suppression of civil liberties, tied for second on supporting general participation rights, and ranked third within the region (behind Hondurans and Panamanians) on rights for regime critics. In contrast, Costa Ricans had the lowest tolerance for civil disobedience within the region. To the extent that opposing disruptive political methods within an established democracy reinforces the democratic regime, Costa Ricans stand out in this regard. This observed pattern fits what one might expect from citizens of a fairly responsive and well-consolidated democratic government.

Correlates of Political Culture

What factors account for Costa Rican's political culture? Education, income, sex, age, religion, and life experiences typically influence citizen attitudes and values. Table 7.5 breaks down four key elements of Costa Rican political culture by various levels of such variables for the 1995 urban sample.

Diffuse Support. Diffuse support (pride in the political system) may also be interpreted as a gross measure of its legitimacy. Only one of the demographic factors—age—revealed a significant relationship to Costa Ricans' levels of diffuse support. Older Costa Ricans, especially those over forty-five years, were more supportive than younger ones. That educational attainment, income, sex, and religion had no significant effects demonstrates that diffuse support was extremely widespread among the society's many socioeconomic subgroups and divisions.

Support for Democratic Principles. Table 7.5 reveals that overall support for democratic norms among Costa Ricans varied significantly and sharply with edu-

TABLE 7.4 Urban Costa Rican Democratic Norms Compared to Other Central American Countries

	Costa Rica	Guatemala	Honduras	El Salvador	Nicaragua	Panama	Region
Democratic principles							
General participation rights[a]	8.22	7.06	8.07	7.47	8.22	8.46	7.94
Oppose suppression of liberties[b]	7.04	6.25	5.82	5.25	6.45	6.78	6.26
Rights for regime critics[c]	6.12	4.60	6.99	5.21	5.69	7.10	5.98
Democratic methodology							
Support for civil disobedience[d]	1.93	2.01	3.41	2.12	2.42	1.96	2.31

sour ce: 1991–1995 surveys.

[a]Index of support for general participatory rights; range 1–10.

[b]Index of opposition to the suppression of civil liberties; range 1–10.

[c]Index of support for participatory rights for regime critics (tolerance); range 1–10.

[d]Index of support for acts of civil disobedience; range 1–10.

TABLE 7.5   Correlates of Political Culture Variables, 1995 Urban Sample

Variable	Diffuse Support[a]	Democratic Norms[b]	Civil Disobedience[c]	Authoritarian Methods[d]
Education				
Up to 6 years	5.11	6.78	1.91	.47
7–11 years	5.01	6.70	1.98	.40
12 years or more	5.98	7.89	1.91	.35
Significance[e]	NS	****	NS	NS
Family income[f]				
Lowest	5.06	6.67	2.02	.47
Medium low	5.00	6.94	1.86	.41
Medium high	5.29	7.36	1.82	.33
Highest	5.00	7.63	2.00	.38
Significance[e]	NS	****	NS	NS
Sex				
Male	5.09	7.35	1.95	.39
Female	5.03	6.94	1.92	.42
Significance[e]	NS	***	NS	NS
Age				
18–25	4.98	6.96	2.42	.47
26–35	4.95	7.14	2.05	.31
36–45	4.91	7.29	1.93	.54
46–55	5.27	7.14	1.48	.33
56 or older	5.48	7.05	1.37	.35
Significance[e]	***	NS	****	**
Religion				
Catholic	5.07	7.07	1.92	.37
Protestant	5.20	7.24	1.77	.49
None or other	4.73	7.55	2.28	.62
Significance[e]	NS	NS	NS	*
Communal activism				
Low	5.10	7.07	1.87	.36
Medium	5.08	7.24	1.95	.35
High	4.92	7.14	2.07	.58
Significance[e]	NS	NS	NS	***
Group activism				
Low	5.05	6.94	1.90	.38
Medium	5.12	7.35	1.99	.44
High	4.95	7.90	2.08	.48
Significance[e]	NS	****	NS	NS
Overall participation				
Low	5.08	6.88	1.84	.32
Medium	5.01	7.34	2.16	.49
High	5.06	7.37	1.85	.48
Significance[e]	NS	***	*	NS

[a]Index of diffuse support for the regime (range 1–7, 1 = low).
[b]Index of overall support for democratic norms (range 1–10, 1 = low).
[c]Index of support for civil disobedience (range 1–10, 1 = low).
[d]Index of support for authoritarian methods (range 0–3, 0 = low).
[e]Significance of difference of means (analysis of variance): * = .05, ** = .01, *** = .001, **** = .0001, NS = not significant.
[f]Family income categories are: lowest = up to 50,000 *colones* per month; medium low = 50,001–110,000; medium high = 110,001–170,000; and highest = over 170,000 *colones* per month.

cation. Ticos with the equivalent of some university education scored over a point higher on the democratic norms index than those with less education. Family income also signaled sharply differentiated support for democratic norms, with a steady increase in commitment as one moved up the income ladder. Sex as well had an impact on a respondent's democratic norms, men scoring higher (7.35) than women (6.94). The difference was modest, and women remained well in the democratic end of the scale, but the gap was statistically significant. Neither age nor religious affiliation affected commitment to democratic liberties.

To evaluate overall support for democratic norms more thoroughly, I ran a multiple regression analysis that included an array of potential attitudinal and participation correlates, including those discussed above.[18] In descending order, the most significant influences upon support for democratic liberties (all positive) were citizens' education, family income, diffuse support, and perceived respect for human rights. High levels of life satisfaction and anticommunism reduced Costa Ricans' support for democratic liberties. It is interesting to note that the inclusion of other variables as controls eliminated the apparent correlation between sex and democratic norms. In the more sophisticated statistical treatment that accounts for the impact of income and education, sex makes no difference in Ticos' commitment to democracy.

From these findings one may conclude that Costa Rica's investments in education and ameliorating poverty and its strong human rights performance have created conditions that undergird mass support for democracy. By educating its population, by helping citizens prosper, and by not abusing them, Costa Rica has reaped enormous benefits in regime legitimacy and a democratic mass culture.

Support for Civil Disobedience. What of civil disobedience, the political tactics of confrontation with government? Overall, Costa Ricans' support for it was quite low—well in the disapproving end of the ten-point scale. Age was the only demographic variable that had a significant impact upon Costa Ricans' propensity to endorse the use of confrontational political tactics. Table 7.5 shows a steady downward progression of support for civil disobedience as respondents' age advances. For example, eighteen- to twenty-five-year-olds scored over a point higher on the civil disobedience scale than citizens fifty-six or older.

Justification of Authoritarian Methods. Table 7.5 indicates that authoritarian proclivities rose and fell across age categories. Citizens aged thirty-six to forty-five were most tolerant of authoritarian political methods, followed by those aged eighteen to twenty-five. Ticos who were forty-six or older scored low on this index. One may smooth out these confusing peaks and valleys somewhat by averaging adjacent groups. Doing so reveals that Ticos aged eighteen to forty-five were more tolerant of authoritarian political methods than those forty-six or older. This finding corroborates the prior finding that tolerance of civil disobedience declined as age advanced.

Why did younger Costa Ricans express more tolerance of confrontational political tactics and more authoritarian political methods? Research has shown that young people all over Central America support civil disobedience more than their older peers.[19] In Costa Rica as elsewhere in Central America, university and high school students often recur to demonstrations and protests. They organize along partisan and ideological lines, especially in the universities. They also mobilize to defend low university tuition and higher education budgets.

Young people in general may also hold other beliefs that might lead them to be more authoritarian and predisposed to civil disobedience. A review of the relationship between age and various other factors reveals three patterns: First, Costa Rican youths perceived themselves as less free to participate than older citizens. Second, they had a lower opinion of the human rights performance of the police and courts than did older citizens. Third, the young supported the political system less than older Ticos. I surmise, therefore, that younger Ticos may well have viewed themselves as more constrained and limited by the political system and thus less supportive and approving of it than their elders. They may have believed that they had fewer tools with which to pursue their goals than their older and better-established fellow citizens. Recall that Chapter 6 demonstrated that protest, agitation, and confrontation often win policy concessions from Costa Rican public officials. Thus greater support for civil disobedience among the young may reflect an instrumentalization of this fact—those who see themselves as relatively powerless turning to civil disobedience because it often works.

Table 7.5 reveals no significant impact of educational attainment, family income, or sex upon tolerance of authoritarian political methods. However, there is a link with religious preference: Catholics were significantly less prone to endorse authoritarian methods than Costa Rica's religious minorities, Protestants, and those of other faiths or without religion.

Does political participation shape Costa Ricans' political attitudes and values? Table 7.5 also examines how levels of political participation affect diffuse support, democratic norms, civil disobedience, and justification of authoritarian methods. Two findings stand out: First, persons most involved in communalism expressed more support for authoritarian methods. Urban activists have developed a political methodology that involves confrontational tactics, and values supporting this appear stronger among younger Costa Ricans. Second, group activism and overall participation levels correlated with greater support for democratic norms.

What has emerged here is a picture of two quite different strains in Costa Rican political culture, each supported by a somewhat different experiential and demographic base. One strongly endorses democratic liberties and appears to be nurtured by higher levels of education, family income, and group and overall participation. The other strain has two components: One endorses civil disobedience; its strongest demographic correlate is youth. The second endorses authoritarian political methodologies; its correlates are youth, experience with communal activism, and minority religious status.

TABLE 7.6   Searching for Antidemocratic Ticos, 1995 Urban Sample (mean scores)

A. Ideological Extremists[a]

| | Ideological Orientation | | |
	Far Left (N = 33)	Far Right (N = 239)	Significance[b]
Perceived respect for human rights index	.76	1.29	**
Perceived freedom to participate index	6.13	7.08	***
Political efficacy index	1.96	2.74	***
Diffuse support index	3.82	5.42	****
Overall democratic norms index	6.69	7.03	NS
Rights for regime critics index	6.02	5.84	NS
Civil disobedience index	2.77	1.71	****
Justification of authoritarian methods index[c]	.65	.27	***

B. Communal Activists

| | Level of Communal Activism[d] | | |
	None (N = 227)	High (N = 149)	Significance
Perceived respect for human rights index	1.25	1.12	NS
Perceived freedom to participate index	6.77	7.40	***
Political efficacy index	2.57	2.53	NS
Diffuse support index	5.16	4.92	NS
Overall democratic norms index	6.98	7.14	NS
Rights for regime critics index	6.10	5.99	NS
Civil disobedience index	1.86	2.07	NS
Justification of authoritarian methods index[c]	.39	.58	**

(continues)

Several questions immediately arise from this observation: Who are these Costa Ricans who favor authoritarian political methodologies? Do they make up some identifiable socioeconomic group or cohort? What are their other political beliefs? Do they represent a core of activists potentially hostile to the current democratic regime? Are there enough Costa Ricans who oppose democratic norms or the democratic rules of the game to undermine the regime?

Searching for Antidemocratic Elements

Answers to the questions just posed are critical to understanding the Costa Rican democratic prospect if political culture supportive of democratic liberties and methods actually undergirds democracy. Table 7.6 further explores the 1995 sur-

TABLE 7.6   (*continued*)

| | C. Age Cohorts | | |
| | Years of Age | | |
	18 to 35 (N = 352)	36 and Older (N = 350)	Significance
Perceived respect for human rights index	1.09	1.29	**
Perceived freedom to participate index	7.08	7.23	NS
Political efficacy index	2.61	2.51	NS
Diffuse support index	4.96	5.15	*
Overall democratic norms index	7.07	7.19	NS
Rights for regime critics index	6.17	6.07	NS
Civil disobedience index	2.20	1.66	****
Justification of authoritarian methods index[c]	.38	.43	NS

[a]Respondents identifying themselves with the far left (positions 1–3 on the ten-point scale) or far right (positions 8–10 on the scale); those on center-left, center, and center-right excluded.

[b]Significance levels: * = .05, ** = .01, *** = .001, **** = .0001, NS = not significantly different.

[c]Index of justification of authoritarian methods constructed by giving one point each for affirmative responses to questions whether a coup d'état might be justified, not indicating a preference for democracy, and preference for radical change in the political system; range 0–3.

[d]Derived from index of communal activism; respondents scoring zero included in "none" category; those scoring 7 or 8 on scale (high end) included in "high" group; others (scoring 1–6) excluded.

vey respondents, subdividing them according to their left-right ideology, level of communal activism, and age.

Costa Rica's anticommunist political culture has long touted the left's alleged threat to democracy. Does having an extreme leftist or, for that matter, an extreme rightist ideology increase the likelihood that citizens might threaten or reject Costa Rica's democratic regime? How serious for democracy is the problem of ideological extremism?

Using a scale that let respondents identify their own positions along a left-right ideological continuum, the 1995 survey found only thirty-three persons who identified with the far left but 239 who identified with the far right. Part A of Table 7.6 presents the differences in scores on various attitudes between these groups. Compared to rightists, leftists perceived Costa Rica to be much less respectful of human rights, viewed themselves as less free to participate and less politically efficacious, and reported much lower diffuse support for the regime. Leftists reported both higher support for civil disobedience and justification of authoritarian political methods. It is striking, however, that no significant differences appeared between leftists' and rightists' commitment to democratic norms and support for the participatory rights of regime critics. Thus we find an intriguing contrast: Costa Ricans of the far left and far right disagree about political methodology but maintain very similar commitment to fundamental democratic principles.

How big are the differences between left and right over political methods? Are those of the far left strongly committed to authoritarian methods and those of the far right not? A look at the values (Table 7.6) on the justification of authoritarian methods index quickly answers the question. The scale ranges from zero to 3.0. The mean response for far leftists (.65) means that on average only about one-fifth of any of the thirty-three self-identifying leftist Ticos gave a positive response to even one of the three items on the scale. That constituted over twice as many justifications of authoritarian methods as occurred among the rightists, to be sure. A similar logic may be followed concerning the civil disobedience index. The leftists scored 2.77; though higher than the rightists, leftists remained strongly disapproving of authoritarian methods.

The potential threat to democracy from the left, however, seems tiny when one notes that fewer than one in twenty of the sample identified with the far left. Moreover, about four-fifths of them rejected all the authoritarian political methodologies, and on average they strongly disapproved of civil disobedience. What one might expect from the Costa Rican left, then, as disgruntled as its members seem to be about the regime and its human rights performance? In short, the left might display a modestly greater penchant for confrontational politics and civil disobedience, tactics widely employed in Costa Rica.

Is there a similar threat from the right? The numbers in Part A of Table 7.6 suggest that the far right tended to support the regime and perceived its human rights performance to be strong and themselves to be free to participate. The far right appeared as supportive of democratic norms and rights for regime critics as the left and was significantly less enthusiastic than the left about civil disobedience or authoritarian methods.

Perhaps because this far right group was so large (over one-third of the sample), it seemed possible that they might have harbored among them a smaller group of antidemocratic extremists. To pursue this possibility, I broke down the far right still further and isolated the sixty-eight Costa Ricans (9.7 percent of the sample) who placed themselves at the extreme right of the ideology scale, with the highest possible score of 10. However, not even this ultrarightist cohort manifested values that seemed menacing to democracy: They were the most system-supportive of all ideological groups and the least supportive of authoritarian methods or civil disobedience—well in the prodemocratic range of each scale. The ultrarightists averaged somewhat below the population mean on both overall democratic norms and support for regime critics but still scored in the democratic end of the scale. Popular ideological extremism, then, at least among the general urban population, seems to offer little menace to Costa Rica's democratic traditions and institutions.

Data in Table 7.5 and in Chapter 6 indicate that communal activists tended to approve of authoritarian political methods more than did other Costa Ricans. This striking finding suggests the opposite of what Putnam predicted about civil society: Instead of increasing support for democratic political tactics, communal activism might do the reverse. Does communal activism encourage an extremism that might threaten Costa Rica's democratic regime?

Table 7.6 (Part B) compares 227 respondents who were inactive in their communities with 149 who reported high levels of activism. It reveals little to distinguish between the groups: No significant differences between communal activists and inactives appeared on perceived respect for human rights, efficacy, or diffuse support. More important, no significant differences appeared between them on overall commitment to democratic liberties, respect for the rights of regime critics, or even support for civil disobedience. Communal activists perceived themselves as far more free to participate than inactives and manifested themselves somewhat more willing to endorse authoritarian methodologies (.58) than inactives (.38).

Only about one in five urban Ticos was highly active in communal affairs, and only 5 percent of these activists endorsed any of the three antidemocratic methodologies. These communal activists both strongly endorsed democratic liberties and disapproved of civil disobedience at rates similar to the inactives. Communal activism, therefore, does not incubate antidemocratic values in Costa Rica, although communalists appeared slightly more likely to embrace antidemocratic methods.[20]

What is the impact of age? Evidence shown in Table 7.5 revealed that younger Ticos supported both the regime and democratic norms less and antidemocratic methods more than their elders. This raises a most serious question, because Costa Rica experienced severe strains during the 1980s and early 1990s that could well have influenced the beliefs of a whole generation. Citizens under the age of thirty-five when the 1995 survey was taken were politically socialized during serious economic crisis, retrenchment of public services, and geopolitical crisis. One might reasonably surmise that such strains could undermine younger Costa Ricans' support for the regime or their commitment to democratic liberties and methods. How committed are the youth of Costa Rica to democracy?

Part C of Table 7.5 addresses these questions by separating Costa Ricans into two age groups: those under thirty-five and those older. The younger group corresponds rather neatly to the generation that reached majority during the turbulent 1980s and early 1990s. The older group had come of age in more stable decades of economic growth and expanding public services. There were few statistically significant differences between these generations in perceived freedom to participate in politics or perceived political efficacy. The younger cohort, however, perceived human rights performance as worse and had lower diffuse support than the older cohort.

But the impact of age upon democratic norms appears modest. Although the younger group was markedly more favorable toward civil disobedience, the mean of the index remained well in the end of the scale signifying disapproval of such tactics. Moreover, there were no significant differences in either commitment to democratic liberties, rights for regime critics, or justification of authoritarian methods between younger and older Ticos.

On balance, then, younger urban citizens were slightly less approving than their older peers of human rights performance, less supportive of the regime overall, and more approving of civil disobedience than older citizens. Nevertheless, the young on average disapproved of such confrontation. Thus younger Ticos as a group seem to pose no threat to Costa Rican democracy.[21]

The Stability of Support for Democracy

A further question arises as to the persistence of Ticos' support for democratic government: How stable is the public's commitment to the democratic regime? Costa Rica in the 1980s experienced a severe economic downturn that sharply lowered incomes, increased unemployment, and raised poverty levels. Such stresses intensified political mobilization and turmoil.

Mitchell Seligson and Miguel Gómez B. examined the possibility that the 1980s economic crisis might also have undermined citizen commitment to democracy.[22] They traced voting for the left, voter turnout rates, citizen evaluation of incumbent government performance, approval of violent political protest, and support for national institutions (diffuse support) across the late 1970s through the mid-1980s. This enabled them to track both behavior and attitudes through the worst years of the economic crunch.

Assuming that voting for the radical left might demonstrate Ticos' disenchantment with the constitutional regime, they found that voting for the left grew throughout the 1970s to peak in 1978 at 7.7 percent, then declined (rather than rose) in the 1982 and 1986 elections. Abstention from voting, another possible sign of disenchantment, also remained stable at around 20 percent during this period. They concluded that these elections, even though held in very trying times, were quite ordinary.

They then looked for attitudes reflecting disenchantment with democracy by comparing surveys taken in 1978 and 1985. They found that evaluations of the government's performance were substantially better for the precrisis Oduber administration than for the crisis-era Monge administration. Despite hard times and despite such manifest disapproval of the performance of the incumbent president in 1985, support for violent political methods showed no increase from 1978 to 1985. Ticos' pride in and support for national institutions either remained high or rose between 1978 and 1985.

Seligson and Gómez concluded that even though the 1980s crisis had badly shaken Costa Rica and citizens were both very aware of the crisis and held their leaders accountable for it, "those feelings have not spilled over into a more generalized dissatisfaction with the basic system of government. . . . In short, Costa Ricans have developed a political culture supportive of democracy."[23] A full decade of continuing economic difficulties has elapsed since this assessment, but

Costa Ricans still reject political violence and authoritarian methods, and still show high support for their political system (see Tables 7.2 and 7.5). Their democratic political culture appears very stable.

Elite Political Culture

Elites control or influence key social, political, and economic resources within a society. It is perhaps ironic that they greatly influence both the establishment and maintenance of representative democracies—systems nominally ruled by their citizens. Elites enjoy such influence because they can deploy critical power resources to shape institutions and either reinforce or disrupt their operations. Widespread elite agreement with democratic rules of the game appears critical to the consolidation and survival of constitutional democracy.

Elites do not control everything within a polity; masses also play critical roles. Indeed, we have seen in Chapter 3 that contemporary Costa Rican democracy took shape when competing elites forged a settlement on a new set of political rules after two decades of economic and political conflict with the increasingly combative working- and middle-class sectors. One may reasonably suppose that a polity in which elites and masses concur on the rules of the existing political game would be much more stable than one with a pronounced mass-elite disjuncture. Data just presented confirm that urban Ticos generally and strongly support the national political system, democratic norms, and democratic political methods. But what of elites? Are they more or less democratic than the general public?

Mario Carvajal Herrera addressed this question of the consonance between elite and mass attitudes. In 1971 he surveyed a group of particular Costa Rican elites—100 political party and pressure group leaders—and compared them with 305 party followers drawn from the general population.[24] He reported that elites had lower diffuse support for the political system and a higher propensity for change—even revolutionary change—than partisan citizens. Party followers were ill informed, politically inactive, and fickle—more committed to party alternation in power every four years than to having their own party always win. Elites knew more and participated more.

Carvajal's findings suggested an elite-mass disjuncture on diffuse support, propensity for change, and political knowledge and participation. He thus raised the possibility that change-oriented elites and conservative masses in Costa Rica might disagree substantially on the rules of the political game, opening up the prospect of instability driven by activist elites. How divergent are mass and elite values and behavior in Costa Rica?

It is not possible here to replicate Carvajal's study, but some of the same issues may be explored employing an elite-mass comparison based upon the 1995 urban sample. I have isolated a socioeconomic elite subsample within the 1995 survey consisting of thirty-nine individuals who fell in the highest family income category, had at least three years of university education, and were at least twenty-eight years of age.[25] Respondents not meeting these criteria constituted the mass public control group for purposes of comparison.

Table 7.7 presents data on these groups' respective demographics, some of the traits Carvajal examined, and other political culture variables. The elite subsample averaged five more years of education than the mass public and enjoyed double the modal family income of the mass sample. Elites were considerably more prone to be non-Catholics or nonbelievers (though still 75 percent Catholic), and far less religiously fundamentalist. As Carvajal reported, elites had much higher political knowledge scores and were overall more politically active (especially in organizations and communal affairs) than masses. However, contrary to Carvajal's finding (using a similar but differently worded question), Tico elites were not significantly more favorable toward change, whether radical (Table 7.7) or gradual (not shown in the table, although 86 percent of elites favored reforms compared to 75 percent among the mass public). Nor were the elites significantly less supportive of the regime, as Carvajal found.

This elite-mass comparison reveals sharp differences in income, education, political information, religion, religious fundamentalism, and overall participation levels but fails to find significant elite-mass differences in diffuse support or preference for change. More important, however, Table 7.7 shows these elites to have strongly embraced both democratic principles and tactics, with elites scoring slightly higher than masses on support for democratic norms. Elites supported civil disobedience significantly less than the mass public.

A Costa Rican elite subsample largely matches or exceeds the mass public in embracing fundamental civil liberties and repudiating antidemocratic political methods. Such harmony seems likely to promote continued political stability. It bears emphasizing, however, that the elite group isolated here was defined socioeconomically rather than drawn from among key strategic institutional leaders in government, the parties, the church, corporations, and interest and pressure groups. It cannot, therefore, reveal the values of those with real operational control over critical resources.

A story told by former president Oduber (1974–1978) during a series of lectures he delivered at the School of International Relations of the National Autonomous University of Costa Rica in mid-1979 illustrates the importance of strategic elites.[26] Oduber, also a founder of the National Liberation Party and Legislative Assembly member, discussed many problems of Costa Rican government, democracy, and foreign relations. His most striking statement, however, was that on multiple occasions of difficulty during his presidency he had been encouraged by unnamed parties (presumably advisers) to overthrow or suspend the constitution. That persons close to the president would recommend a coup d'état dramatically emphasizes how fragile democratic governance may be in the hands of elites, irrespective of mass preferences. That President Oduber declined to toss aside democracy puts in bold relief how important it is that key power holders remain faithful to democratic methods.

TABLE 7.7 Characteristics of Elite Subsample Compared to Other Urban Costa Ricans, 1995

	Elite[a] (N = 39)	Others (N = 616)	Significance[b]
Demographics			
Education (mean years)	16.25	9.79	****
Family income (modal group)[c]	8 of 8	3 of 8	****
Religion (percent)			*
Catholic	75.0	79.9	
Protestant/evangelical	7.1	13.5	
Other or none	17.9	6.5	
Attitudes and values and cognitions			
Religious fundamentalism index	6.04	7.68	****
Political knowledge index[d]	1.46	.79	****
Percent supporting radical change[e]	3.6%	2.3%	NS
Anticommunism index	4.52	4.32	NS
Perceived respect for human rights index	1.48	1.15	*
Perceived freedom to participate index	7.54	7.14	NS
Political efficacy index	2.63	2.57	NS
Diffuse support index	4.86	5.05	NS
Overall democratic norms index	7.89	7.07	**
Support civil disobedience index	1.43	1.94	*
Justify authoritarian methods index	.29	.42	NS
Political participation			
Contacting public officials index	.57	.38	NS
Campaign activism index	1.19	1.24	NS
Group activism index	2.79	1.10	****
Communal activism index	2.54	1.80	**
Overall participation index	9.11	6.22	****

[a]The elite subsample consists of all respondents in the 1995 urban survey meeting all of these three conditions: (1) in the highest family income category (over 200,000 *colones* per month); (2) at least three years of higher education; and (3) at least 28 years of age. Respondents not meeting these criteria were coded as "others."

[b]Significance levels: * = .05, ** = .01, *** = .001, **** = .0001, NS = not significantly different.

[c]Group 3 income = 50,001–80,000 *colones* per month; group 8 income = 200,000 *colones* or more per month.

[d]Political knowledge index based upon correct answers to several domestic and foreign information items; 0 = low score.

[e]Percent preferring radical change in the political system to gradual reform or no change at all.

Conclusions

Returning to the theories about political culture in Latin America, we see just how Costa Rica stands out as an anomaly in the region. Giving lie to the pessimism of certain academic pundits, Costa Rica has developed both a successful and long-standing democratic regime, and its population and elites share a democratic political culture despite roots in Spanish authoritarianism. Moreover, it has arrived at both democracy and democratic culture despite Inglehart's contention that predominant Catholicism, poverty, and low interpersonal trust would impede democratic culture and thus necessarily prohibit structural democracy.

Costa Rica may, however, constitute less of an anomaly than these theorists believe. Political culture evolves. One key role of culture, after all, is to permit societies and their populations to adapt to their circumstances. All around Latin America and even in the former "banana republics" of Central America, political regimes have repudiated military rule and dictatorship and embraced democratic rules of the game. The urban mass publics of Central America by the early 1990s had adopted democratic liberties as solutions to domestic repression. Elites had complied, too, most likely bending to international example and pressures. That Costa Rica developed a democratic political culture early in comparison to the rest of the region may not signify that it is an anomaly in Latin America. Rather, it may mean only that the structural conditions for the development of democratic norms and methods developed first in Costa Rica and are now following elsewhere.

Costa Rican urban mass political culture reveals several striking features: The legitimacy of the Costa Rican political system is high and support for it widespread. Ticos strongly support fundamental democratic liberties and oppose disruptive tactics and antidemocratic methods. The political culture is decidedly conservative: Citizens wish to retain the democratic system. The public supports the alternation of parties in office, which is seen as a way to restrain party power.[27] Ticos are strongly anticommunist, though political elites have not systematically denied political rights to the left, nor would a majority deny rights to regime critics.

There are certain strains that seem somewhat dissonant with the desire to conserve democracy. Some Ticos support political confrontation, demonstrations, and even violent protest and justify antidemocratic political methods. However, such values appear largely instrumental rather than constituting an antidemocratic subculture. That is, endorsing civil disobedience derives not from hostility to democracy but from citizens' knowledge that government often responds favorably to confrontation. Indeed, even members of those social sectors that most endorse such views (the far left, communal activists, and youth) are on balance mostly opposed to such tactics and strongly endorse democratic liberties.

Elites and masses largely share the same political values. Elites manifest even more commitment to democratic liberties than the general urban public and approve less of antidemocratic tactics. Our elite subsample, contrary to expectations, did not appear greatly more inclined toward change than the mass public.

Institutions and shared norms appear to work together to restrain elites with anti-democratic impulses.

Notes

1. See, for instance, Gabriel Almond and Sidney Verba, *The Civic Culture* (Princeton: Princeton University Press, 1963); Ronald Inglehart, *Culture Shift in Advanced Industrial Society* (Princeton: Princeton University Press, 1990); Larry Diamond, "Introduction: Political Culture and Democracy," in Larry Diamond, ed., *Political Culture and Democracy in Developing Countries* (Boulder: Lynne Rienner Publishers, 1993), pp. 1–33.

2. Michael Burton, Richard Gunther, and John Higley, "Elite Transformation and Democratic Regimes," in John Higley and Richard Gunther, eds., *Elites and Democratic Consolidation in Latin America and Southern Europe* (Cambridge: Cambridge University Press, 1992); Mitchell A. Seligson and John A. Booth, "Political Culture and Regime Type: Evidence from Nicaragua and Costa Rica," *Journal of Politics* 55 (August 1993): 777–792; and John A. Booth and Mitchell A. Seligson, "Paths to Democracy and the Political Culture of Costa Rica, Mexico, and Nicaragua," in Diamond, *Political Culture and Democracy,* pp. 107–138.

3. Edward N. Muller and Mitchell A. Seligson, "Civic Culture and Democracy: The Question of Causal Relationships," *American Political Science Review* 88 (September 1994): 645–652.

4. Guillermo A. O'Donnell, *Modernization and Bureaucratic Authoritarianism* (Berkeley: Institute of International Studies, University of California, 1973).

5. Glen C. Dealy, "The Tradition of Monistic Democracy in Latin America," in Howard J. Wiarda, ed., *Politics and Social Change in Latin America: The Distinct Tradition* (Amherst: University of Massachusetts Press, 1974), p. 73.

6. Howard J. Wiarda, "Social Change and Political Development in Latin America: Summary, Implications, Frontiers," in Wiarda, *Politics and Social Change in Latin America,* pp. 269–270, 274. Wiarda's pessimism about democracy in Latin America has diminished somewhat more recently; see Howard J. Wiarda, *The Democratic Revolution in Latin America* (New York: Holmes and Meier, 1990.)

7. Ronald Inglehart, "The Renaissance of Political Culture." *American Political Science Review* 82 (November 1988): 1203–1230; and Inglehart, *Culture Shift.*

8. John A. Booth and Mitchell A. Seligson, "The Political Culture of Authoritarianism in Mexico," *Latin American Research Review* 19, 1 (1984): 106–124; Booth and Seligson, "Paths to Democracy"; and Seligson and Booth, "Political Culture and Regime Type."

9. Martha Honey, *Hostile Acts: U.S. Policy in Costa Rica in the 1980s* (Gainesville: University Press of Florida, 1994), p. 8.

10. Ibid., pp. 9–10.

11. Richard Biesanz, Karen Zubris Biesanz, and Mavis Hiltunen Biesanz, *The Costa Ricans* (Englewood Cliffs, N.J.: Prentice-Hall, 1982), p. 188.

12. Ibid., pp. 187–189.

13. Although Catholics and Protestants reported similar levels of religious fundamentalism and frequency of prayer, Protestants reported far higher levels of church attendance.

14. John A. Booth and Patricia Bayer Richard, "Repression, Participation, and Democratic Norms in Urban Central America," *American Journal of Political Science* 40 (November 1996): 1205–1232; see table 5.

15. Breaking the index down by its components, 53.0 percent of those responding regarded the police as not respecting human life. In contrast, only 31.0 percent had this negative view of judges. This strongly suggests that the periodic violence against protesters by the Costa Rican police has undermined the trust of much of the populace. Indeed, the police forces have long been plagued by disorganization, political meddling, poor training, and incompetence, giving sound reason for public skepticism See Mavis Hiltunen de Biesanz, Richard Biesanz, and Karen Zubris de Biesanz, *Los costarricenses* (San José, Costa Rica: Editorial Universidad Estatal a Distancia, 1979), pp. 615–620; and Honey, *Hostile Acts*, p. 294.

16. Diffuse support was regressed on perceived treatment by government and the indexes of perceived efficacy, freedom to participate, and institutional respect for human rights, as well as demographic controls for education, standard of living, sex, and age.

17. Indeed, a factor analysis of the democratic norms items indicates a distinct pattern of interaction among six of these eight variables. Support for general participation rights, rights for regime critics, and opposition to the suppression of civil liberties cluster together into a democratic principles factor. Justification for a coup, preference for democracy over dictatorship, and support for civil disobedience group together into a distinct democratic methods factor.

18. The trimmed model, having dropped all insignificantly contributing independent variables from the first run, was highly significant, with an R^2 of .21; $N = 524$.

19. Booth and Richard, "Repression, Participation, and Democratic Norms."

20. A two-stage multiple regression analysis confirmed this finding. I regressed both the justification of authoritarian methods index and the support for civil disobedience index on a panoply of attitudinal, demographic, and participation variables. A trimmed model of each was developed by deleting insignificant independent variables in the second stage. Communal activism contributed very modestly and positively to support for civil disobedience but was weaker than age, diffuse support, education, and anticommunism (all with negative beta weights). Communal activism made no independent contribution to justification of authoritarian political methodology.

21. Two-stage multiple regression analysis confirmed this finding. I regressed both the justification of authoritarian methods and support for civil disobedience indices on several attitudinal, demographic, and participation variables. A trimmed model of each was developed by deleting insignificant independent variables in the second stage. Age made no significant independent contribution to the justification of authoritarian methods but did contribute markedly negatively to support for civil disobedience. Recall, however, that the average values for civil disobedience support were well in the disapproving end of the scale for the younger cohorts, so they are less against such tactics than older Ticos but against them all the same.

22. Mitchell A. Seligson and Miguel Gómez B., "Ordinary Elections in Extraordinary Times: The Political Economy of Voting in Costa Rica," in John A. Booth and Mitchell A. Seligson, eds., *Elections and Democracy in Central America* (Chapel Hill: University of North Carolina Press, 1989), pp. 158–184.

23. Ibid., p. 179.

24. Mario Carvajal Herrera, *Actitudes políticas del costarricense* (San José: Editorial Costa Rica, 1978), especially pp. 137–149.

25. This is a socioeconomic-status-based definition of elite membership rather than the positional definition (leadership role in parties and pressure groups) that Carvajal Herrera employed. When speaking of elites, I generalize only to these wealthier, best-educated,

older citizens (age was included on the assumption that no one under twenty-eight would be likely to have attained much influence over institutions or resources, irrespective of education).

26. I attended these lectures as a Fulbright visiting faculty member at the school.

27. Carvajal Herrera, *Actitudes políticas,* p. 156; Biesanz et al., *The Costa Ricans,* pp. 186–187.

8

POLITICAL ECONOMY IN TRANSITION

This chapter examines Costa Rica's political economy, the relationship between the nation's economy (in the world economic context) and its politics. It reviews the nation's political economic evolution, focusing principally upon successive development models and their implications for politics and public policy.

The intersection of politics and economics raises important questions for economic development: What should the nation produce—what mix of primary products, manufactured goods, and services? How should economic growth be promoted—by the state, by private initiative, or by some combination of both? What relationship should the economy have to the world economy—should it remain insular or embrace vigorous trade? Who should provide the capital necessary for investment in economic growth—citizens through taxes paid to the state, private initiative, or foreign investors? Who should benefit from growth—investors through profits or the citizenry through tax-financed services? The answers to many such questions are obviously determined by national circumstances such as size, location, climate, natural and human resources, population, and the existing level of development. National political economic models, however, represent nations' attempts to influence as many of these variables as possible.

Political economy may also affect democracy and social justice. One fundamental democratic question concerns who shall influence decisions about the economy—the people acting directly, a representative government influenced by popular opinion, or the owners and managers of capital alone. Shall the array of economic questions subject to popular influence through governmental control be small or large? There are also critical distributive issues at stake in a political economic model. To what extent should the state intervene to redistribute costs and benefits? Who should pay for the operation of the government and services?

How egalitarian should the burden of taxation be? And who should reap the benefits of the economy and services?

The political and economic actors of a nation (classes, parties, interest and pressure groups, and institutions, including the state itself) contend for influence over these issues. At any particular moment, the struggle to shape an economic development model is partly determined by the existing distribution of power resources among political actors. The distribution and nature of political and economic power evolve, which sometimes produces critical shifts in a development model with major implications for democracy.

Evolution of the Political Economy

Costa Rica's colonial history and position in the world economy set the small and relatively mineral-poor country on a modern quest to produce exportable agricultural commodities that might generate increased wealth, especially for those who controlled the key resource of cultivable land. More recently, new political forces such as organized labor and the middle class have gained political power and used it to wrest some benefits away from the wealthy and to promote industrialization. However, because modern Costa Rica has evolved as a trade-dependent economy, its economic health (and some of its politics) have been quite sensitive to external economic and geopolitical forces.

Two critical economic problems for Costa Rica have always been its terms of trade and its trade balance. "Terms of trade" refers to the relative value of the nation's exports versus its imports. Other things equal, when Costa Rica's main exports of coffee and bananas have brought high prices compared to the cost of imported manufactured goods and oil, Ticos have found it easier to prosper.

When Costa Rica's trade balance has been positive (exports exceeding imports), both government and private sector have tended to have the resources they needed to keep the economy growing. When terms of trade have remained unfavorable, Costa Rica has often imported more than it exported (a trade deficit), and both government and private sector have experienced shortages of foreign currency. Because disposable foreign currency is essential to keep vital imports flowing, a persistent trade deficit, by exhausting foreign currency reserves, can choke off key imports (such as oil and machinery) and slow the entire economy. The government can borrow abroad the foreign currency it needs, but if it builds up too much foreign debt, paying the interest and principal on it (servicing the debt) becomes a burden that can itself impede imports. Thus excessive debt service can curtail the spending and investment that promote growth.

When Costa Rica's trade balance has been in deficit for extended periods, the ensuing economic difficulties have often caused political turmoil. For example, economic difficulties in the 1930s and 1940s undermined the Liberal development model that had prevailed for over a century. The adoption of a new, social democratic development model brought more democracy and more social justice to Ticos. Likewise, beginning in the late 1970s the social democratic model began to fail because of renewed trade imbalances and their domestic repercussions. Costa Rica now struggles to consolidate a new development model that might restore economic stability. This political economic restructuring since the 1980s has been driven by external actors more than it has by Costa Ricans, but it does have important domestic allies. The determinative role of outsiders in the struggle over Costa Rica's development model represents a significant loss of sovereignty and of democratic influence on public policy.

The Liberal Era

From independence through 1949, landed elites dominated a state with a modest economic role.[1] Inequalities between larger, wealthier landowners and poorer producers intensified with the spread and evolution of the coffee industry. The coffee-growing-processing-exporting elite dominated the state, which modernized the law and governmental apparatus to facilitate agroexports. This Liberal agroexport model became fully consolidated with the development of banking (1858–1877) and the railroads and ports (Chapter 3). "The state apparatus . . . concentrated its attention on guaranteeing satisfactory delivery of the essential services and the creation of the basic infrastructure that capital required."[2]

As the twentieth century began, several processes started to transform the national economy: concentration of landownership driven by coffee, government-promoted modernization, urbanization, and the increasing economic complexity stimulated by Costa Rica's integration into the world economy. These forces expanded the middle and lower classes. In the late nineteenth century, banana production provided jobs that partly attenuated growing landlessness and poverty among peasants. But the accelerated social strains of the twentieth century—especially economic turbulence during World Wars I and II[3]—brought these new classes forcefully into politics in labor unions and new political and ideological groups. Their mobilization ultimately undermined the *cafetaleros'* dominance of the polity.

Elite efforts to politically reform the Liberal system failed (Chapter 3). This divided the agroexport elite and gave rise to the unstable 1940s populist alliance of *cafetalero* president Calderón Guardia, the Catholic Church, and the communist-led union movement. Calderón Guardia attempted to retain power by co-opting organized labor with social security and labor reforms on the one hand and by placating his political adversaries with further political reforms on the other. This strategy proved ineffective. Disgruntled sectors of the bourgeoisie and middle class rebelled in 1948 and defeated the regime.

Social Democracy

The victorious National Liberation junta, led by José Figueres Ferrer, ruled by decree for a year and a half. It was abetted enormously by the larger geopolitical environment in the wake of World War II. By ending communist and union participation in Costa Rica's government, the junta had won some leeway for its policy agenda from the United States, which at the time was preoccupied with the early stages of the cold war and the reconstruction of Europe.

This enabled the Liberation junta to put in place the foundations of an unusual new development model while a new constitution was being written. Figueres and the junta quickly offset their weakness and stripped the *cafetaleros* of a weapon by dismantling the army. They also retained the Calderonista labor and social security reforms to placate organized workers but tried to divide the union movement and temporarily suppress the communist Popular Vanguard Party. The junta seized powerful economic tools by nationalizing the banking and insurance systems. It reached out to the middle and working classes by writing extensive social protections into the new constitution. By eventually turning power over to conservative Otilio Ulate Blanco and converting itself into a party, the National Liberation movement helped consolidate Costa Rican formal democracy and forge an interelite consensus on the rules of the political game.

After Ulate's term, the newly constituted National Liberation Party won the 1953 election. Led by Figueres, the PLN elaborated the new development model: An economically activist state would redistribute income toward the middle class, provide more social services, regulate the economy more, and more aggressively promote economic growth.[4] By the 1960s Costa Rica had committed itself to import substitution industrialization and to regional economic integration, promoted and managed through the Central American Common Market. The government assumed new functions, provided new services, broadened educational opportunity to assure itself trained workers, and expanded public-sector employment.

The social democratic development model, coinciding with several decades of growth of the world economy, transformed Costa Rica. The CACM era brought foreign aid (Appendix, Table A.5) to improve roads, ports, and public services. Domestic and foreign investment increased sharply. GDP quintupled between 1950 and 1975, and GDP per capita more than doubled, from $372 to $779 (Table 8.1). Although agriculture remained crucial to export earnings, its share of overall economic activity shrank steadily after 1950. In contrast, investment stimulated by the CACM raised the manufacturing sector's share of GDP. The government's portion of GDP also boomed after 1950, peaking around 12 percent in 1970 (Table 8.2).[5]

The social democratic development model remarkably improved the well-being of citizens and politically strengthened the state. During its heyday, unemployment and consumer prices stayed low (Table 8.3), income inequality declined (Table 5.1), and real wages, infant mortality, literacy, life expectancy, and educational attainment all improved (Appendix, Tables A.2 and A.3). Even the PLN's conservative political adversaries did not attack the social democratic development model when they held power. None of the radical left parties pressed truly revolutionary demands or struggled to overthrow a system that was generally improving workers' standards of living.

TABLE 8.1   Economic and Population Growth of Costa Rica, 1920–1996

	Population (1,000s)	GDP (millions of 1970 dollars)	GDP per capita (1970 dollars)
1920[a]	420	119	284
1925	460	134	291
1930	500	142	284
1935	550	147	267
1940	620	191	308
1945	700	198	282
1950	800	298	372
1955	1,030	444	431
1960	1,250	593	474
1965	1,490	814	546
1970	1,730	1,139	659
1975	1,970	1,543	779
1980	2,220	1,981	892
1985	2,642	1,969	789
1990[b]	3,035	2,439	851
1995[b]	3,424	3,046	935
1996[b]	3,502	3,029	909

[a]Values through 1980 are calculated directly from data in Bulmer-Thomas, expressed in constant 1970 dollars.

[b]Values for 1990, 1995, and 1996 are extrapolated from Bulmer-Thomas's 1980 base, based upon growth rates reported by the IADB.

sour ces: Victor Bulmer-Thomas, *The Political Economy of Central America Since 1920* (Cambridge: Cambridge University Press, 1987), tables A1 and A9; Inter-American Development Bank (IADB), *Latin America After a Decade of Reforms: Economic and Social Progress in Latin America, 1997 Report* (Baltimore: Johns Hopkins University Press, 1997), tables A-1, B-1, and B-18.

The Crisis of the Social Democratic Model

Despite its successes, the social democratic model failed badly by the 1980s and was attacked from within and abroad. By the early 1990s, a neoliberal political economic model began to emerge and restructure economy-state relationships. What happened to undermine the social democratic regime?

Costa Rica imports all of its oil, making the economy sensitive to petroleum prices. When oil prices rose drastically in 1973 and thereafter because of the oil cartel's embargo, the sudden growth of the trade deficit created a balance-of-payments problem and depressed the economy well into the 1980s.[6] Virtually everything consumed in the country became more costly. Oil price rises hit transport and shipping especially hard. Other inflationary effects quickly rippled across the economy. For example, the prices of industrial inputs (many of them petroleum

TABLE 8.2   Selected Costa Rican Economic Sectors as Percentage of GDP, 1920–1995

	Agriculture (%)	Manufacturing (%)	Government (%)
1920[a]	47.3	7.3	2.9
1925	43.6	8.3	4.0
1930	43.3	8.7	4.8
1935	40.0	10.4	4.6
1940	33.5	13.2	5.1
1945	34.0	10.5	8.1
1950	38.5	11.6	5.9
1955	32.1	12.3	8.7
1960	29.7	12.5	10.7
1965	27.4	13.5	11.5
1970	25.0	15.1	12.0
1975	22.4	16.3	11.5
1980	19.2	16.9	11.2
1985[b]	20.1	17.0	11.1
1990[b]	18.1	16.9	9.9
1995[b]	15.4	20.1	8.7

[a]Values through 1980 are calculated directly from sectoral data in Bulmer-Thomas, expressed in constant 1970 dollars.

[b]Values for 1985–1995 are extrapolated from Bulmer-Thomas's 1980 base, based upon growth rates reported by the IADB.

sources: Victor Bulmer-Thomas, *The Political Economy of Central America Since 1920* (Cambridge: Cambridge University Press, 1987), tables A1 and A9; Inter-American Development Bank (IADB), *Economic and Social Progress in Latin America: Overcoming Volatility, 1995 Report* (Baltimore: Johns Hopkins University Press, 1995), tables B-1 and B-18.

derived) jumped, raising consumer prices, but agricultural export prices remained low. Inflation then rose sharply while real wages fell (Table 8.3). This badly reduced demand for goods and services, causing private-sector layoffs that further depressed demand for consumer goods.

The government responded with policies that cushioned the oil shock in the short run but eventually created a worse problem. The tax system relied heavily upon regressive, indirect taxes upon consumption (around 70 percent of revenues) in the 1970s and much less upon direct income or property taxes.[7] Rather than raise taxes on the middle or upper classes or scale back spending to fit revenue (and thus deepen the already sharp recession), the government maintained its spending and made up budget deficits by borrowing internationally.

Two examples of how much the government exceeded its means help illustrate the reasons for the borrowing binge: (1) In the late 1960s, the government usually ran a small budget surplus, but spending began to outstrip revenues from the mid-1970s on. The national budget deficit peaked in 1980 around 8 percent of

TABLE 8.3   Unemployment, Consumer Prices, and Real Wages, 1970–1996

	Unemployment (%)	Annual Change Consumer Prices (%)	Real Wage Index (1973 = 100)
1970	3.5	2.5[b]	96
1975	5.0[a]	14.08[b]	91
1979	4.7	5.7[b]	128
1980	5.9	18.1	129
1981	8.1	37.1	114
1982	15.0	90.1	92
1983	8.6	32.6	102
1984	6.6	12.0	110
1985	6.7	14.6	120
1986	6.7	11.8	127
1987	5.9	16.8	120
1988	6.3	20.8	114
1989	3.7	16.6	118
1990	–	19.0	121
1991	–	28.7	118
1992	–	21.8	119
1993	–	9.8	129
1994	4.2	13.5	131
1995	–	23.2	128
1996	–	17.5	132

[a]Estimate.

[b]Values for 1970 and 1975 are means for the five-year period ending in each year; value for 1979 is a mean for the four-year period ending that year.

sour ces: Data through 1989 from John A. Booth and Thomas W. Walker, *Understanding Central America* (Boulder: Westview Press, 1993), appendix tables 4 and 5; later data from Inter-American Development Bank (IADB), *Latin America After a Decade of Reforms: Economic and Social Progress in Latin America, 1997 Report* (Baltimore: Johns Hopkins University Press, 1997), p. 276.

GDP (Table 8.4). Major deficits continued into the mid-1990s.[8] (2) Firms operated by the state holding company, the Costa Rican Development Corporation (Corporación Costarricense de Desarrollo, or CODESA), originally conceived as an enterprise and revenue generator, performed badly. Rather than let these firms fail, the government increased their subsidies, from \$337,000 to \$19.1 million between 1977 and 1983.[9]

Costa Rica financed this burgeoning fiscal deficit by borrowing heavily from abroad. Foreign loans permitted the government to keep up its own consumption and to subsidize state enterprises, the private sector, and consumers. Foreign loans maintained the foreign currency liquidity in national accounts—critical for trade—and thus staved off a deeper recession. Borrowing abroad also financed

TABLE 8.4   Costa Rican Deficit and External Debt, 1970–1996

	Budget Deficit (% of GDP)	Total External Debt ($ millions)[a]	External Debt as % of GDP[b]	Interest Payments/ Exports[c]
1970	0.1	227	11.5	1.0
1975	−2.3	732	–	–
1976	–	1,002	–	–
1977	–	1,295	–	–
1978	−4.3	1,622	35.0	–
1979	−6.5	1,924	43.0	6.6
1980	−8.0	2,735	47.0	18.0
1981	−4.6	3,286	115.0	28.0
1982	−3.2	3,627	147.0	36.1
1983	−3.6	4,136	135.0	33.0
1984	−3.1	3,971	105.0	26.6
1985	−2.0	4,401	108.1	24.9
1986	−3.3	4,576	105.3	21.8
1987	−2.0	4,721	101.8	21.2
1988	−2.5	4,545	93.1	21.6
1989	−4.1	4,603	86.7	20.0
1990	−4.4	3,772	66.6	15.4
1991	−3.1	4,049	68.2	10.0
1992	−1.9	3,966	56.5	8.6
1993	−1.9	3,872	51.2	7.4
1994	−6.9	3,873	54.5	6.4
1995	−4.4	3,769	51.5	6.2
1996	−5.2	3,667	49.0	–

[a]In current dollars

[b]Disbursed total external debt outstanding.

[c]Interest payments due/exports of goods and nonfactor service.

sources: Inter-American Development Bank (IADB), *Economic and Social Progress in Latin America: Natural Resources, 1983 Report* (Washington, D.C.: IADB, 1983, tables 6, 22, 59, and p. 195; IADB, *Economic and Social Progress in Latin America: Working Women in Latin America, 1990 Report* (Washington, D.C.: IADB, 1990), tables B-6, C-4, E-1, and E-9; IADB, *Economic and Social Progress in Latin America: Overcoming Volatility, 1995 Report* (Washington, D.C.: 1995), tables B-6, C-4, E-1, E-10, and E-11 and p. 276; IADB, *Latin America After a Decade of Reforms: Economic and Social Progress in Latin America, 1997 Report* (Baltimore: Johns Hopkins University Press, 1997).

subsidies on public services such as transport and utilities, helped keep the public payroll filled, and permitted the restoration of wages lost to inflation.

Such policies at first eased the recession, but they eventually had several bad effects: Costa Rica sank deeply into debt. Foreign debt, expressed as a percentage of GDP, rose from 11.5 percent in 1970 to 147.0 percent in 1982 (Table 8.4). The interest payments on this external debt consumed one-third of export earnings by the early 1980s (Table 8.4), heavily burdening the economy and government. The entire Central American economy went into recession with Costa Rica in the mid-1970s because of the oil price shock. Soon political turmoil in the region frightened away domestic and foreign capital and collapsed the CACM and Costa Rica's regional export markets.

The exchange rate, stable at around 8.6 *colones* to the dollar since the early 1960s, had to be repeatedly devalued under these pressures. Devaluation raised prices of imports (including industrial inputs and petroleum itself), which curtailed imports but also further slowed the commercial sector and aggravated inflation. Exchange controls and higher interest rates imposed to prevent capital flight further retarded growth and increased unemployment.

By July 1981 Costa Rica's terrible trade and foreign reserve situations forced the Carazo administration to default on the payment of the foreign debt, and the *colón* was devalued to 21.7 to the U.S. dollar. From there the value of the *colón* continued to erode, eventually falling to 157 to the dollar in 1994. This plunge made exports and labor cheaper on international markets and thus eventually stimulated the domestic economy. But in the short run it raised import and consumer prices and further depressed real wages (Table 8.3).[10] With the CACM out of commission and a full-blown regional depression under way, recovery was very slow.

The administration of Luis Alberto Monge Alvarez took office in May 1982 and found the economy and public treasury in dire straits. Monge moved swiftly to stabilize the economy. He found a temporary escape valve in the escalating regional geopolitical crisis. From the advent of the Reagan administration in 1981, the United States sought to overthrow the Sandinista revolutionary government of Nicaragua and to contain the Marxist-led insurgency in El Salvador. President Monge collaborated broadly with U.S. anti-Sandinista efforts by permitting widespread *contra* and U.S. covert operations in Costa Rica.[11] The United States handsomely compensated the Ticos with $1.14 billion in economic aid between 1981 and 1988—a tenfold increase over the previous eight-year period (Appendix, Table A.5). A big share of the aid consisted of outright grants (gifts).

With such abundant foreign aid, the Costa Rican government from 1982 through 1985 enacted macroeconomic controls and promoted a quick recovery "derived principally from stimulating internal demand with increases in real wages."[12] The recovery, however, was artificial and thus merely postponed confronting various Achilles' heels of the social democratic development model—Ticos' massive appetite for imports, persistently unfavorable terms of trade, the trade deficit, and ballooning external debt.

From 1985 on a second and more drastic phase of economic transformation began, based upon "structural adjustment programs [developed] via agreements with the World Bank. The emphasis from then on would be to reactivate and transform the economy beginning with its reinsertion into the international market, based upon exporting nontraditional products to areas outside of Central America."[13] This initiated a concerted neoliberal attack upon the social democratic development model, engineered mainly by powerful external economic actors with the help of influential national economic interests. The neoliberals wanted to reduce the size of the state and its economic role as entrepreneur, regulator, and service provider; to stimulate new exports; and to open up Costa Rica to foreign capital, both to reduce imports and to attract investment by lowering labor costs through currency devaluations.

The international banking community's leverage was the massive external debt (still over 100 percent of GDP by the mid-1980s). Costa Rica desperately needed to refinance the debt on more favorable terms. In exchange for further assistance, the international bankers (a consortium of private banks holding about one-third of Costa Rica's debt, the Paris Club of major creditor nations, and international banks such as the World Bank–International Monetary Fund [IMF], and the Inter-American Development Bank [IADB]) plus the United States in effect forced Costa Rica to abandon the social democratic development model for a neoliberal one.

Structural Adjustment and the Neoliberal Model

The international bankers who would guide Costa Rica's recovery from its economic crisis viewed structural adjustment as a sort of twelve-step program for ending foreign debt addiction. In exchange for treatment (new loans to provide liquidity and an extended repayment schedule), Costa Rica would change its behavior and, indeed, its entire political economy. Costa Rica made three successive agreements on structural adjustment programs (*programas de ajuste estructural,* or PAEs) with the IMF, World Bank, and other international lenders.

PAE I, approved in 1985, pursued the objectives of reducing the state's economic role, the number of government employees, and public spending.[14] PAE I froze public-sector employment, encouraged early retirements of public employees, permitted public-sector wage rises only to match cost-of-living increases, began privatization of CODESA, and eliminated or reduced such subsidies as crop price supports and below-cost public utilities pricing. Bilateral external debt was rescheduled with major foreign lenders (the Paris Club) in 1983 and 1985. Costa Rica also reached agreement with foreign commercial banks to reschedule the nation's private debt.[15]

PAE II, signed in 1989, continued PAE I objectives and policies and added new goals: increased property taxes; improved sales tax collection; elimination of subsidies to public services, railroads, and the national refinery, the Costa Rican Petroleum Refinery (Refinadora Costarricense de Petroleo, or RECOPE); promotion of production (especially nontraditional products) for export; and an opening the economy through tariff reduction. The government made further agreements with the Paris Club countries and with private commercial banks in 1989 to again reschedule a significant portion of its still massive debt. In May 1990 Costa Rica signed a debt reduction agreement, permitting the country to "buy back 64 percent of its debt at 16 cents on the dollar with $253 million provided by concessional lending."[16]

PAEs I and II had notable effects: The government's contribution to GDP diminished from 11.1 percent in 1985 to 9.9 percent in 1990 (Table 8.2). CODESA privatized numerous firms.[17] The government reduced (but did not eliminate) the budget deficit and substantially eased its debt service burden (the ratio of interest payments to exports; see Table 8.4). Public services such as the electric and telephone company (the Costa Rican Electrical Institute [Instituto Costarricense de Electricidad, or ICE]) and RECOPE raised prices enough to break even. Under heavy pressure from the U.S. Agency for International Development (USAID), banking—a state monopoly since 1948—was partially privatized. New private banks quickly assumed a substantial share of investments.

PAE I and II effectively dismantled the Costa Rican social democratic development model and replaced it with a neoliberal model.[18] Yet despite the extent of the reforms, the economy remained deeply troubled and the new model unconsolidated. Even though external debt as a percentage of GDP shrank somewhat in the late 1980s, the overall foreign debt continued to rise until 1989 (Table 8.4). Perhaps most worrisome were sharp increases in deficit spending for 1988–1991 and again in 1994–1996, each of which again pushed up interest rates and debt. The government suddenly stepped up its borrowing to replace a big cut in U.S. economic assistance after 1987. President Arias (1986–1990) had reversed several years of cooperation with U.S. anti-Sandinista efforts and helped engineer the Central American (Esquipulas) peace accord of August 1987. Because the Reagan administration had pressured Arias not to push the accord, the United States punished Costa Rica by cutting its economic aid by 56 percent for the 1989–1992 period (Appendix, Table A.4).[19]

The external advocates of structural adjustment who had forced Costa Rica to abandon the social democratic development model during the 1980s by means of PAE I and II hoped to consolidate the neoliberal model with PAE III in the mid-1990s. The task proved politically difficult, as certain domestic political forces rallied against PAE III in protest of its high social costs.

Economic conditions worsened again in the early 1990s. In negotiations with the Calderón administration (1990–1994) for PAE III, external lenders including the IMF, IADB, Paris Club countries, and USAID pressed Rica for even greater reductions of public spending and employment, further privatization of banking and insurance, lowered trade barriers, and greater stimulation of nontraditional exports.[20]

There were some positive developments in the economy in the early 1990s. Tourism surged as revolutionary turmoil in Nicaragua and El Salvador declined after 1990. By 1995 an estimated 765,000 visitors came to Costa Rica. Tourism came to employ 15 percent of workers and surpassed coffee and bananas in generating foreign exchange.[21] Foreign and domestic investment also recovered with increased geopolitical stability. Export prices rose, exports grew, and the government privatized the rest of CODESA. Costa Rica joined the General Agreement on Tariffs and Trade (GATT) and promised to end most of its remaining trade barriers.

On the negative side, however, were several problematic trends: Ticos were shocked (and the public deficit greatly aggravated) when in 1993 the government-owned Banco Anglo-Costarricense collapsed from mismanagement and graft. Inflation rekindled because of an expanding money supply and the government's granting of wage increases in anticipation of the 1994 election. In 1995 and 1996, inflation rose further (Table 8.3). The government's deficit jumped from 1.9 percent to 6.9 percent of GDP between 1993 and 1994 and remained high during much of the Figueres Olsen administration (Table 8.4). Both interest rates and the volume of imports rose in the early 1990s. To curtail imports and encourage exports, the Calderón government allowed the *colón* to devalue freely, greatly eroding its worth, a policy that continued under Figueres Olsen.

Costa Rica worked out PAE III with the IMF and IADB in protracted negotiations in 1994 and 1995. The IMF and IADB required that Costa Rica cut its fiscal deficit to 0.5 percent of GDP by 1996, immediately pay $79 million to the Paris Club creditors, cut 8,000 more public-sector jobs, and enact large tax hikes. Other goals included further bank privatization and deregulation and privatization of ICE. In exchange for these and other reforms, the international lenders would provide critically needed additional credit.[22] Ultimately, then, PAE III would finish the reorganization of the Costa Rican political economy, leaving a government much less involved as a service provider, regulator, entrepreneur, and redistributor of wealth. Individuals and firms would have to assume much more responsibility for their own fortunes. For this, they would gain much in risk but also greater freedom of initiative, less government regulation, and (potentially, at least) more profitability.

Several vexing problems arose in meeting PAE III's conditions, however. Because President José Maria Figueres Olsen's PLN was one seat short of a majority in the 1994–1998 Legislative Assembly, the government found itself vulnerable to opposition party demands. The Social Christian Party held up the tax hikes required by the IMF and IADB and also demanded full privatization of banking and ICE. A protracted stalemate eventually forced President Figueres to negotiate an accord with the opposition, after which critical legislation (budgets, pension reforms, further privatization legislation), passed the assembly.

Various domestic groups balked at the drastic cuts they would have to sustain. Teachers struck for over a month in mid-1995 but failed to win most of their goals. Other public-sector unions, chastened by the teachers' failure, nevertheless decried the impact of budget cuts on public employees and especially on pension plans. The national human rights ombudsman criticized past and projected program cuts as harmful to the middle class. Traditional social democratic elements within the PLN resisted fully privatizing ICE, which forced the president to backtrack to a proposal of only partial privatization. Citizens of Limón, hit hard by port privatization and the railroad closure, protested violently in June 1996.

The Figueres administration's inability to deliver on taxes, privatization, and budget reforms and its increased domestic borrowing to cover a growing budget deficit dismayed and angered international lenders. The IMF escalated compliance pressure by holding up the loans and sending new negotiating and monitoring teams to San José. The United States, miffed at Costa Rica's acceptance of a banana import quota from the European Union and certain property and contract disputes involving U.S. interests, terminated USAID programs and refused to support Costa Rica in its critical negotiations with the IMF and IADB. On the positive side, the Paris Club creditors' group reached an accord with Costa Rica on its arrears.

All in all, the implications of neoliberalism became clearer in the mid-1990s. The Figueres Olsen administration took the full brunt of Ticos' anger over what they were losing. Figueres had the lowest presidential approval ratings of any president in memory as citizens assessed their bleak economic prospects.[23] Many angry Ticos also took to the streets in protest. Hamstrung as he was without a PLN majority, Figueres had the grimly ironic task of cajoling the Legislativa Asamblea and his own PLN into dismantling the social guarantees and development model built by his father and the party.

Neoliberalism has had important implications for Costa Rican entrepreneurs. Under the social democratic model, "the Costa Rican businessman was not, for the most part, forged in commercial struggles but emerged as a product of state intervention. He was the creature of government policy, and his education did not teach him to be creative, accept risks, or anticipate trends."[24] The new development model, long advocated by some economic elites, would provide great new opportunities and much new risk. The state would no longer regulate, control, subsidize, plan for, buy from, sell to, compete with, invest with, grant monopolies to, or tax the private entrepreneur nearly so much as before—both a gain and a loss for many firms. This newfound freedom will provide much opportunity, but success in the new environment will also demand much of the entrepreneur: more courage, risk taking, planning, and perspicacity to compete not only at home but with a world full of hungry competitors.

Policy Implications of Neoliberalism

One could dedicate chapters to the impact of the neoliberal development model, but a few policy areas illustrate the dramatic changes being wrought. Because the transformations are still occurring, the longer-term effects must remain partly conjectural. Nevertheless, certain features have begun to emerge.

Size and Scope of Government

As already noted above, the government's share of GDP has shrunk by almost 30 percent of its peak contribution to the economy. This has meant a dramatic reduction in the role of government that has affected all policy areas. The government's share of the national workforce fell 18.9 to 16.2 percent between 1980 and 1989 (Table 8.5). This brought "a deterioration of the efficiency and quality of [public] services, juxtaposed against a growing population demanding attention."[25]

TABLE 8.5   Impact of Neoliberal Reforms in Costa Rica, 1980–1990

A. Distribution of Social Expenditures
(as percent of GDP)

	Education	Health	Social Assistance	Housing	Sector Total
1980	6.9	11.3	3.6	1.5	23.3
1984	5.2	7.1	3.2	1.0	16.5
1987	4.7	5.5	7.4	2.5	20.1
1989	4.5	5.7	6.9	2.3	19.4

B. Tax Revenue Structure (percent of total revenue)

	Income	Property	Sales	Imports	Exports
1981	21.4	1.0	36.3	12.9	27.2
1984	19.2	0.6	46.1	16.9	12.8
1987	15.4	0.7	51.4	22.9	7.9
1990	16.7	3.1	50.0	25.3	3.1

C. Real Wage Indexes, by Sector (1979 = 100)

	Public Sector	Central Government	Autonomous Agencies	Private Sector
1980	89	86	91	98
1983	66	61	69	79
1987	98	88	110	115
1990	100	90	113	109

D. Other Indicators

	Nontraditional Exports ($ millions)		Percent of Workforce in Public Sector
1980	380.9	1980	18.9
1983	315.2	1983	17.8
1986	368.1	1987	15.7
1989	654.6	1990	16.2

SOURCES: Carlos Castro Valverde, "Sector público y ajuste estructural en Costa Rica (1983–1992)," in Trevor Evans, ed., *La transformación neoliberal del sector público* (Managua, Nicaragua: Latino Editores, 1995), tables 2.3, 2.4, 2.7, 2.9; José Manuel Salazar X., "El Estado y el ajuste en el sector industrial," in Claudio González Vega and Edna Camacho Mejía, eds., *Políticas económicas en Costa Rica,* vol. 2 (San José, Costa Rica: Academia de Centroamérica–Ohio State University, 1990), table 20.3.

Shifting Policy Priorities

The import of such reductions in the size and scope of government grows when one considers that from 1970 to 1994, ever more of the public budget went to interest payments on the burgeoning public debt. "The payment of the foreign debt has in effect become the principal public institution in Costa Rica."[26] The share of the public budget dedicated to interest payments rose from 12.9 percent in 1984 to a high of 23.2 percent in 1991. Even after favorable debt restructuring, it declined only to 18.7 percent in 1994. Another recession and renewed deficit spending in 1994–1996 pushed debt service back up to 27.6 percent by 1996.[27]

Social and education spending once contributed importantly to Ticos' exceptional social and demographic quality of life. Structural adjustment, however, seriously undermined these programs. Table 8.5 presents data on the evolution of the government social spending under PAEs I and II. Social spending, expressed as a percentage of GDP, declined by 25 percent from 1980 to 1989. Education spending eroded from 6.9 to 4.5 percent of GDP (off by 43 percent), and health care spending fell 54 percent. Education suffered gravely: The Ministry of Education cut the length of the school year by one-third and the school day by half, and many schools ran double (in some cases triple) sessions daily.[28] The cumulative effect of such cuts upon the literacy, numeracy, and knowledge of Costa Rica's children will become fully known only over time, but it can hardly be anything but detrimental to individuals and to the nation alike.

During the 1980s the government tried to ease the impact of the severe recession upon the poor. Housing spending grew by 36.7 percent and social assistance (welfare) rose by 72.7 percent. As Chapters 5 and 6 have shown, Costa Rican governments have a tradition of responding to social mobilization and popular demands. These sudden jumps in social assistance represented government attempts to mollify with public handouts the nation's many angry, newly impoverished citizens. An obvious further implication for social policy was that as the government moved from social democracy to neoliberalism, it traded long-term human capital investment in health and education for the immediate relief of crises of poverty, hunger, and housing. This policy no doubt had humanitarian merit and clearly made political sense to incumbent politicians, yet one must question its impact upon future individual and societal welfare.

Investment

Government investment in building and maintaining such critical infrastructure as roads, ports, and utilities constitutes an important key to future economic growth.[29] Neoliberalism forced Costa Rica to cut investment in basic public works by 54 percent from 1980 to 1990. Public infrastructure such as roads and bridges deteriorated quickly. During most of the 1980s, school construction and maintenance were slashed. From 1981 through 1983, water, sewer, electricity, and telephone utility investments were also trimmed drastically. Despite continuing population growth, between 1980 and 1990 investment of the National Urbanization and Housing Institute (Instituto Nacional de Vivienda y Urbanismo, or INVU) was cut by 66 percent. INVU's housing and urbanization programs, which had traditionally benefited the middle sectors, were sacrificed to provide housing assistance to the very poor. Investment by the National Production Council (Consejo Nacional de Producción, or CNP) fell by 18 percent, and that of the Ministry of Health declined by 6 percent.

Not all areas of investment were cut. The government invested more during the 1980s to support neoliberal development objectives: nontraditional exports, export promotion in general, and facilitation of private enterprise. Beneficiaries included the Ministry of Agriculture, the Agrarian Development Institute, and the telephone–electric utility ICE. ICE's investments grew by 46 percent between the 1980 and 1990 budgets, and the National Bank of Costa Rica's by 53 percent. The grand prize winner for increased development was the Atlantic Development Junta, the operator of key port facilities, into which the government poured 148 percent more investment in 1990 than it had in 1980.

Taxation

Costa Rica has long had a regressive tax structure in which consumers and poorer citizens have carried the bulk of the state's revenue burden, mainly through sales taxes. Better-off Ticos (salaried employees and property owners) have traditionally shouldered little of the load. Taken by itself, the regressivity of the pre-1980 tax structure appeared inconsistent with the social democratic development model because it taxed the poor most heavily. However, the social democratic state somewhat compensated for this tax regressivity with various subsidies (on basic foodstuffs, health care, utilities) that disproportionately benefited the poor. The social democratic state also collected much of its revenue from taxes on imports and exports (thus shifting the tax burden abroad).

Changes in tax policy under PAEs I and II brought taxes more into line with neoliberal preferences. Table 8.5 shows that from 1981 to 1990 sales taxes increased by one-third, whereas income taxes fell by about one-fifth, aggravating tax regressivity. In a slightly contrary trend, property taxes have increased fourfold, to 3.1 percent of revenue, which reduced the formerly virtually free ride of the propertied classes.

The most dramatic tax changes affected trade. Consistent with the neoliberal export orientation, the government cut export taxes by almost 90 percent between 1981 and 1990. This reduced foreigners' and increased Ticos' relative contributions to Costa Rican state revenue. It also made national exports cheaper, a substantial stimulus for the export market and to foreign capital considering export-oriented investments in Costa Rica. Import taxes, which should also have been cut under neoliberal goals, were actually raised sharply (to the chagrin of the international lenders) in order to reduce the deficits and curtail the voracious demand for imports that persisted despite the rapid devaluation of the *colón*.

Wage Policy

Table 8.5 demonstrates the wage effects of the neoliberal transformation. All workers lost ground in real earnings from 1979 through the early 1980s. Policymakers, sensitive to popular pressure, responded predictably with policies that restored most Ticos' wages within a few years, aided for a while by massive

U.S. assistance. This wage recovery alleviated some of the worst effects upon living standards of the economic slump of the early 1980s.

Not all sectors suffered, or recovered, equally. Overall public-sector wages recovered 1979 levels by 1990. However, within the government sector the central ministries dependent upon the assembly for their budgets recovered only to 90 percent of 1979 wage levels by 1990. In contrast, employees of the autonomous agencies won back and even bested 1979 real wages. Indeed, autonomous agency wages seemed to be outperforming even the fairly successful private sector by 1990. All in all, therefore, workers in traditional government sectors (the central ministries) suffered most under the neoliberal policy ax.

Export Promotion

One positive aspect of the neoliberal model has been the growth of nontraditional exports. Coffee and bananas once dominated Costa Rica's exports but left the nation vulnerable to unfavorable prices cycles and eroding terms of trade. The government began to encourage the diversification of exports even under social democracy. Nontraditional exports eventually caught fire during the 1980s. Between 1980 and 1990, Costa Rica's nontraditional exports (flowers, plants, wood, paper, and textiles) almost doubled in value (Table 8.5). A sharp reduction of tariffs (Table 8.5) and the steady devaluation of the *colón,* both supported by external lenders, assisted this growth by making Costa Rican products (especially those with a significant labor component) relatively cheaper abroad.

Increased export diversity meant less reliance upon coffee and bananas, although coffee remained a key export (Photo 8.1). New exports also brought new private-sector jobs that absorbed some of the shrinkage of the public-sector work-force. On the negative side of these policies, of course, was Ticos' relative loss of purchasing power for imported goods as the national currency steadily lost value. By 1996 the *colón* reached 208 to the dollar, down from 92 to the dollar in 1990.[30] Moreover, the nation's greater exposure to the highly price competitive world labor market will likely exert continuing downward pressure on Costa Rican wages and living standards.

Other Likely Effects

The list of public programs and social and environmental problems likely to be affected by Costa Rica's neoliberal development model could well be virtually endless. Two linked problems warrant at least passing mention.[31]

Urban areas have developed rapidly.[32] For decades, urban population growth has exceeded that of rural areas. The urban population rose from its 1960 level of 33 percent to 52 percent in 1998.[33] Metropolitan San José and its environs have sprawled out virtually to engulf the nearby provincial capitals of Heredia and Alajuela. Perhaps 1.9 million of the nation's 3.7 million people live in this central metropolitan area, many of them recent migrants from rural areas.

PHOTO 8.1   Traditional export coffee remains strong despite efforts to promote new products (photo by Julio Laínez, courtesy *Tico Times*)

The rapid urbanization of the metropolitan center has caused complex problems. Rapid growth continuously strains the urban service infrastructure (roads, water and sewer treatment, and other utilities). Rural in-migrants and the urban poor, unable to find affordable housing, establish squatter homes on private and public land. They often occupy such dangerous and inappropriate locations (typically bereft of basic utilities) as railroad and road rights-of-way, farmland, and terrain under bridges, in overly steep canyons, and along riverbanks. These spontaneous neighborhoods have generated unexpected and unplanned-for demand for schools, roads, utilities, and social services. The political mobilization of the urban poor demanding housing and services has become an important part of the national political landscape (Chapter 5).

The national government and the weak, resource-poor municipal governments have fought an often losing battle to cope with this anarchic urban growth. The government dramatically shifted resources toward the squatters and away from the urbanization institute INVU, which once built orderly, planned working- and middle-class subdivisions. Shrinking resources and new investment priorities have stripped the government of critical funds to address urbanization problems. Structural adjustment and changing development models, in short, have undermined Costa Rica's ability to manage its rapid and disorderly urbanization. As a consequence, by the late 1990s urban and environmental problems—manifold social pathologies, waste management problems, and seriously worsening air and water quality—accumulated at a daunting pace.

The natural environment has suffered mightily under the onslaught of population, urbanization, agriculture, and industry. Costa Rica remains a breathtakingly beautiful country, despite the damage centuries of export agriculture have wreaked upon the natural environment: deforestation, erosion, loss of biodiversity, and serious contamination of water and soil.[34] Population growth, industrialization, and urbanization have all tended to aggravate these problems.

On the positive side, Costa Rica has excelled in aspects of environmental protection, especially in awareness of these problems. The country has set aside several national biological reserves and parks to protect species and endangered environments. The very lightly populated indigenous reserves that cover a significant fraction of the national territory probably also help conserve environments and species.[35] The Legislative Assembly has enacted laws to protect certain endangered species and regulate logging and slash-and-burn agriculture in many tropical forests. Efforts are under way to promote sustainable and ecologically responsible economic activities in the interest of conserving the burgeoning ecotourism industry.

These advances notwithstanding, Costa Rica's fragile environment faces enormous threats and continued degradation from uncontrolled urbanization, deforestation, misuse of agricultural chemicals, poaching, untreated sewage, legal and illegal landfills and waste disposal, and a host of other problems (Photo 8.2). Transition to the neoliberal development model has considerably disarmed a state once much more capable of enforcing environmental regulations. Resources to devote to environmental protection and conservation may depend more and more upon private initiative and less upon government.

Conclusions: Political Economy and Democracy

Costa Rica has largely completed a virtual revolution in its political economy, the transition between the social democratic and neoliberal development models. Those concerned principally about the macroeconomic health of the nation are rejoicing. The intrusive, regulatory, clunkily bureaucratic state and its myriad restrictions upon business have been dramatically scaled back. Economic freedom has increased. Although the new freedom brings new risks, a smaller, leaner government and freer private sector may help Costa Rica find a new and advantageous niche in the international economy. Years of fiscal profligacy combined with the power of external lenders to force the debt-addicted state to address its financial weaknesses and operate the economy somewhat more responsibly. Nevertheless, continuing weakness in the economy, a declining *colón*, and a doubling of the inflation rate in 1995–1996 once again led Costa Rica to boost foreign borrowing and deficit spending. The vulnerability of the economy was not eliminated.

For those concerned mainly about social justice, the neoliberal revolution in Costa Rica represents a catastrophe. Transition to the neoliberal model brought

PHOTO 8.2   Environmental
damage from deforestation
(photo courtesy *Tico Times*)

no dramatic short-term changes in income distribution (Table 5.1), but some early evidence suggests that income may shift back toward the wealthy. The new model, however, threatens social and economic justice because it limits the state's ability and will to redistribute income toward the middle and poorer classes, shifts social costs down rather than up the socioeconomic ladder, and promotes new inequalities. Structural adjustment immediately reduced and promises continuing restrictions upon public spending, investment, and program quality in education, health, and other public services. To many critics, such policies will inevitably worsen, both absolutely and relatively, the standards of living, resources, health, and skills of middle-class and poorer Ticos. They thus undermine the very national traits that make Costa Rica so distinctive among developing nations.

What does the transition to the neoliberal development model imply for democracy? Democracy might benefit in two ways: First, a leaner and less debt-reliant government and economy offer a stronger and healthier state, which should fortify democratic institutions. Second, the proliferation of economic interests caused by the privatization and the reduction of regulation will create new interests. This new civil society should broaden and deepen democracy by making the government more responsive and stimulating citizen participation. Indeed, the government's backsliding on the deficit in 1995–1996 likely reflects Tico policy-makers' sensitivity to public opinion.

Some significant possible costs to democracy also warrant consideration. First, structural adjustment was imposed mainly by external actors. Although Costa Rican officials technically enacted and implemented it, outside forces dictated the details of neoliberal reforms. External imposition of the new political economic model thus completely fails to meet any reasonable test of democratic decisionmaking.

Second, in order to implement structural adjustment presidents and the executive branch resorted increasingly to legislation by decree (see Chapter 4). This took away from the representatives of the people in the Legislative Assembly much of their constitutionally assigned lawmaking responsibility. Such a decline in popular influence (even if indirectly exercised through representative government) over public policy clearly reduces the depth of democracy.[36] This loss of democracy as the people's representatives ceded policy influence to technocrats and foreign institutions represents a considerable setback for Costa Rican democratic governance.

Finally, Costa Rica's neoliberal retreat from statism has relinquished the electorate's potential to influence critical aspects of national economic activity. Government's withdrawal from much of the economic arena also reduces the range of Costa Rican democracy. Indeed, one may reasonably surmise that the many protests of the 1990s and the sharp drop-off in election turnout in 1998 expressed the anger of many Ticos about two things: their polity's losses in democratic range and depth, and how palpably and quickly neoliberalism had eroded their well-being.

A quiet revolution in Costa Rica's political economy occurred in the 1980s and early 1990s. Government lost size, power, and responsibilities. Private initiative gained freedom, and the burden of financing government, social welfare, and debt repayment shifted away from the economically comfortable and toward middle- and working-class citizens. As the state shrank, the power of the executive branch over public policy decisions grew greatly while that of the people's legislative branch waned. Time alone will reveal whether the losses in the depth and range of Costa Rican democracy brought about by these changes will be partially offset by the strengthening of civil society. The once great ability of the Costa Rican middle sector to influence and benefit from economic policy through the social democratic model has diminished. In stark contrast, neoliberalism has shifted political and economic power to economic elites and appears to offer them disproportionate benefits and influence over the long run.

Notes

1. This section is drawn mainly from Victor Hugo Acuña Ortega and Iván Molina Jiménez, *Historia económica y social de Costa Rica (1750–1950)* (San José, Costa Rica: Editorial Porvenir, 1991); Ciro F. S. Cardoso and Héctor Pérez Brignoli, *Centro América y la economía occidental (1520–1930)* (San José: Editorial Universidad de Costa Rica, 1977); Rodolfo Pastor, *Historia de Centroamérica* (Mexico City: El Colegio de México, 1988); Mitchell A. Seligson, *Peasants of Costa Rica and the Development of Agrarian Capitalism*

(Madison: University of Wisconsin Press, 1980); and John Peeler, *Latin American Democracies* (Chapel Hill: University of North Carolina Press, 1985).

2. Acuña Ortega and Molina Jiménez, *Historia económica y social,* p. 97.

3. Between 1920 and 1945, there were two major slumps in Costa Rica's per capita GDP (Table 8.1), resulting in a net change of roughly zero.

4. Jorge Rovira M., "El nuevo estilo nacional de desarrollo," in Juan Manuel Villasuso, ed., *El nuevo rostro de Costa Rica* (Heredia, Costa Rica: Centro de Estudios Democráticos de América Latina, 1992), pp. 242–245.

5. By the early 1980s, the Costa Rican public sector included the central government (presidency, ministries, judiciary, electoral tribunal, comptroller); the municipalities; twenty autonomous bureaucracies delivering services; twenty-seven public corporations, including all banks, insurance, and public utilities; and some fifty government-owned corporations, forty of them subsidiaries of the state holding company, CODESA. See Thelmo Vargas, "Eficiencia del sector público en Costa Rica," in Claudio González Vega and Edna Camacho Mejía, eds., *Políticas económicas en Costa Rica,* vol. 1 (San José, Costa Rica: Academia de Centroamérica–Ohio State University, 1990), pp. 273–276.

6. Victor Bulmer-Thomas, *The Political Economy of Central America Since 1920* (Cambridge: Cambridge University Press, 1987), table A14.

7. Inter-American Development Bank (IADB), *Economic and Social Progress in Latin America: Natural Resources, 1983 Report* (Washington, D.C.: IADB, 1983), tables 27–30. Regressive taxes disproportionately levy the poor; progressive taxes do the opposite.

8. IADB, *Socio-Economic Progress in Latin America, Annual Report 1971* (Washington, D.C.: IADB, 1971), tables 46, 48; IADB, *1983 Report,* table 22; IADB, *Economic and Social Progress in Latin America: Overcoming Volatility, 1995 Report* (Baltimore: Johns Hopkins University Press, 1995), table C-4.

9. Expressed in nominal *colones,* converted at the official exchange rate to U.S. dollars; from Vargas, "Eficiencia," p. 279.

10. Sebastián Edwards, "Ajuste económico y equilibrio macroeconómico en Costa Rica: Lecciones y perspectivas," in González Vega and Camacho Mejía, *Políticas económicas,* vol. 1, pp. 93–135; "Costa Rica," in IADB, *1983 Report,* pp. 197–202.

11. See Martha Honey, *Hostile Acts: U.S. Policy in Costa Rica in the 1980s* (Gainesville: University Press of Florida, 1994); Dario Moreno, *The Struggle for Peace in Central America* (Gainesville: University Press of Florida, 1994), ch. 4.

12. Carlos Castro Valverde, "Sector público y ajuste estructural en Costa Rica (1983–1992)," in Trevor Evans, ed., *La transformación neoliberal del sector público* (Managua, Nicaragua: Latino Editores, 1995), p. 49. For an excellent overview of this period, see Jorge Rovira Mas, *Costa Rica en los años '80* (San José, Costa Rica: Editorial Porvenir, 1989), pp. 57–141.

13. Castro Valverde, "Sector público," p. 51.

14. This section is drawn mainly from ibid., pp. 51–56.

15. IADB, *Economic and Social Progress in Latin America: Working Women in Latin America, 1990 Report* (Baltimore: Johns Hopkins University Press, 1990), p. 89.

16. "Costa Rica," in IADB, *1990 Report,* pp. 91–92.

17. Between 1980 and 1989, Costa Rica fully privatized twenty-seven firms and subsidiary enterprises, and the government divested its partial ownership of nine more firms. Vargas, "Eficiencia," pp. 273–276.

18. Rovira M., "El nuevo estilo," pp. 245–254; see also Lucía Chinchilla, "Cambios en la agricultura costarricense en los últimos años," pp. 457–470; Anabelle Ulate Q., "Aumento

de las exportaciones: Obsesión del ajuste estructural," pp. 471–492; and Rafael Trejos S., "Desarrollo del sector servicios en Costa Rica," pp. 493–516; all in Villasuso, *El nuevo rostro;* and González Vega and Camacho Mejía, *Políticas economicas,* vols. 1 and 2, passim.

19. Moreno, *The Struggle for Peace,* pp. 85–87.

20. "Costa Rica," in IADB, *1990 Report,* p. 92; Castro Valverde, "Sector público," pp. 55–56.

21. IADB, *1995 Report,* p. 75; "Costa Rica," *Mesoamerica,* January 1996, p. 7.

22. "Costa Rica," *Mesoamerica,* May 1995, pp. 7–8.

23. Ibid., November 1995, p. 4.

24. Alvaro García B., "El sector empresarial en una década de cambio," in Villasuso, *El nuevo rostro,* p. 521.

25. Castro Valverde, "Sector público," p. 101.

26. Ibid.

27. IADB, *Economic and Social Progress in Latin America: 1994 Report* (Baltimore: Johns Hopkins University Press, 1994), table C-13; and IADB, *Latin America After a Decade of Reforms: Economic and Social Progress in Latin America, 1997 Report* (Baltimore: Johns Hopkins University Press, 1997), tables C-4, C-13. See also Sergio de la Cuadra, "Los principales desequilibrios macroeconómicos en Costa Rica: 1989," in González Vega and Camacho Mejía, *Políticas económicas,* vol. 1, table 4.3.

28. Yolanda M. Rojas, "Transformaciones recientes en la educación costarricense," pp. 107–122, and Jorge Rovira M., "Las universidades en los años ochenta," pp. 133–135, both in Villasuso, *El nuevo rostro.*

29. Data for this section are from Castro Valverde, "Sector público," appendix 2.2.

30. IADB, *1997 Report,* p. 276. Inflation rose sharply in 1995 and 1996, when consumer prices escalated 23.2 percent and 17.5 percent, respectively.

31. The brevity of this discussion should not be read as a measure of the lack of importance of these problems. They are merely too extensive to address sufficiently in the space available here.

32. Vargas C., "Los movimientos urbanos"; and Marlon Yong Ch., "Sinópsis de las patologías sociales en Costa Rica," in Villasuso, *El nuevo rostro,* pp. 71–96.

33. IADB, *1990 Report,* table A-2; and IADB, *1997 Report,* table A-2 (1998 figures are estimates based on the urban growth rate).

34. Robert G. Williams, *Export Agriculture and the Crisis in Central America* (Chapel Hill: University of North Carolina Press, 1986), pp. 48–51, 114–116; Andrea Simpson, "The Rise and Fall of Trees—A Reflection on Development," *Mesoamerica,* July 1994, pp. 7–9; Timothy Griffiths, "Campesino Logging Cooperative: New Guardian of the Tropical Forest," *Mesoamerica,* May 1996, pp. 10–11.

35. However, the government itself has repeatedly violated their conservation value by issuing mineral and logging permits.

36. Not all of the loss of Legislative Assembly influence nor all of the rise of executive decree and rule making stems from structural adjustment pressures, but structural adjustment has contributed significantly to the process.

9

COSTA RICA
IN THE WORLD

This chapter examines Costa Rica's foreign relations and policy. As a small and relatively poor nation situated near the large and powerful United States, Costa Rica experiences the problems typical of all small powers. Its proximity to a great power often limits Costa Rica's freedom in foreign affairs. Despite such constraints, the nation's foreign policy makers consistently strive to maximize economic and political advantage.

Foreign policy making tends to be undemocratic. It is a policy arena to which most nations assign little influence to the public and interest groups and only modest influence to the legislature representing the people. Foreign policy power typically resides in executive branches, particularly in the hands of presidents. Costa Rica's constitution follows this pattern but also gives considerable shared influence over foreign policy to the foreign and public security ministers.

Despite centralization of decisionmaking, various domestic political forces struggle to shape Costa Rican foreign policy. And foreign policy makers sometimes reach out to domestic and external actors for support. Never in its national life has the interaction among Costa Rica's foreign policy establishment, external forces, and domestic actors been more contentious or complex than during the turbulent 1980s. Indeed, some observers believed that the witch's brew of economic crisis, the geopolitics of the Nicaraguan revolution and its U.S. opposition, and powerful domestic ideological pressures on foreign policy actually imperiled Costa Rican democracy during the 1980s.

General Characteristics of Foreign Policy

Isolated by great distance and difficult terrain from the other power centers of Central America, Costa Rica early on developed distinctive features of its foreign policy and relations.[1] First, its position on the far southern margin of Central America and its civilian political traditions made early governments reluctant to share the political life of its more powerful, praetorian, and violent northern neighbors. After the Central American Federal Republic collapsed in 1839, Costa Rica repeatedly evaded nineteenth-century efforts to rebuild it. More recently, Costa Rica was the last Central American nation to enter the Central American Common Market and declined to elect representatives to the Central American Parliament in the 1990s.

Second, foreign policy has historically tended to be reactive and pragmatic rather than proactive or idealistic. With their limited resources, Costa Rican governments have mainly sought to manage and limit damage from challenges arising from the external environment. Rather than acting assertively to reshape its external environment, as larger powers might, Costa Rica usually accepted the general contours of its geopolitical and economic environments and, when possible, manipulated them for national advantage.

Third is the long and pragmatic tradition of friendly cooperation with the United States, the Caribbean region's geopolitical equivalent of the fabled 900-pound gorilla. Recognizing the risks of antagonizing such a powerful neighbor, Costa Rica has usually supported U.S. policy both in the hemisphere and in the world at large. The United States has not always reciprocated with the respect and support that the two nations' common democratic, constitutional traditions warrant.[2] Indeed, U.S. efforts to contain Nicaragua's Sandinista revolution, including the promotion of the Nicaraguan *contras* and efforts to remilitarize Costa Rica during the 1980s, often violated Costa Rican law and tradition.[3]

Fourth, the nation's lengthy civil, democratic tradition and its demilitarization in 1949 have shaped its foreign policy: Its democratic tradition has long moved Costa Rica to offer political asylum to those fleeing oppression elsewhere in Latin America. Costa Rica delayed its entry into the CACM out of reluctance to subordinate its economic policy to neighboring dictatorships. Two-time president and leading citizen José Figueres Ferrer helped exiles attempting to unseat Nicaraguan dictator Anastasio Somoza García during the late 1940s and early 1950s.[4]

Costa Rica has usually tempered this preference for democracy with pragmatism. Although official Costa Rican rhetoric has often proclaimed "an adherence to a code of immutable and essentially 'democratic' values [with] a certain messianic moralism, a great practical sense has prevailed ultimately to prevent the sacrifice of the national interest to dogma."[5] It did eventually join the CACM when convinced that its national economic interest outweighed its democratic scruples. Other recent examples of such pragmatism include President Oduber's policy of "cohabitation" with regional dictators, President Carazo's "support for the Sandinista insurrection, and the benevolent tolerance of the Monge administration of the [Nicaraguan] 'contras' followed by his subsequent proclamation of neutrality that saved the nation's sovereignty."[6]

Demilitarization bolstered Costa Rica's preference for negotiated solutions to international conflicts. Boundary conflicts once caused repeated strains in relations with Panama and Nicaragua, but even though Costa Rica then had an army, it settled these disputes with arbitration. "Costa Rica has been a strong advocate of the pacific settlement of disputes and has participated in international conventions and organizations established for that purpose."[7] Once it demilitarized, of course, Costa Rica pragmatically strengthened its commitment to peaceful conflict resolution, nominal neutrality with respect to its neighbors' internal politics, and international security arrangements. Indeed, Costa Rica has largely relied upon the Organization of American States (OAS) and the security umbrella of the United States and other democratic regional powers such as Venezuela to guarantee its security on the few occasions when it has been threatened.[8]

Finally, despite their pragmatism and usual reserve toward the rest of Central America, Costa Rican foreign policy makers have occasionally displayed the quite contradictory penchant of isthmian leaders to meddle in each other's internal affairs. Part of this tendency arose in the colonial and early republican eras, when the five Central American peoples belonged to the same political systems. Costa Rica's four most egregious modern cases of intervention have all involved northern neighbor Nicaragua: (1) José Figueres Ferrer's commitment to the social democratic, anticommunist Caribbean Legion made Costa Rica host to rebels conspiring against dictatorial regimes in Venezuela, Nicaragua, and the Dominican Republic.[9] (2) President Carazo Odio, troubled by the atrocities under Nicaragua's Somoza regime and the growing instability there, allowed the Sandinista-led revolutionary coalition's guerrilla forces and shadow government to operate freely in Costa Rica in 1978 and 1979. Costa Rican officials even helped smuggle arms to the Nicaraguan rebels.[10] (3) Carazo changed his opinion of the Nicaraguan revolution in the early 1980s and began to assist its opponents. With enthusiastic U.S. encouragement, Carazo's successor, Monge, extensively aided Nicaraguan counterrevolutionaries. (4) Assistance to the *contras* had grave repercussions for Costa Rica's domestic and foreign affairs. President Arias (1985–1990), struggling to restore domestic order and promote regional stability, withdrew Costa Rican support for the *contras* and promoted a regional peace agreement, actions that annoyed the United States.[11]

Foreign Economic Policy

As explained in Chapter 8, during the era of the social democratic development model, Costa Rica promoted its prosperity in part by protecting its economy from external challenges. It rejected the contention of classical liberal economic theory that free domestic and external markets and relatively unfettered capital should determine the nation's economic fate with minimal interference by government. Rather, in an attempt to boost prosperity and reduce uncertainty, the government managed the state, the economy, and individual citizens' interactions with the external economic world.

One such strategy was to promote import substitution industrialization (ISI), a policy Costa Rica pursued from the 1950s through the 1980s. ISI encouraged manufacturing by protecting local industry with high tariffs (import taxes) to raise the cost of competing foreign goods. Tariffs thus encouraged domestic capitalists to manufacture goods by permitting new industry to operate inefficiently and thus sustain the relatively high wages that contributed to income redistribution and labor peace. When local capital was too timid or insufficient, the state itself would enter into joint ventures or wholly owned manufacturing enterprises rather than freely allow imports.

Under social democracy the Costa Rican government practiced currency controls and managed its exchange rate. Costa Rica kept the exchange rate for the *colón* artificially high against other currencies for various reasons: One was to keep down the relative cost of the imported foreign petroleum, raw materials, and technology that kept agriculture producing and supplied the new factories developing in the country. (The exchange rate policy thus amounted to another form of protection for manufacturing under ISI.) A valuable and stable *colón* constituted an element of national pride and made daily life and economic decisions predictable. Paradoxically, a valuable *colón* also permitted, even subsidized, consumption of foreign goods and travel abroad by the middle and upper classes—benefits that promoted their loyalty to the system.

During the social democratic period, Costa Rica established state monopolies in banking and insurance. These monopolies permitted the government to manage investment, interest rates, and currency flows and barred or made it difficult for foreign capital to gain a foothold in the Costa Rican economy. Although these policies brought the benefits of international financial independence and investment control, they also meant economic bureaucratization and sluggishness.

In the 1960s Costa Rica joined the newly formed CACM, which sought to open regional economies to each other and to rationalize their collective industrialization. The United States assisted in this effort with loans for economic and social infrastructure development through the Alliance for Progress. Costa Rica saw the CACM and the alliance as consistent with its social democratic development strategy in that they helped manage and protect the economy, but in collaboration with the other nations of the isthmus. The CACM's industrial policy involved regionally planning the allocation among countries of key industries (modern tire manufacturing, for instance) to maximize utilization of plant capacity, prevent excessive competition, and extend markets to the entire region's population. Central American goods received lower tariffs than did goods from outside the region. These policies made the region more attractive to private foreign capital seeking to invest in manufacturing.

The CACM contributed greatly to industrial and economic growth in the booming 1960s and 1970s as Tico products gained freer access to the region. Despite the early success of the CACM, economic policy tensions among the member nations were common. They argued about the allocation of plants, tariff reduction and adjustment schedules, and balance-of-trade problems. Early on, because of its high labor costs, Costa Rica tended to import more manufactures from other CACM countries and ran an irritatingly consistent trade deficit with them. However, Costa Rica's political and labor stability ultimately corrected much of this problem in the 1970s as Guatemala, Nicaragua, and El Salvador's instability worsened. Foreign industrial investment diverted into the more secure environment of Costa Rica. By the late 1970s, though, the CACM's advantages for Costa Rica evaporated. Political turmoil in the region effectively collapsed most of the remaining trade in a CACM whose economies had been already depressed by escalating oil and industrial input costs.

The oil price shocks and regional instability of the 1970s and early 1980s frightened many prosperous Ticos into converting their *colones* into dollars and investing them more safely abroad. Higher oil and industrial input costs also drew down Costa Rica's foreign currency reserves. To counter these problems, the government restricted the purchase of and payments in foreign currencies. It also set high interest rates on foreign currency (U.S. dollar) accounts to keep these funds in Costa Rica. Capital flight and escalating import costs, however, so outpaced export earnings that foreign reserves vanished anyway (see Chapter 8).

Costa Rica borrowed heavily abroad to keep its foreign currency accounts liquid, but in 1981 the reserve problem became so severe that the nation defaulted on payment of the foreign debt. The default placed national economic policy at the mercy of international lenders and wrought major changes in foreign economic policy already outlined in the previous chapter. One was the progressive devaluation of the *colón*, which by increasing the relative cost of foreign goods sought to discourage their consumption.

Other policies flowed from the gradual adoption of the neoliberal economic model under structural adjustment agreements: The government reduced tariffs to force Costa Rican manufacturers to compete with the world market for goods and thus either become more competitive or fail (many failed). The government also eliminated subsidies for public-sector industries and eventually privatized almost all governmentally owned enterprises. It thus divested itself of an economic burden but also diminished its economic power. The government eliminated much of the state's banking monopoly, permitting private capital to assume a major share of the national investment portfolio.

Other Foreign Economic Policies

Costa Rica began to project itself more vigorously into the international arena during the early 1970s.[12] This had several effects upon foreign economic policy worthy of brief mention. First, Costa Rica participated in two cartels—those of coffee-exporting and banana-exporting countries—in hopes of stabilizing the prices of its exports. The coffee cartel (the International Coffee Producers Agreement) used marketing quotas to regulate the world supply of coffee to keep coffee prices stable and high. The agreement's demise in 1980 undermined coffee prices and thus reduced Costa Rica's export earnings and tax revenue.[13]

Costa Rica also joined the Organization of Banana Exporting Countries, but this organization did little to effectively control prices. The banana-exporting group and Costa Rica energetically protested the European Economic Community's (EEC) system of quotas on banana imports during the early 1990s. They argued that the EEC quotas unfairly protected inferior banana production in Europe's former African and Caribbean colonies. In negotiations on GATT in early 1994, Costa Rica and Colombia wrangled a much more favorable banana export quota from the EEC. This deal, however, prompted an energetic protest by the United States that such quotas violated GATT policies and harmed the economic interests of the U.S.-based fruit company Chiquita Brands.[14]

Costa Rica ratified the international Law of the Sea Treaty, part of which extended national territorial waters to 200 miles offshore. This, too, precipitated a lengthy conflict with the United States during the 1980s when Costa Rica impounded U.S. tuna fishing vessels and arrested their crews for illegally fishing in Costa Rican waters. The United States had not ratified the Law of the Sea Treaty, nor did it accept the 200-mile territorial limit. There ensued the U.S.–Costa Rican "tuna war" in which the United States demanded the release of American boats and crews and unimpeded fishing rights under former boundary waters conventions. The issue remained an irritant between the United States and Costa Rica throughout the 1980s.[15]

In order actively to promote its national economic interests and to protect itself from threats developing elsewhere, Costa Rica has also signed various economic accords. Particularly noteworthy was GATT, a worldwide trade agreement tending to reduce tariffs and promote free markets. In the latest (Uruguay Round version), signed by 124 nations including Costa Rica in early 1994, major economic powers like the United States and the EEC nations promoted and agreed to major tariff cuts. But they made concessions for lesser tariff reductions by developing nations in order to protect their smaller economies and firms. Although even such moderated GATT tariff cuts may harm some parts of Costa Rica's economy, the nation could not stay out of the agreement because of the easier access it will offer Tico exports.[16] Viewing GATT membership as a necessary evil, Costa Rica fought for specific concessions to minimize possible damage. It won special tariff allowances on chicken parts and milk products and negotiated the side agreement for a larger (and disputed) banana quota with the EEC.[17]

Costa Rica viewed the development of the North American Free Trade Agreement (NAFTA) among Canada, Mexico, and the United States as a considerable economic threat. NAFTA sought to lower trade barriers among the three great economic powers of the region well below the levels required by GATT. This would have disadvantaged Costa Rica with two of its principal foreign markets, Mexico and the United States. During the early 1990s, therefore, Costa Rica sought entry into NAFTA but was rebuffed. To protect itself, Costa Rica forged a bilateral free trade agreement with Mexico that effectively permitted Costa Rica to enjoy the benefits of NAFTA via the back door of Mexico.[18]

Geopolitics

Small and disarmed, Costa Rica during the 1950s and 1960s pursued its national sovereignty and interest by aligning itself with the great hegemonic power of the hemisphere and Western bloc, the United States. By the 1970s the discipline of the cold war's power blocs began to loosen as new centers of economic and political power moved the world toward multipolarity. Costa Rica reacted to these changes by seeking new, collaborative spaces for the promotion of its interests, and "beginning with the second government of José Figueres [1970–1974], the foreign policy of Costa Rica universalized itself. . . . Its ambits of action broadened to include . . . all of Latin America, and beyond the continent, the European Community, socialist Europe, and the Soviet Union."[19]

These changes partly reflected Figueres's pretensions as an international promoter of democracy. They were assisted by the continuity afforded by several successive (or virtually so) National Liberation Party governments, the first great détente of the cold war, and Latin America's efforts to break free from U.S. foreign policy dominion in such venues as the OAS. Costa Rica developed stronger ties with other developing countries, hosted international conferences, took a larger role in the United Nations, supported Panama in its canal treaty negotiations with the United States, and began working with other Latin American nations on common problems.

This universalization of Costa Rican foreign policy began in the early 1970s, encouraged by the maneuvering room created by East-West détente and the Watergate crisis in the United States. Costa Rica opened relations with the Soviet bloc, and even defied U.S. preferences by advocating the readmission of Cuba to the OAS. The cold war intensified again, however, and during the late 1970s and 1980s Central America became a main theater of conflict. For Costa Rica, the resulting geopolitical turmoil was as traumatic as its nearly simultaneous economic travails.

For the most part, Costa Rica pragmatically tolerated military dictatorship elsewhere in Central America, but by the late 1970s the situation in Nicaragua became deeply troubling. The administration of Jimmy Carter in Washington advocated human rights improvements in Nicaragua and even withdrew its support from the dictatorship of Anastasio Somoza Debayle. This signaled that Costa Rica might oppose its vexatious and violent neighbor to improve its own security. Somoza's excesses and the growing civil war in Nicaragua in 1978 prompted President Carazo (Photo 9.1) to reverse field. Costa Rica embraced the insurrection against Somoza; permitted Sandinista guerrillas to operate and recruit in Costa Rica; helped Venezuela, Panama, and Cuba supply arms to the Sandinistas;

PHOTO 9.1   Rodrigo Carazo
Odio, president, 1978–1982 (photo
by Julio Laínez, courtesy *Tico
Times*)

and harbored the rebels' shadow government. The policy paid off with the collapse of the Somoza regime in July 1979.

Carazo soon developed grave reservations about the revolution in Nicaragua. As anti-Somocista exiles left Costa Rica, other Nicaraguans—former allies of the dictator—flowed in to replace them. Within months the Marxist-Leninist Sandinistas assumed dominance over the new regime there. Moderate former allies of the Sandinistas broke with the revolution, and many returned to Costa Rica.[20] The Nicaraguan counterrevolution developed a powerful wing in Costa Rica and attracted anticommunist allies who began agitating against Nicaragua's revolution. Carazo's growing apprehension about the leftward shift of the Nicaraguan revolution (and thus Costa Rica's own security) paralleled U.S. president Carter's. Carazo's last year in office overlapped the first of Ronald Reagan, who expressed open antagonism toward the Sandinistas.

Despite Carazo's open break with the Sandinistas and the support he lent to U.S. policy in El Salvador, his prior backing of the Sandinistas, clashes with IMF negotiators,[21] and the "tuna war" all deeply angered the new administration in Washington. Despite his best efforts, Carazo thus in 1982 bequeathed to his successor, Monge (Photo 9.2), strained relations with the United States, several major foreign policy crises, an economic catastrophe, and growing domestic turbulence.

Contending Policy Options

Three contending proposals to solve Costa Rica's geopolitical dilemmas had taken form by the start of the Monge administration: anticommunist, neutralist, and peacemaking.[22] According to Carlos Sojo, each approach had advocates from a strong political base within Costa Rica, and each would eventually have some influence. A protracted struggle over the anticommunist and neutralist strategies

PHOTO 9.2   Luis Alberto Monge Alvarez,
president, 1982–1986 (photo courtesy *Tico
Times*)

dominated the Monge government. Monge, caught in this debate with enormous
implications for national security, seemed to vacillate between anticommunism
and neutrality or simultaneously to embrace both. The peacemaking approach
gathered support near the end of Monge's term, partly in reaction to his decisions
and to growing fears about Costa Rica's prospects.

The advocates of the anticommunist approach included conservative ideological groups, some labor unions affiliated with the PLN, and key entrepreneurial
sectors, including the mass media. Pressing the anticommunist line from outside,
of course, was the United States. These foreign policy anticommunists, many
Monge administration insiders, justified a hard line toward Marxist-led revolutionary movements in Central America, especially Nicaragua, with several facts:
Nicaraguan armed forces pursuing *contra* rebels had interfered with navigation
on the San Juan River, the border between the two nations. Nicaraguan forces attacked Costa Rica's Las Crucecitas border station, killing two guards.[23] Police attributed to Nicaraguan agents a bombing at a Honduran airline office in San José.
The hard-liners also blamed Nicaraguan and Salvadoran rebels for efforts to
destabilize Costa Rica, taking as evidence street protests and incipient armed activity by Tico leftists. To the anticommunists, all these events demonstrated a
growing Soviet- and Cuban-backed revolutionary threat to democracy.

Monge adopted several policies that reflected the anticommunist line early in
his administration. He accused the Sandinistas of provoking domestic unrest in
Costa Rica, vigorously protested the border problems to Nicaragua, proposed a
Forum for Peace and Democracy among isthmian nations that would have ex-
cluded Nicaragua, and opposed the efforts of the Contadora Group (made up of
Mexico, Panama, Colombia, and Venezuela) to negotiate a settlement of the
Central American imbroglio. Monge also aligned Costa Rica with the Reagan ad-
ministration, persuaded by copious U.S. economic aid (Appendix, Tables A.4 and

A.5). He gave both *contras* and U.S. intelligence operatives considerable freedom to operate on national soil. His National Security Council, an advisory body of key foreign policy and security officials, contained outspoken anticommunists who coordinated Costa Rica's help to the *contras*.[24] The nation's security forces were substantially strengthened with U.S. assistance. Finally, Monge opposed negotiating with "illegitimate" (unelected) governments, which almost scuttled the Costa Rican–Nicaraguan Mixed Commission that President Carazo had set up to resolve border conflicts.

In contrast, the neutrality approach argued that Costa Rica should remain neutral toward the internal political arrangements of other isthmian countries (as it usually had) and toward the great East-West geopolitical clash. Neutrality advocates advanced several arguments: The most obvious was that a disarmed Costa Rica could not effectively confront neighboring revolutionary regimes and would be better served by relying upon existing multilateral security arrangements. Second, democratic Costa Rica should employ diplomacy, not force and confrontation, to maintain peace with its neighbors. Third, submission to U.S. anti-Sandinista policies had undermined national sovereignty and promised greater downstream risks should the Nicaraguan revolution survive. Finally, Costa Rica had strong economic ties to Mexico and Venezuela, both members of the peace-promoting Contadora Group, and to Great Britain, and all preferred a negotiated resolution of the region's problems.

The social base of the neutrality policy included several of Monge's PLN party advisers, PLN deputies in the Legislative Assembly, and a proneutrality consultative group that developed within the government. Many public employees' unions and university student groups advocated neutrality and mobilized public demonstrations in its favor. Finally, opinion polls revealed that a majority of the public supported neutrality.

Neutrality advocates struggled within the foreign policy apparatus to counteract the anticommunist line. Their most important initiative was a legislative effort to enact neutrality into either statutory or constitutional form. Despite media hostility to neutrality, public support for it grew. The legislative effort ultimately failed because anticommunism advocates in the Legislative Assembly held hostage other legislation vital to the structural adjustment agreements and pending international loans.

Monge, persuaded by popular sentiment and neutrality advocates and hoping to "detain the U.S. on its runaway course toward converting Costa Rica into a second aircraft carrier against the Sandinistas,"[25] on November 17, 1983, used his executive authority to proclaim neutrality to be Costa Rica's policy. The United States reacted negatively: USAID held up disbursal of scheduled loans. Washington pressured Costa Rica hard to continue its alignment with U.S. efforts to topple the Sandinistas.[26] Responding to U.S. criticism, the Monge government organized a demonstration "against war and for peace and neutrality" held on May 15, 1984; 50,000 people attended.[27]

Monge also endured blistering criticism from the anticommunist hard-liners after the neutrality proclamation. They employed rhetoric that some observers read as threatening a coup d'état should Monge refuse to recant on neutrality. Monge formally stood his ground, however, in part by rallying European endorsements and attempting to "boost Costa Rica's tarnished image as an unarmed, neutral country."[28] Nevertheless, Monge also pragmatically continued to cooperate with U.S. initiatives against Nicaragua in many ways.

Under arch-conservative [Security Minister Benjamín] Piza, U.S. influence over the police and security apparatus greatly increased. The most controversial of Washington's military programs was the creation of the U.S.-run civil guard military base located just ten miles from the Nicaraguan border.... The base was to be run by Green Beret instructors and used to train a new Costa Rican battalion to patrol the border with Nicaragua.[29]

The base, El Murciélago, accessible by sea, land, and air, was situated and equipped so as to inspire Nicaraguan fears that it might also serve the launching point for a U.S. invasion. El Murciélago complemented the extensive, simultaneous buildup of U.S.-Honduran military facilities on Nicaragua's northern border.

When the El Murciélago base opened in 1985, there began a debate whether this constituted remilitarization, but another violent border incident muted the discussion and for a time rallied Ticos behind the anticommunist hard-liners. As the Monge administration ended, Costa Rica's foreign policy remained stalemated between formal neutrality and practical anticommunism in cooperation with the United States. The conflict with Nicaragua, the ongoing economic crisis and strains with international lenders, incidents of terrorism, domestic turmoil, and revelations of espionage and skulduggery by foreign agents remained the daily stuff of Ticos' lives. It elevated their apprehensions about the geopolitical forces at the root of so many problems. The 1986 presidential campaign and election of Arias eventually helped break this stalemate by opening the domestic political way to the third foreign policy alternative—peacemaking.

The peacemaking option had less political support in the Monge administration than anticommunism and neutrality but eventually garnered strong backing. Peacemaking had two variants: The first was pacifistic; it argued that Costa Rica should coexist with any regime, no matter what its political characteristics, and should completely eschew military options. The second option—the "peacemaking via democratization" variant—advocated taking the initiative to promote peace within Central America via the full democratization of each nation.

The initial expression of the peacemaking option was the pacifist one, which appeared in the early 1980s. Its social base was in the popular organizations of urban Costa Rica, influenced by leftist social organizers; leftist political parties and unions, including the PVP and CUT; and Costa Rica's small cluster of peace groups—many involving idealistic foreigners, including religiously motivated pacifists—attracted to Costa Rica by its demilitarization and democracy. Because

PHOTO 9.3   Oscar Arias Sánchez, president, 1986–1990, and Nobel Peace laureate (photo by Julio Laínez, courtesy *Tico Times*)

the pacifists found neutrality more palatable than the anticommunist hard line, they tended also to endorse Monge's neutrality policy. Thus when the government held the May 1984 rally for peace and neutrality, many demonstrators were pacifism supporters from leftist labor and community organizations.

The peacemaking via democratization variant first emerged as a campaign proposal of PLN presidential candidate Oscar Arias, who ran against the PUSC's Rafael Angel Calderón Fournier, son of the 1940s populist. Powerful entrepreneurs, the media, the United States, and the Nicaraguan exile community (indeed, much of the hard-line anticommunist community) backed Calderón. During his campaign Arias had criticized *contra* activity within Costa Rica as harmful and promised to end it while taking care not to appear pro-Sandinista. Arias's polling, moreover, revealed a strong desire for peacemaking among the electorate. Late in the race—a very close one—Arias heavily emphasized his peacemaking intentions. This rallied undecided voters to him, and he eked out a narrow victory.

Upon taking office in April 1986, President Arias (Photo 9.3) elaborated his conception of promoting peace through democratization. He advocated the active promotion of regional peace. To this end he proposed a peace initiative to replace the failed Contadora attempt: This effort would seek to end conflict both within and between nations. He proposed that all isthmian nations (1) cease harboring rebels against other nations, (2) settle their internal armed conflicts, and (3) hold free elections to bring about full democratization. Arias portrayed Nicaragua's Sandinista regime as undemocratic (discounting its 1984 election) and understood that his proposed accord would require Nicaragua to hold fair elections.[30]

Arias withdrew Costa Rican support for the *contras,* despite the fierce opposition of the Reagan administration. In late 1996 the Iran-*contra* scandal broke in the United States and began to undercut U.S. pressure upon Arias. The unfolding Iran-*contra* story revealed that the Reagan administration had violated U.S. law against providing military support to the *contras:* A White House–based operation of the U.S. National Security Council, managed by marine lieutenant Oliver North, had secretly sold U.S. arms to Iran and transferred the proceeds to the *contras.*[31] The scandal tied up and undermined much of the administration's drive to overthrow the Sandinistas by forcing the White House to defend itself against massive press and congressional scrutiny. The scandal also weakened the administration's already troubled relations with Congress and its Democratic Party leadership and collapsed a tenuous bipartisan agreement on Nicaragua.

Iran-*contra* and its ramifications in Congress suggested to Central American governments that the United States would promote its anti-Sandinista agenda much less vigorously, signaling Central American foreign policy makers that they would have relatively greater freedom to act independently of the United States for some time. This was particularly important to Arias, who was trying to break with his predecessor's policies. To Honduras and El Salvador, it meant that they could not count on an indefinite extension of Reagan's energetic efforts to contain communism and the enormous largesse that flowed from it. To Guatemala's new president, Vinicio Cerezo Arévalo, wavering U.S. élan in Central America provided an opportunity to collaborate with Arias and thus improve a national image terribly tarnished by human rights abuses. To Nicaragua it meant that the *contras* might lose ground with diminished U.S. military support.

Iran-*contra,* in short, disrupted the Reagan administration's policy juggernaut and opened up the entire geopolitical equation in Central America. Arias's proposal had other obvious potential benefits. Three isthmian nations were enduring devastating civil wars that had killed hundreds of thousands, created millions of refugees, and demolished their economies. Exhausted by these wars, Guatemala, El Salvador, and Nicaragua each saw enormous potential benefit from peacemaking, especially if it would undermine support for its rebellious enemies. The insurgents in El Salvador and Guatemala, and even the *contras* of Nicaragua, also spent by years of stalemated combat, saw potential advantages from trading arms for political legitimacy and policy reforms.

Outside the isthmus other nations applauded the Arias proposal. The long-frustrated Contadora countries and their supporters embraced it. European nations who had criticized U.S. policy in Central America and had repeatedly called for peace also endorsed the notion. Pro-peace Democrats in the U.S. Congress, including House Speaker Jim Wright, encouraged Arias in his efforts.[32] The external situation thus seemed ripe for creative change in early 1987.

Arias found that his peace via democratization proposal had strong political legs within Costa Rica. Extreme anticommunists, including Nicaraguan exiles and the Tico far right, continued attacking Arias. But many of the more moderate members of this coalition saw in Arias's proposal for democratization and his determinedly anti-Sandinista rhetoric prospects for an end to the Nicaraguan revolution. Neutrality supporters, frustrated by Monge's de facto cooperation with U.S. policy on Nicaragua and with the *contras*, viewed the Arias plan as having the potential to reduce regional tensions. The peace proposal thus co-opted key segments of the anticommunist and neutralist camps. The pacifists, of course, had nowhere else to go, and many were delighted at improved prospects for peace. Arias's plan quickly garnered strong domestic backing.

Arias invited the other isthmian presidents (without Nicaragua's Daniel Ortega) to San José to discuss his proposal in February 1987.

> The importance of the Arias peace plan was that by agreeing to Arias's emphasis on democratization, regional leaders discovered a formula for resolving the decade-long conflict. At the San José summit Arias restored Costa Rica's moral authority on the issue of democracy and peace. In addition to his country's legitimacy as an honest broker, Arias had another important advantage over Contadora: a shift in the balance of power in Washington.[33]

Tentative agreement among the presidents led to the presentation of the proposal to Nicaragua with an invitation to a full regional summit. Nicaragua agreed, its revolutionary leaders confident that they could win another election (one was already scheduled for 1990).

A summit of all five Central American presidents was scheduled to take place in Esquipulas, Guatemala, in early August 1987. In Washington Reagan's Central American policies remained in shambles, but the administration scrambled to regain control. Attempting to head off Arias's ambitious proposal and regain initiative, the White House sought U.S. House Speaker Jim Wright's help. After consultations, Wright and Secretary of State James Baker drafted the Wright-Reagan Peace Plan aimed mainly at Nicaragua.[34] Wright, encouraged by the White House actions, went outside normal U.S. diplomatic channels and urged the Central American presidents to press ahead at Esquipulas. Reagan, however, then failed fully to support the Wright-Reagan proposal during the summit itself. An incensed Wright dispatched his aide Richard Peña to Guatemala "to give the Central Americans the green light in regard to the Arias peace plan. Peña and Guido Fernández, the Costa Rican ambassador to Washington, transformed the Wright-Reagan plan into a blank check for Arias to use as he saw fit at the summit."[35] Wright thus convinced even the more reluctant presidents to agree to the draft accord. Arias persuaded the Sandinistas to accept it with the provision that each country would deny aid to rebel forces from neighboring nations. This plank would undercut the *contras* in Honduras and Costa Rica and thus greatly offset their continued U.S. financing and political support.[36]

The presidents made numerous revisions to Arias's initial draft, but on August 7, 1987, all five signed the Central American peace accord, also called the Esquipulas accord.[37] It required each nation of Central America, following a common timetable, to undertake internal reconciliation and dialogue, pursue a cease-fire with rebels, move toward "authentic" democratization including political plu-ralism and full press freedom, hold free elections monitored by international ob-servers, terminate aid to insurgents and refuse the use of national territory for aggression against neighboring states, hold further negotiations on security is-sues, aid with refugee relocation, and set up an international verification commis-sion monitored by the UN, OAS, and several Latin American nations. This pro-vided the framework to end the region's three civil wars, successfully concluded by agreements in Nicaragua (1988) and subsequent demobilization agreements in El Salvador (1992) and Guatemala (1996).

The Central American peace accord, several regional presidential summits that followed, and the events that flowed from them had immediate payoffs for Costa Rica. They promptly restored much of its prestige as a pacific and democratic na-tion, its status confirmed when President Arias won the 1987 Nobel Peace Prize. Relations with Nicaragua improved right away, and difficulties along their border essentially ceased. The Nicaraguan peace agreement, signed at Sapoá in 1988 by a *contra* movement debilitated and disillusioned by wavering U.S. support, largely eliminated the *contras* as a source of Costa Rica's internal and foreign difficulties. In Nicaragua's February 1990 election, a domestic opposition coalition led by moderate conservative Violeta Barrios de Chamorro (not the *contras*) unseated the FSLN. This fully vindicated Arias's claim that his strategy of peace via democ-ratization would end the Sandinista revolution and its related security threats.

A Reagan White House stunned by the Central American peace accord contin-ued to cling to the hopes of reviving the *contras* militarily. The administration put heavy but fruitless pressure on Honduras, El Salvador, and Costa Rica to disrupt the accord. U.S. aid to Costa Rica was cut again, leaving a frustrated and angry Arias, normally circumspect in his comments about the United States, to note in an interview: "We want an intelligent friend, not a stupid ally."[38]

Relations with the United States improved when pragmatic George Bush be-came U.S. president in 1989 and as the cold war subsequently ended—especially that part of it taking place in Central America. Thanks to Arias's political skill and vision and to the Iran-*contra* scandal's impact on U.S. policy, Costa Rica emerged from this challenging decade with its security enhanced and its international prestige restored. Arias's perspicacity and the traditional values of Costa Rican foreign policy—pragmatism, unarmed and activist neutrality, and preference for democracy—allowed the government to extract itself from its geopolitical bind. In the process Costa Rica helped its neighbors restore peace and move toward democracy.

Persisting into the 1990s are the foreign economic policy issues discussed above and several bilateral problems with the United States. Arias's successors Calderón Fournier (PUSC) and Figueres Olsen (PLN) continued to struggle with structural adjustment programs and such issues as tuna fishing rights, confiscation of the property of U.S. citizens, and Costa Rica's EEC banana import quotas.

Conclusions

The international environment can be very harsh to small nations, as Costa Rica's plight in the 1970s and 1980s so amply demonstrates. Powerful international forces menaced it sufficiently to threaten the nation's democratic traditions and institutions. Because decisions are made by elites, Costa Rica's foreign policy making typically takes little account of the mass public. The conflict over approaches to the Central American crisis, however, reveals just how much its foreign policy can be shaped by interest groups and political pressures. Indeed, the way out of the crises of the 1980s involved finding a policy option that built a strong coalition of supporters. Oscar Arias's peacemaking via democratization formula calmed domestic turmoil and restored some of the initiative that Costa Rica had lost to the United States.

In terms of national sovereignty and democracy, the crises of the era produced mixed results. During the 1980s Costa Rica ceded considerable authority over itself to the United States and international lenders because of overpowering geopolitical and economic difficulties. Costa Rica reclaimed some of its political autonomy under Arias, but the ongoing debt crisis eventually overwhelmed the ability of Costa Rica's elected institutions and leaders to determine the national development model. Under the threat of economic catastrophe, the executive and legislative branches swept away social democracy and implemented neoliberalism. The government did so despite persistent public resistance and protest. This external pressure helped shift much ruling power from the people's branch of government, the Legislative Assembly, to the executive. This further reduced popular influence on policy and made Costa Rican democracy shallower.

Notes

1. This section draws heavily on Luis Guillermo Solís R., "Costa Rica: La política exterior y los cambios en el sistema internacional en los ochenta," in Juan Manuel Villasuso, ed., *El nuevo rostro de Costa Rica* (Heredia, Costa Rica: Centro de Estudios Democráticos de América Latina, 1992), pp. 341–356; Charles D. Ameringer, *Democracy in Costa Rica* (New York: Praeger, 1982), ch. 5; and Gonzalo J. Facio, "Política exterior," in Chester Zelaya, ed., *Costa Rica contemporánea,* vol. 1 (San José: Editorial Costa Rica, 1979), pp. 159–187.

2. For instance, on several occasions since the 1970s the U.S. government has pressured Costa Rican presidents to allow U.S. armed forces into Costa Rican territory without first obtaining the constitutionally mandated permission from the Legislative Assembly. Even more alarming, U.S. law officers have suborned Costa Rican police to kidnap wanted fugitives and deliver them to the United States, rather than taking the trouble to extradite them properly through the courts.

3. See, for instance, Martha Honey, *Hostile Acts: U.S. Policy in Costa Rica in the 1980s* (Gainesville: University Press of Florida, 1994), chs. 8–13.

4. Ameringer, *Democracy in Costa Rica,* pp. 81–85.

5. Solís R., "Costa Rica: La política exterior," p. 343.

6. Ibid.

7. Ameringer, *Democracy in Costa Rica*, p. 80.

8. In both 1949 and 1955, Costa Rica invoked the Inter-American Reciprocal Assistance Treaty and called upon the OAS when the nation appeared threatened by Nicaraguan dictator Anastasio Somoza García. In each case José Figueres Ferrer had angered Somoza by supporting Nicaraguan exiles seeking to overthrow the tyrant. In retaliation, Somoza gave military aid to anti-Figueres rebels involving former Costa Rican president Calderón Guardia and his supporters. OAS intervention successfully ended each crisis. See, for instance, Ameringer, *Democracy in Costa Rica*, pp. 81–85; Miguel Acuña, *El 48* (San José, Costa Rica: Librería Lehmann, 1974), pp. 367–374; and Miguel Acuña, *El 55* (San José, Costa Rica: Librería Lehmann, 1977).

9. Ameringer, *Democracy in Costa Rica*, pp. 81–88.

10. John A. Booth, *The End and the Beginning: The Nicaraguan Revolution* (Boulder: Westview Press, 1985).

11. This maneuver, further discussed below, was interventionist because it sought to topple the Sandinistas through the accord's provisions for elections. The United States preferred continued support for the military strategy—the *contras*. See Carlos Sojo, *Costa Rica: Política exterior y sandinismo* (San José, Costa Rica: Facultad Latinoamericano de Ciencias Sociales, 1991), pp. 173–205.

12. Solís R., "Costa Rica: La política exterior," p. 341.

13. Lucía Chinchilla, "Cambios en la agricultura costarricense en los últimos años," in Villasuso, *El nuevo rostro*, p. 459.

14. *Mesoamerica*, December 1993, p. 10; March 1994, p. 13; December 1994, p. 7; and Sara Campbell, "No Such Thing as Free Trade," *Mesoamerica*, May 1994, pp. 3–4.

15. Solís R., "Costa Rica: La política exterior," pp. 342–352.

16. For example, Costa Rican products received the following import tariff reductions in the EEC: papaya, guava, and mango from 6 percent to tax free; coffee from 5 percent to tax free; and houseplants from 13 percent to 6.5 percent (Campbell, "No Such Thing," p. 3).

17. Ibid., pp. 3–4.

18. *Mesoamerica*, May 1994, p. 2; June 1994, p. 11; November 1994, p. 8.

19. Solís R., "Costa Rica: La política exterior," p. 341. See also Facio, "Política exterior," pp. 171–180.

20. Booth, *The End and the Beginning*.

21. The terms proposed by the IMF team angered Carazo.

22. This analysis is drawn mainly from Sojo's excellent *Costa Rica: Política exterior*.

23. The San Juan River defines most of the border between Nicaragua and Costa Rica; the river is Nicaraguan territory, but by treaty Costa Rica has free navigation rights. Both interference in navigation and the border attack arose from the *contra* presence and activity on Costa Rican soil. Nicaraguan forces often pursued *contras* who crossed the river or who harassed them with fire from inside Costa Rican territory.

24. For extensive details on these matters, see Honey, *Hostile Acts*.

25. Solís R., "Costa Rica: La política exterior," p. 353.

26. Honey, *Hostile Acts* (pp. 303–338), spells out in detail aspects of this campaign. It included efforts to have U.S. military engineers upgrade roads in northern Costa Rica; increased U.S. military assistance, equipment, and training for the Civil Guard and rural police; and CIA-provoked *contra* attacks on Nicaragua from Costa Rica that brought a Nicaraguan military incursion inside the northern border.

27. Quote from Honey, *Hostile Acts*, p. 309; see also Sojo, *Costa Rica: Política exterior*, pp. 12–164.

28. Honey, *Hostile Acts*, p. 309.

29. Ibid., p. 310.

30. Solís R., "Costa Rica: La política exterior," pp. 353–355; Honey, *Hostile Acts*, ch. 14; Sojo, *Costa Rica: Política exterior*, ch. 4; and Dario Moreno, *The Struggle for Peace in Central America* (Gainesville: University Press of Florida, 1994), ch. 4. The draft of Arias's peace proposal is in Moreno's appendix 4.

31. John Tower, Edmund Muskie, and Brent Scowcroft, *The Tower Commission Report* (New York: New York Times Books, 1987).

32. Jim Wright, *Balance of Power: Presidents and Congress from the Era of McCarthy to the Age of Gingrich* (Atlanta: Turner Publishing, 1996), chs. 32–34; Solís R., "Costa Rica: La política exterior," p. 355.

33. Moreno, *The Struggle for Peace*, p. 87.

34. The administration clearly interpreted this document not as a serious peace proposal but as a mechanism with which to co-opt Speaker Wright and the Democrats in Congress and to block the more ambitious Arias proposal.

35. Moreno, *The Struggle for Peace*, p. 89.

36. Ibid., p. 91.

37. Ibid. Moreno presents the full text of the accord, actually entitled "Procedure for the Establishment of a Firm and Lasting Peace in Central America," as his appendix 5.

38. Quoted in ibid., p. 97.

10

ANALYSIS AND CONCLUSIONS: CAN DEMOCRACY SURVIVE?

The overview of Costa Rican politics and its historical, social, and economic foundations in the preceding chapters has covered considerable territory. The complex mixture of theories about democracy and data about Costa Rican politics, economics, social structure, and history almost overwhelms one with ideas and opportunity, much as the Mercado Central (Central Market) of San José envelopes the first-time visitor. In the market a jumble of products surrounds the visitor from floor to ceiling. Riotous color and voices and an incomparable array of odors from flowers to butchered meat, from soap to new leather to the delightfully pervasive odor of roasting coffee assail the senses. But to the repeated visitor the market begins to take form—its apparent chaos reveals clear and stable patterns of order in its activity, products, venues, and personalities. The first goal of this chapter is to review and summarize a bit in order to pull together Costa Rica's blurred portrait into a more coherent picture.

To begin, recall that in classical terms democracy involves the governance of a community by its members. Democracy's extent may be evaluated by how much and how well citizens participate in politics. Because governments can abuse citizens and restrict their participation and because citizens can abuse each other, democratic constitutions spell out limits on government and rights and protections for citizens. At the national level, representative democracy's specialization places practical limits on citizens' participation and influence. Nevertheless, in operational terms democracy minimally involves free and fair elections among competing candidates for leadership in which citizens may freely participate in politics.

Costa Rica clearly and by far exceeds the minimal operational conditions for democracy. It has a fair and competitive electoral system in which citizens enjoy extensive freedom to participate, criticize officials, organize to oppose incumbents, compete for ruling power, and influence policy. The constitution and an effective court system provide meaningful restraints upon governmental power.

These basic facts reflect well upon Costa Rica but contain no surprises. So why devote so much discussion to something so commonplace, to this seemingly ordinary national-level democracy? The answer is that Costa Rica became an ordinary democracy in a place, time, and cultural milieu when it was not ordinary at all. Costa Rican democracy intrigues us precisely because it developed when most theories about Latin America and about democratization would not have predicted it. This raises the questions of how democracy arose in Costa Rica, how it survives, and whether it offers a model or lessons for democratization for other developing countries.

Democratization

How did democracy arise in Costa Rica? Costa Rica's great national myth—that democracy grew upon the colonial foundation of a uniquely racially homogeneous, egalitarian, rural protodemocracy—has many flaws. Costa Rica clearly shared much of the origin, history, social culture, and political and economic traits of Central America. The colony had considerable socioeconomic inequality, including racial and cultural diversity. A wealthy social and economic aristocracy took control of national political life at independence; ordinary citizens had no political role. However, there were differences from its neighbors: Poor and isolated, Costa Rica developed more of a free yeomanry, a tradition of civilian rule, local self-government, and less-militarized politics.

During the second half of the nineteenth century, Costa Rica deviated even further from the images of the foundation myth. Wealthy coffee growers dominated national politics, usually competing via indirect, fraudulent, and elitist elections. After 1857 the democratic prospect dimmed further as Tomás Guardia and others used a growing military to disrupt the political hegemony of the *cafetaleros*. Costa Rica experienced militarization and authoritarian rule quite like those in the rest of the isthmus. However, increasing education, economic diversity, and immigration created new popular political forces near the century's end, some of them activated by the 1880s recession. After the 1889 Catholic Union and popular uprising, the *cafetaleros* gradually regained political ascendancy. They reduced the military's role and reconstructed a system of personalistic elite factions competing for power through electoral fraud and imposition.

Contrary to the foundation myth's contention of the virtual classlessness and egalitarianism of Costa Rica, world economic and political forces stimulated further class differentiation, mobilization, and conflict in the early twentieth century. Direct popular participation in elections after 1913 intensified rather than relieved pressures from below for real economic and political reform. Ruling elites attempted institutional reforms (especially in elections) to salvage their political and economic hegemony, but several rebellions betrayed the inconsistency of elite commitment to democratic norms.

In the 1940s Calderón Guardia enlisted the communists, their unions, and the Catholic Church in his attempt establish a new, more inclusive regime with himself at the helm. This provoked the countermobilization of anticommunist forces from the middle and upper classes and the 1948 civil war. The resolution of the class, ideological, and political forces at play during the civil war and its critical aftermath gave shape to the modern Costa Rican democratic regime. Although militarily victorious, the middle-class National Liberation forces of Figueres Ferrer could not control the constitutional revision in 1949. They had to compromise with their more conservative erstwhile allies from the upper class led by Ulate Blanco. By the early 1950s, this cooperation had laid the foundations of an inclusive elite settlement in which the emergent National Liberation Party and the conservative political elite agreed to compete for power through fair elections, mass (including union) participation in politics, and a social democratic development model.

In sum, Costa Rica established its democratic system in the 1940s and early 1950s through a protracted struggle among working- and middle-class political forces and an entrenched political and economic elite. The process was complex. First, a coalition of the communists and union movement with the Catholic Church and Calderón Guardia's breakaway upper-class faction implemented social and labor reforms. Then a coalition of middle-class and upper-class forces rebelled and defeated that coalition in 1948. Neither working- nor middle- nor upper-class forces subsequently had sufficient power to prevail alone after the civil war, so the resulting political system permitted the participation of all three forces under democratic rules.

What does the Costa Rican case reveal about contending political science theories about democratization? This democratic foundation best supports two complementary theories of democratization—the structuralist and elite settlement approaches. The structuralists contend that elites relinquish exclusive ruling power and democracies develop only when forced to do so by the growth in the power and resources of competing nonelites.[1] Chapter 3 relates how Costa Rica's system of *cafetalero* rule succumbed, after decades of fruitless tinkering with political rules, to just such overpowering structural forces (first to the Calderón-communist-labor coalition and then to the middle-class forces in the civil war).

Elite settlement theory contends that elites forge democracies through agreements, whether explicit or tacit, to play by democratic rules and tolerate mass participation.[2] Chapter 3 relates how an elite settlement emerged in Costa Rica during the years following the civil war.[3] The middle-class-based National Liberation movement and the upper-class forces behind Ulate each had some impact on the 1949 constitution. Together they dismantled the military, a stroke of brilliant constitutional engineering given the armed forces' checkered past in both Costa Rica and throughout Latin America. They retained the 1940s social security and labor reforms to placate the defeated but still potentially potent organized working class. The National Liberation forces let Ulate assume the presidency and reorganized themselves into the PLN to compete for power in 1953. Led by Figueres, the PLN then developed and consolidated the social democratic political economy model that prevailed until the 1980s. Both PLN and more conservative elites effectively embraced and honored democratic rules of the political game.

The process theories of democratization, which invoke causes such as regime breakdown, economic crisis, and demonstration effects, have at least some relevance to Costa Rica's case.[4] In the mid- and late 1940s, prodemocracy movements arose in several Central American countries (Guatemala, Honduras, Nicaragua, and El Salvador). Two of them succeeded, in Guatemala in 1944 and in Costa Rica in 1949. The Great Depression of the 1930s and its effects had undermined the legitimacy of *cafetalero* rule in Costa Rica. Cooperation with the Western allies in the war energized middle-class aspirations for democracy, whereas prewar and postwar economic difficulties mobilized working- and middle-class elements to seek reform. The *cafetalero* regime broke down definitively when Calderón Guardia defected from his upper-class allies to unite with the communists and labor.

Culturist theories of democratization appear less persuasive in accounting for Costa Rican democratization. Catholic, poor, and heir to the Iberian authoritarian tradition, Costa Rica should probably never have become democratic at all were culturist theories correct.

Costa Rica's own democratic foundation myth also has a cultural component—the argument that egalitarian social conditions and civilian rule bred democratic, civilist norms into Costa Rican elites and masses by the early nineteenth century. As noted in Chapter 3, the facts of Costa Rica's development and history do not support this argument. The country developed a large and politically intrusive military in the nineteenth century. Pronounced inequalities existed in the colonial era and grew in the nineteenth century. Class inequality intensified further in the twentieth century. It is indisputable that Costa Rican masses and elites have developed a political culture supportive of democracy (Chapter 7). However, whatever its origins, this democratic culture cannot have arisen either from socioeconomic equality or an absence of militarism—both of which were far more mythical than real.

In sum, Costa Rica's democratic development provides good empirical support for the structural theory of democratization, and there is evidence that an elite settlement contributed to democracy's eventual consolidation.[5] The contagion of democratic ideals in the isthmus during the 1940s and the clear breakdown of the Tico *cafetalero* ruling coalition in the early 1940s suggest that process theories may help outline some of the forces that shaped democratization. Cultural theories of democratization seem to explain little of what occurred.

Operation of Democracy

The Costa Rican constitution of 1949 sets up a government in the classical liberal mold: popular sovereignty, representative government, separation of powers, and checks and balances to divide and restrain authority. Ticos enjoy quintessential participatory rights: freedom of opinion, expression, and the press; freedom of association, assembly, and to petition and criticize the government. The constitution grants other fundamental social and economic rights, including prohibition of both discrimination against minorities and gender discrimination in the workplace.

These constitute fundamentally democratic rules for the national political game. Many nations, of course, have similarly lofty constitutional provisions yet fail to honor them, engaging in repression or plagued by corruption that effectively undermines the essential democratic liberties.

How well do constitutional restrictions on state power and citizen rights ensure Ticos' opportunity to participate? Very effectively. Costa Rica's human rights performance permits citizens freely to take part in politics. This is confirmed by outside observers' evaluations of political freedom in Costa Rica and by Ticos' own perceptions (as measured in surveys) of their freedom to participate. Further confirmation comes from the energetic role of the independent judiciary, to which citizens regularly have recourse in disputes with each other and with the government. Finally, the electoral system governed by the Supreme Electoral Tribunal provides regular, free, and honestly counted elections. Thus citizens may compete openly and without fear of repression in choosing their leaders and may count upon the TSE accurately to reflect and implement their wishes as expressed in elections.

Costa Ricans exercise periodic influence over the deputies who make their laws and have changed the party with the majority in the Legislative Assembly several times since 1949. The structure of the representation system—multimember electoral districts and proportional representation in the assembly—permits some role in government for smaller groups such as regional and ideological parties.

Despite the opportunity for party diversity in the formal rules of representation, the party system has become steadily less diverse. The PLN and its rival, the Social Christian Unity Party, dominate the presidency and have progressively squeezed smaller parties out of seats in the assembly. The PLN has recently shifted considerably rightward toward the ideological center, leaving voters with less choice among public policy proposals. The modernization of political campaigning through greater use of television advertising has lessened campaigning politicians' direct contact with voters. The burgeoning cost of elections driven by television and public opinion polling has made the parties increasingly reliant upon special interest funding and undermined much of the former leveling effect of public campaign financing. So at this level there has occurred some loss in the depth and breadth of democracy. Indeed, this loss has aroused popular criticism and stimulated political action. Many citizens (a seventh of the usual electorate) in 1998 heeded critics' calls to abstain in protest of such problems. Such efforts by Ticos to protest democratic decay may become keys to the consolidation and future quality of Costa Rican democracy.

Given this reduction of direct popular involvement in elections and in ideological diversity in the policy arena, one must ask, How responsive is the Costa Rican government to citizen participation? The government seems to listen to and consider citizen demands when making public policy. Legislators clearly respond to citizen pressure for policy change and for pork barrel benefits to communities. Yet the rule against self-succession in office combines with the weakness of assembly staffing to prevent the people's branch of government from acquiring much policy expertise of its own. This leaves the assembly vulnerable to the technical advantages of the executive branch in policymaking. The Legislative Assembly in recent decades has ceded considerable policy influence, especially over the economy, to the presidency and has apparently consoled itself by distributing small community improvement grants.

In striking contrast, the Costa Rican executive branch has gained power in recent decades. Foreign policy and economic crises have contributed to an ever more activist presidency that increasingly governs the nation by decree and regulation. Reforms of autonomous bureaucracies have strengthened the presidency within the executive branch. External actors—foreign governments and international lending agencies—have imposed far-reaching changes upon Costa Rica that have strengthened the relative power of the executive branch but narrowed the executive's economic policy options. In sum, while Costa Rican citizens are largely free to participate and have a potentially powerful and responsive legislature, the range of public decisions dominated by the Legislative Assembly—and therefore the range of democracy shaped by the citizenry's representatives—has dwindled of late.

How do economic and social divisions within Costa Rican society affect citizens and their relations with the state? From the 1950s through the early 1980s, a politically powerful middle-class movement led by the PLN used the state to redistribute income, wealth, and public services toward the middle sectors under a social democratic development model. These policies gave many Ticos from working-class backgrounds the education and social mobility that permitted them to improve their standards of living. Income inequality diminished and the quality of life improved for many, undoubtedly undergirding popular support for the democratic political system.

But powerful and ideologically conservative interest groups, aided by a national economic crisis and international actors (Chapters 8 and 9) succeeded by the early 1990s in revamping the national economic development model. A reduced government cut back on investment, education, and health and social service spending in ways that decreased the quality of life of many Ticos. In the short run, poverty increased, education quality eroded for those reliant upon public schools, public-sector employment fell, and government wages declined. Over the longer run, these factors, combined with the opening of the economy to international competition and early trends indicating the upward redistribution of income, strongly suggest that the poorer and working classes stand to lose much of the ground they once gained under social democracy. Narrowly defined special interests have already gained in freedom and political influence and will likely continue to do so. This raises two questions: Will the diminished range of democracy (and the increased freedom of capital) produce sufficient economic growth and well-being to offset these negative effects? Will the benefits from anticipated economic growth be sufficient to prevent an erosion of Ticos' long-standing and widespread support for democracy?

Political Participation and Culture

Political participation and political culture shape democracy in at least three important ways: Participation places demands upon government and determines who among competing candidates will rule. Political culture provides legitimacy to the system and to some extent defines and limits how government should function. If harmonious, both citizen participation and political culture can contribute to the consolidation of a democratic system.

Costa Ricans actively engage in political participation of many kinds, and their activities appear enduring and similar to those in other representative democracies. The government itself encourages political participation, both conventional (voting, campaigning, and contacting officials) and unconventional (protest and confrontational activity). In these regards democracy in Costa Rica seems both reasonably broad and reasonably deep. Many citizens become involved in politics. Government regularly responds positively to initiatives, whether channeled or confrontational.

Some Ticos participate in politics more than others, inequalities that arise partly from corresponding disparities in income and education. To the extent that education and income inequities grow in the future, as present trends suggest they will, participation inequalities among Costa Ricans seem destined to grow as well in ways that may affect the political system. The poor and less-educated will participate less in conventional activism as their resources dwindle, winning fewer regularly supplied public goods from the state. Under such circumstances, however, the poor and less-educated may also become more prone to protest and confrontation. Indeed, some Ticos did just that during the 1980s and 1990s in defense of their economic interests when the tectonic shift in development models left them worse off.

To what extent does this prospect that some Ticos might become more confrontational in their participation threaten political stability? Evidence on Costa Rican political culture points to some possible effects. Surveys reveal that the typical urban Costa Rican is a political conservative and an anticommunist, embraces fundamentalist religious ideas, and generally distrusts other people but is nevertheless still fairly satisfied with his or her situation in life despite recent economic turmoil. Most Costa Ricans strongly endorse democratic principles and democratic political methods. Substantial majorities of urban Costa Ricans perceive themselves as completely free to participate in the political arena and as treated acceptably or well by government. They view their participation as either somewhat or very efficacious. Such perceptions probably explain why Ticos express high levels of pride in their political system. Despite this generally positive image, over half of those responding expressed reservations about institutional respect for life (especially by the police).

The preference for democracy among Ticos, though strong, is not universal. A detectable undercurrent of authoritarian values exists even here in Latin America's oldest and strongest democracy. However, the search for authoritarian and antidemocratic strains in Costa Rica's political culture (Chapter 7) noted several patterns that should encourage supporters of democracy: First, the polity enjoys a generally high degree of legitimacy among the urban population; only a small number of extreme leftists and some communal activists seem disenchanted with the system. Second, support for fundamental civil liberties and disapproval of disruptive and antidemocratic tactics hold strong across all urban social and economic groups and sectors. Third, analysis of three groups—ideological extremists, communal activists, and youth—that might be reservoirs of antidemocratic sentiments shows almost no consistent, mutually reinforcing repudiation of democracy among them. On the contrary, their commitment to democratic liberties remains statistically indistinguishable from that of other key groups or the general population. Leftists, communal activists, and younger citizens reveal only modestly higher tendency to embrace either civil disobedience or authoritarian means.

Confrontational political methods have become part of the political ethos of some groups, but serious threats to democracy in Costa Rica have not yet arisen from the sectors studied here and even less from among the wider urban mass public. Whether the growth of such inequality and erosion of mass living standards over the longer term will lead some Ticos to withdraw support from the regime or to intensify and spread antidemocratic attitudes remains to be seen.

The political system not only tolerates but encourages some mass support and use of confrontational political tactics. This confrontational ethos and the state's responsiveness to it do not, in my opinion, destabilize the system. Rather, the two operate together to provide a safety valve for frustrated groups (whose members generally appear strongly committed to democratic principles) by providing a way to have the state meet some of their needs.

The political culture of elites also reflects commitment to democratic liberties and democratic political methods. As shown in Chapter 7, elites seem little more inclined toward change than does the urban mass public. Overall, Costa Rica's elite and mass political cultures share in a great democratic consensus: They both embrace democratic principles and methods.

This national consensus on the rules of the political game constitutes a critical element of democratic consolidation and stability in Costa Rica. In the absence of dissensus about democracy, one must ask whether there exist other forces capable of straining or undermining Costa Rica's democratic consensus. External economic and political problems are important possible sources of such stress.

External Strains and Democracy

The economic crises of the 1970s and 1980s, driven largely by the interaction of uncontrollable external factors such as energy costs and regional economic decline, led to understandable but ultimately very harmful governmental decisions to maintain consumption and living standards. The government's efforts to borrow its way through the difficulty contributed to massive external debt, which then compounded the other strains and led to deep economic decay. The solution to these economic difficulties brought about a remarkable revolution in Costa Rica's political economy—the abandonment of the social democratic development model for a neoliberal one.

As already noted, this transformation has begun to improve the health of the Costa Rican government in accounting terms and may ultimately produce a more flexible and energetic national economy. However, the short-run impact of the neoliberal revolution and economic crunch included a generalized deterioration of the economy. The longer-run impact of neoliberalism upon social equity—income, wealth, and public service distribution—appears likely to be increased inequality and eroded living standards for the working and middle classes. This will undermine some of those very traits—high literacy, longevity, and widespread well-being—that make Costa Rica so distinctive in Central America.

Undeniably decisive in Costa Rica's adoption of neoliberalism was foreign pressure. The debt crisis and default of 1981 threw the nation's economic management upon the tender mercies of international lenders, who promoted the neoliberal economic model as a panacea for developing economies. As a condition for the loans needed to rescue the Ticos from their economic catastrophe, the international bankers and major economic powers pushed Costa Rica into structural adjustment and the neoliberal development model. Gradually, grudgingly, and with much pain, the state of necessity trimmed its own size and scope, reduced regulation and management of domestic economic management, curtailed social spending and investment, made itself more open to trade and foreign capital, and promoted new exports.

The economic and social effects of these pressures and reforms are fairly clear, but what are their implications for Costa Rican democracy? There appear to be two main ones: First, the neoliberal reforms reduced the range of citizen and legislative influence over economic matters and relinquished state economic power to the domestic and international private sectors. It was mainly external actors, not Ticos, who imposed the neoliberal development model. Costa Ricans and their elected representatives had little choice but to accept these policies or sink further into their economic quagmire. National officials shaped certain details but not the general outlines of the new model, which the international lenders had already determined. Costa Rican citizens participated only on the margins of the new policies, relegated mainly to protesting their effects upon living standards and public services. This clearly curtailed the range of democracy by reducing the array of policies over which citizens held direct or indirect influence.

Second, the loss of national autonomy represented by the external imposition of the new development model and the shift of power away from the people's representatives in the Legislative Assembly to the executive branch each diminished the depth of Costa Rican democracy. Major decisions about the future direction of national economic policy were made in ways that largely denied the Costa Rican public and its constitutionally elected officials meaningful influence.

Foreign affairs raised a second, major set of stresses for Costa Rican democracy during the 1980s (Chapter 9). The revolutionary movements in Central America and the U.S. response to them brought enormous pressures upon unarmed Costa Rica. Foreign radicals of the far left and far right used Costa Rica as a platform from which to wage their own national conflicts. The United States promoted many of these activities by its anticommunist allies, even many that were illegal in Costa Rica, and heavily pressured Costa Rica to accept them, rearm itself, and align openly against Nicaragua. Domestic actors in Costa Rica became deeply embroiled in this messy geopolitical struggle, mobilizing supporters, taking up arms, intimidating their opponents, and committing acts of terrorism. Some explicitly threatened to overthrow the government.

Constrained by Costa Rica's military weakness, diminutive size, and dependency upon foreign help with its ballooning economic troubles, the nation's leaders experienced years of deep frustration while they struggled to find a favorable policy direction. For a time, even democracy itself appeared menaced by the violence and disloyal rumblings of certain ideological and economic groups emboldened by the geopolitical ruckus and the support of foreign actors. But then President Arias skillfully developed a political strategy that coalesced domestic anticommunists, neutralists, pacifists, and the general public behind his peace initiative for Central America. When the Iran-*contra* scandal in the United States sapped American initiative in 1987, Arias seized the moment and with other regional presidents forged the Central American peace accord. The region eventually cooled down, and Costa Rica's internal turmoil abated with it.

One may reasonably surmise that the peace accord not only helped end wars and promoted democratization elsewhere in Central America but may have saved Costa Rica's own democracy as well. It is risky to speculate about such things, but an indefinite prolongation of violent geopolitical conflict in the isthmus, especially in Nicaragua, might eventually have undermined Costa Rica's democratic regime. Had the geopolitical imperative not shifted, democratic breakdown in Costa Rica could have happened in various ways: Increasingly disgruntled elites might have staged a coup. Popular unrest and mobilization driven both by economic trouble and ideological demagogues might have spawned violent civil disorder. The reestablishment of a politicized Costa Rican military could have facilitated a coup or violent conflict. Most likely would have been some combination of all three of these scenarios. Fortunately, events, personalities, and political skills and vision provided a way to avoid such a catastrophe.[6] To those who might argue that the United States would not have permitted Costa Rica's democracy to collapse, I suggest that the U.S. record in this regard has not been good, especially when geopolitical stakes were high.[7]

In sum, external stress put enormous pressure on Costa Rican democracy in the 1980s and 1990s. The nation weathered those of geopolitical origin with a combination of good fortune and skilled political leadership. The adoption of neoliberal economic reforms under external duress did not in the short run threaten the democratic regime per se. It did, however, erode both the range and the depth of Costa Rican democracy. The sharp abstention increase in the 1998 election demonstrated that the domestic political effects of neoliberal reforms had not yet run their course. Whether over the long term the effects of the development model change will strengthen Costa Rica's democratic consensus or undermine it remains to be seen.

Evaluation and Prospects

Contending class and political forces in Costa Rica in the 1950s established the contemporary democratic polity. It has operated with extensive and open participation by citizens and with a system of fair elections and a restrained, policy-responsive government. For decades, Costa Rica has enjoyed a quite successful national-level democracy—broad in citizen involvement, with a fairly wide range of policies subject to citizen input, and relatively deep in actual or potential citizen impact.

Certain changes in recent decades have nibbled away at some of the dimensions of Costa Rican democracy. Among the more important are four:

1. The legislature's loss of policymaking influence to the executive;
2. The diminishing ideological and organizational diversity of the party system;
3. The decline of citizen involvement in campaigning and the growing power of monied special interests in election campaign finance; and
4. The government's externally imposed relinquishment of authority over the economy.

In combination, these changes have somewhat reduced the breadth and even more reduced the range and depth of democracy. They have not, however, undermined the democratic regime, which remains remarkably resilient and stable despite these changes and the intense geopolitical and economic strains to which it has been subjected.

Costa Rica's overall prospects for continued institutional democracy appear fairly good. It meets many items in Chapter 1's checklist of conditions contributing to democratic consolidation:[8] Costa Rica has a presidential system dominated by two competitive, centrist parties. Its electoral agency is highly competent and honest, and the security forces pose little threat to civilian rule. The state is capable, legitimate, and able to govern with little repression. Despite some internal racial and religious differences, Costa Rica is relatively homogeneous culturally and ethnically; many of its social cleavages are cross-cutting. Most elites and most of the populace share a consensual set of democratic rules. The nation is surrounded by other civilian democracies, and major international actors affecting Costa Rica appear strongly to prefer democracy in the region.

Yet certain consolidation factors do pose risks for Costa Rica: There are significant and persistent economic inequalities that have worsened with the recent economic crises and that may intensify in the future. The government retains some ability to ameliorate the effects of poverty, but neoliberalism has stripped it of many of the policy instruments most helpful in such efforts. Economic growth, strong in the 1950s through the early 1970s, has become erratic and unpredictable ever since. Prospects for sustained economic recovery under neoliberalism remain uncertain.

What threats, then, does Costa Rica's democratic polity most likely face in the future? One set of problems stands out. The adoption of the neoliberal development model may invigorate the economy, but it will also make it more volatile and potentially riskier for ordinary citizens. The government will do less for Ticos in the future than it did from the 1950s through the 1980s. Withdrawn as it has from the economic arena, the government will also have fewer policy tools with which to address future economic and social problems. This raises the question of whether the democratic regime can retain the loyalty of its citizens.

During recent hard times, masses and elites have punished incumbent leaders for poor economic performance but remained loyal to democracy in general. Should hard times for the great majority persist and should living standards and opportunities for social mobility further deteriorate, citizens may become frustrated and alienated by weak government response. Or they may not. Democratic norms and external constraints favoring democracy may have become sufficiently entrenched that Costa Rica will remain democratic no matter what economic hardships may arise.

Costa Rican democracy has taken some hard knocks in recent decades and emerged in good condition. The great question for the future of Costa Rican democracy is whether citizens will remain loyal to the idea and practice of a democratic regime should the neoliberal political economy prove unsuccessful.

Lessons

The immense complexity of even small societies and their politics guarantees that no other nation will precisely follow Costa Rica's particular path of democratization and consolidation. Yet from this case one may glean some lessons applicable to other nations in Central America, Latin America, and even other regions.

The first lesson concerns the structural forces that lead to democracy. Democratization in Costa Rica did not occur because of the nation's largely mythical equality, homogeneity, and civil traditions. It occurred because structural changes in society undermined the *cafetalero* regime and created new power contenders. Long-term economic change and short-term economic strains created and mobilized working-class and middle-class political forces that eventually gained enough power to win inclusion in the political arena. Other Central American and Latin American nations have experienced or are undergoing similar structural transformations that have now given them (or will do so) similarly potent political forces. Costa Rica attained this important threshold of democratization at an earlier date than other Central American nations, but much about the evolution of neighboring countries suggests that they may have reached a similar stage in the evolution of class forces.[9]

A second lesson involves the conditions favoring the adoption of democratic rules and the prospects for stable elite settlements on democracy. Costa Rica's insurgent political elites of the 1940s pressed for and eventually settled upon democratic rules of the game in the era during and after World War II when inclusion of the labor and political left and liberal democratic political arrangements were in vogue in the West.[10] Contending players in the constitution-drafting effort of 1949 were undoubtedly aided in designing inclusionary rules by Costa Rica's traditions of co-optation of rural labor and electoralism.

Although other Central American and Latin American countries lack Costa Rica's electoral and labor co-optation traditions, by the 1990s liberal democracy was once again in fashion in the world. The end of the cold war had somewhat reduced the geopolitically driven fear of labor and the left that led to determined repression of such forces from the 1950s through the 1990s. External actors such as the United States, the European Union, the United Nations, and the Organization of American States now advocate national-level democracy and human rights. Evidence suggests that Central American citizens prefer democracy. There are, therefore, many forces that can constrain elites to adopt and maintain democratic rules of the game. This, I believe, markedly increases the possibility of successful democratic elite settlements in Central America.

The last and most difficult lesson concerns one of the grand bogeymen of Latin American democracy: the military. The abolition of a standing army enormously aided in Costa Rica's democratic consolidation. It removed from the political scene a force that had several times upset civilian, constitutional rule. At present the only other country in Central America that has effectively lost its military is Panama.[11] No informed observer would deny the enormous capacity of the region's armed forces, driven by their traditions and institutional cultures, to wreak havoc in Central America's fledgling democracies.

Several encouraging signs exist, however. Military interventions of the 1970s and 1980s had many negative effects on the armed forces themselves, apparently causing the region's soldiers to pull in their horns. Moreover, the recent settlements of Central America's violent civil conflicts have led to significant reductions in the size, budgets, and autonomy of the armed forces of Nicaragua, El Salvador, and Guatemala. Thus militaries—though still present—may be relatively weaker during this critical formative stage of Central America's young democracies. This may reduce the threat of military intervention and give civilian regimes time to consolidate themselves.

Costa Rica's democratization may not offer a blueprint for other countries, but it suggests certain critical variables to consider in other cases. Although enormous caution is greatly in order in such speculation, these lessons concerning structural forces favoring democratization, factors shaping elite settlements, and the military's evolving role give cause for some optimism. Other isthmian and Latin American nations, each having eventually followed Costa Rica into the formally democratic camp by its own path, may remain in the Ticos' good company.

Notes

1. See Georg Sorensen, *Democracy and Democratization* (Boulder: Westview Press, 1993), ch. 2; Tatu Vanhanen, *The Process of Democratization* (New York: Crane and Russak, 1990); Dietrich Rueschemeyer, Evelyne Huber Stephens, and John D. Stephens, *Capitalist Development and Democracy* (Chicago: University of Chicago Press, 1992); Robert D. Putnam, *Making Democracy Work: Civic Traditions in Modern Italy* (Princeton: Princeton University Press, 1993); Robert D. Putnam, "Bowling Alone: America's Declining Social Capital," *Journal of Democracy* 6, 1 (January 1995): 65–78; and Deborah J. Yashar, *Demanding Democracy: Reform and Reaction in Costa Rica and Guatemala, 1870s–1950s* (Stanford: Stanford University Press, 1997).

2. The best exposition of this argument, applied specifically to the Costa Rican case, is that of John Peeler, in his *Latin American Democracies: Colombia, Costa Rica, Venezuela* (Chapel Hill: University of North Carolina Press, 1985). Also see Michael Burton, Richard Gunther, and John Higley, "Elite Transformations and Democratic Regimes," in John Higley and Richard Gunther, eds., *Elites and Democratic Consolidation in Latin America and Southern Europe* (Cambridge: Cambridge University Press, 1992); and Terry Lynn Karl, "Dilemmas of Democratization in Latin America," *Comparative Politics* 23, 1 (1990): 1–21.

3. Peeler provides the definitive study of this process in *Latin American Democracies*.

4. See Samuel Huntington, *The Third Wave: Democratization in the Late Twentieth Century* (Norman: University of Oklahoma Press, 1990), ch. 2; Guillermo O'Donnell, Philippe C. Schmitter, and Laurence Whitehead, eds., *Transitions from Authoritarian Rule: Prospects for Democracy* (Baltimore: Johns Hopkins University Press, 1986); and Sorensen, *Democracy and Democratization*, ch. 2.

5. Yashar's *Demanding Democracy* combines the structural explanation with attention to the role of elites.

6. Not least among the events was the decline of the cold war, which eventually lessened the U.S. perception of threat from Central America's leftist insurgencies.

7. U.S. involvement in numerous coups d'état in Latin America is well documented, especially in the Caribbean Basin. In Guatemala in 1954 and Chile in 1973, the United States encouraged and abetted the overthrow of constitutional, democratic regimes.

8. This list is drawn mainly from Larry Diamond and Juan Linz, "Introduction," in Larry Diamond, Juan Linz, and Seymour Martin Lipset, *Democracy in Developing*

Countries, vol. 4: *Latin America* (Boulder: Lynne Rienner Publishers–Adamantine Press, 1989); Huntington, *The Third Wave;* and Peeler, *Latin American Democracies.*

9. Mitchell A. Seligson, "Development, Democratization, and Decay: Central America at the Crossroads," in James M. Malloy and Mitchell A. Seligson, eds., *Authoritarians and Democrats: Regime Transition in Latin America* (Pittsburgh: University of Pittsburgh Press, 1987), pp. 167–192; John A. Booth and Thomas W. Walker, *Understanding Central America* (Boulder: Westview Press, 1993), chs. 6–8; and Rueschemeyer et al., *Capitalist Development and Democracy.*

10. This era was rapidly ending in the late 1940s with the rise of the cold war, which led many Latin American nations to repress communist parties and the labor left.

11. The United States dismantled the Panamanian Defense Forces following the 1989 U.S. invasion. The army had not been reconstructed by 1997.

Appendix

TABLE A.1   Selected Economic Data for Central America, by Country, 1950–1994

	Costa Rica	El Salvador	Guatemala	Honduras	Nicaragua	Region[a]
Gross Domestic Product (GDP)[b]						
1960	1,646	1,985	4,045	1,112	1,461	10,249
1970	2,932	3,437	6,911	1,905	2,849	18,034
1980	5,975	4,723	11,987	3,243	2,950	29,978
1990	6,313	6,334	12,923	3,985	2,587	32,143
1994	7,647	8,029	15,175	4,550	2,702	38,166
GDP per capita[c]						
1960	1,332	772	1,020	575	879	891
1970	1,694	958	1,373	725	1,388	1,207
1980	2,222	1,044	1,732	886	1,065	1,393
1990	2,094	1,210	1,404	775	663	1,209
1994	2,283	1,423	1,470	827	631	1,312
Percent change in GDP per capita						
1960–1970	27	24	31	26	58	35
1970–1980	31	9	26	22	−23	15
1980–1990	6	16	−18	−13	−38	−13
1990–1994	9	18	5	7	−5	9
Percent[d] employed in agriculture						
1960	51	62	67	70	62	63
1980	29	50	55	63	39	47
c. 1992	27	40	60	62	44	50
Percent[d] employed in manufacturing						
c. 1950	11	11	12	6	11	10
1983	16	14	15	13	15	15
Percent GDP from manufacturing						
1960	14	15	13	12	16	14
1980	22	18	17	16	25	18
1994	20	22	14	14	16	16
External debt[e]						
1980	2,737	915	1,166	1,486	1,172	7,746[f]
1990	3,772	2,132	2,778	3,480	10,676	22,838[f]
1994	3,831	2,245	3,112	4,172	10,704	24,064[f]

(*continues*)

211

TABLE A.1 (*continued*)

	Costa Rica	El Salvador	Guatemala	Honduras	Nicaragua	Region[a]
Debt as a percent of GDP						
1970	11.5	5.2	3.6	9.5	10.9	8.2[g]
1982	110.3	42.0	17.6	69.4	121.5	72.2[g]
1991	73.0	36.7	29.8	118.9	649.1	181.5[g]
1994	55.9	33.4	33.6	128.1	432.5	136.7[g]
Debt service ratio						
1990	15.4	13.0	11.2	18.0	58.3	23.8[g]
1994	6.6	8.2	4.1	18.1	105.5	25.1[g]

[a]Weighted averages unless otherwise specified.

[b]In millions of 1986 U.S. dollars; regional value is sum for all nations.

[c]In 1986 U.S. dollars.

[d]Of economically active population.

[e]Disbursed total external debt, in millions of U.S. dollars.

[f]Regional total for all five nations in nominal U.S. dollars.

[g]Unweighted mean.

sour ces: Based on John A. Booth and Thomas W. Walker, *Understanding Central America* (Boulder: Westview Press, 1989), appendix table 2; Inter-American Development Bank (IADB), *Economic and Social Progress in Latin America: 1988 Report* (Washington, D.C.: IADB, 1988); table E-1 and country tables; IADB, *Economic and Social Progress in Latin America: 1983 Report* (Washington, D.C.: IADB, 1983), tables 3 and 58; IADB, *Economic and Social Progress in Latin America: 1992 Report* (Baltimore: Johns Hopkins University Press, 1992), tables B-2, E-11, and country tables; IADB, *Economic and Social Progress in Latin America: 1994 Report* (Baltimore: Johns Hopkins University Press, 1994); IADB, *Economic and Social Progress in Latin America: Overcoming Volatility, 1995 Report* (Baltimore: Johns Hopkins University Press, 1995), tables B-1, B-2, and country tables; Central Intelligence Agency, *The World Factbook, 1993* (Washington, D.C.: CIA, 1993), country reports.

TABLE A.2   Selected Social Data for Central America, by Country, 1950–1995

	Costa Rica	El Salvador	Guatemala	Honduras	Nicaragua	Region[a]
Population[a]						
1960	1,236	2,570	3,964	1,935	1,493	11,198
1980	2,284	4,525	6,917	3,662	2,771	20,159
1995 (est.)	3,395	5,911	10,614	5,986	4,555	30,461
Population density (persons/km²)						
1993	64.2	263.5	92.1	47.6	34.8	70.5
Mean annual population growth						
1961–1970	3.4	3.4	2.8	3.1	3.2	3.3
1971–1980	2.8	2.3	2.8	3.4	3.0	3.0
1981–1990	2.8	1.6	2.9	3.4	3.4	2.8
1991–1995	2.4	2.4	2.9	3.1	3.3	2.8
Percent indigenous population						
1978	1	2	60	2	2	14
Percent urban population						
1960	33.2	36.4	34.0	22.5	41.7	33.6
1993	48.0	46.8	40.6	46.1	65.8	48.3
Percent literate						
1960	86	42	40	30	32	42
c. 1990	93	73	55	73	87	70
University enrollment[a]						
1950	1.5	–	2.1	0.7	.05	4.8[b]
1980	51.0	27.1	37.8	20.4	19.8	156.1[b]
Primary school enrollment ratio						
1990	93	78	79	108	98	89
Life expectancy at birth						
1980–1985	73	57	59	60	60	60
1993	76	66	65	65	67	67
Infant mortality/1,000 live births						
c. 1993	14	40	62	49	56	55
Religious identification c. 1985 (percent)						
Catholic	97	93	79	94	88	90
Protestant	3	4	6	3	8	5
Average income for population strata (c. 1980)[c]						
Poorest 20%	$176.7	46.5	111.0	80.7	61.9	95.3[d]
Next 30%	500.8	155.1	202.7	140.0	178.2	235.4[d]

[a]Thousands.

[b]Total for region.

[c]In constant 1970 U.S. dollars.

[d]Unweighted averages.

sources: John A. Booth and Thomas W. Walker, *Understanding Central America* (Boulder: Westview Press, 1989), appendix table 2; Inter-American Development Bank (IADB), *Economic and Social Progress in Latin America: 1988 Report* (Washington, D.C.: IADB, 1988), pp. 384, 408, 416, 440, 464; IADB, *Economic and Social Progress in Latin America: 1992 Report* (Baltimore: Johns Hopkins University Press, 1992), country tables; IADB, *Economic and Social Progress in Latin America: 1994 Report* (Baltimore: Johns Hopkins University Press, 1994), country tables; Maria Eugenia Gallardo and José Roberto López, *Centroamerica: La crisis en cifras* (San José, Costa Rica: Instituto Interamericano de Cooperación para la Agricultura [IICA]–Facultad Latinoamericana de Ciencias Sociales [FLACSO], 1986), tables 2, 4, 7, 8, and 10; Tom Barry and Deb Preusch, *The Central America Fact Book* (New York: Grove Press, 1986), p. 129; Central Intelligence Agency, *The World Fact Book, 1993* (Washington, D.C.: CIA, 1993), country reports.

TABLE A.3 Real Working-Class Wage Indices, Central American Countries, 1963–1994 (1973 = 100)

	Costa Rica	El Salvador[a]	Guatemala[b]	Honduras[c]	Nicaragua[d]
1963	80	90	–	–	92
1965	–	92	109	–	125
1967	94	93	115	–	137
1970	96	92	109	–	121
1971	107	93	109	–	119
1972	103	94	107	96	114
1973	100	100	100	100	100
1974	108	98	96	94	100
1975	91	90	95	91	106
1976	103	95	97	102	106
1977	113	85	81	95	97
1978	123	87	84	101	88
1979	128	84	84	103	77
1980	129	82	84	97	64
1981	114	76	86	93	64
1982	92	68	92	101	56
1983	102	60	85	92	49
1984	110	57	84	89	46
1985	120	49	72	86	35
1986	126	45	59	83	14
1987	125	49	63	81	15
1988	124	44	66	77	1[e]
1989	131	42	70	70	1[e]
1990	130	40	57	86	2[e]
1991	122	37	53	86	2[e]
1992	123	37	62	72	2[e]
1993	134	35	69	49	2[e]
1994	137	35	74	44	2[e]

[a]Excludes construction (after 1974); for 1980s data are for private sector only.

[b]Unweighted average of all sectors.

[c]Unweighted average wages in manufacturing, construction, and agriculture (agricultural wages not included in 1972 and 1973 figures).

[d]Includes wages in manufacturing, transportation (only), and construction.

[e]Hyperinflation and collapse of Nicaraguan exchange rate in the late 1980s render the wage index functionally meaningless. Many Nicaraguans relied upon nonwage resources (food distribution at workplaces) and informal-sector activities to cope with the collapse of effective real wages.

source: John A. Booth and Thomas W. Walker, *Understanding Central America* (Boulder: Westview Press, 1989), appendix table 4. See original source for notes on data. Data since 1985 drawn from Inter-American Development Bank (IADB), *Economic and Social Progress in Latin America: 1994 Report* (Baltimore: Johns Hopkins University Press, 1994), country tables; and IADB, *Economic and Social Progress in Latin America: Overcoming Volatility, 1995 Report* (Baltimore: Johns Hopkins University Press, 1995), country tables.

TABLE A.4   Mean Annual U.S. Military Assistance to Central America, 1946–1992 (in millions of dollars)

	Costa Rica	El Salvador	Guatemala	Honduras	Nicaragua	Region[a]
1946–1952	–	–	–	–	–	–
1953–1961	.01	.03	.19	.14	.24	.62
1962–1972	.16	.72	3.31	.90	2.36	7.45
1973–1976	.03	2.08	.83	2.23	.28	5.45
1977–1980	1.25	1.60	1.25	3.13	.85	6.98
1981–1984	3.95	98.85	.00	41.48	.00	144.28
1985–1988	3.93	112.78	5.20	57.73	.00	179.64
1989–1992	.10	63.10	2.35[b]	25.60	.00	91.15
Overall mean, 1946–1992	.83	23.86	1.63	12.38	.69	38.24

[a]Includes only Costa Rica, El Salvador, Guatemala, Honduras, and Nicaragua.

[b]The Bush administration cancelled Guatemala's 1990 military assistance of $3.3 million for human rights reasons. That left the aid delivered at less than originally appropriated for the period.

sour ces: Based on G. Pope Atkins, *Latin America in the International Political System* (New York: Free Press, 1977), tables D and E; G. Pope Atkins, *Latin America in the International Political System* (Boulder: Westview Press, 1989), tables 10.2 and 10.4; and Office of Planning and Budgeting–U.S. Agency for International Development, *U.S. Overseas Loans and Grants and Assistance from International Organizations: Obligations and Loan Authorizations, July 1, 1945–September 30, 1992* (Washington, D.C.: Congressional Information Service, 1993).

TABLE A.5   Mean Annual U.S. Economic Assistance to Central America, 1946–1992 (in millions of dollars)

	Costa Rica	El Salvador	Guatemala	Honduras	Nicaragua	Region[a]
1946–1952	1.00	.40	1.65	.42	1.03	4.50
1953–1961	5.80	1.23	13.48	3.90	3.73	28.14
1962–1972	9.41	11.95	14.52	8.42	12.95	56.07
1973–1976	14.10	6.10	19.60	24.43	26.90	91.13
1977–1980	13.65	21.85	17.28	27.88	18.63	99.56
1981–1984	112.75	189.43	21.13	79.53	16.55	419.39
1985–1988	171.13	383.38	135.90	179.33	.10	869.84
1989–1992	75.83	287.68	116.73	150.18	206.80	837.22
Overall mean, 1946–1992	36.48	78.72	32.73	42.06	26.83	216.83

[a]Includes only Costa Rica, El Salvador, Guatemala, Honduras, and Nicaragua.

sour ces: Based on G. Pope Atkins, *Latin America in the International Political System* (New York: Free Press, 1977), tables D and E; G. Pope Atkins, *Latin America in the International Political System* (Boulder: Westview Press, 1989), tables 10.2 and 10.4; and Office of Planning and Budgeting–U.S. Agency for International Development, *U.S. Overseas Loans and Grants and Assistance from International Organizations: Obligations and Loan Authorizations, July 1, 1945–September 30, 1992* (Washington, D.C.: Congressional Information Service, 1993).

TABLE A.6   Growth of the Costa Rican Public Sector, 1920–1995 (value added to GDP by government, in thousands of dollars)

	Total GDP[a]	Value Added by Government[a]	Percent of GDP Added by Government
1920	119,208	3,475	2.9
1930	142,154	6,757	4.8
1940	191,138	9,706	5.1
1950	297,600	17,622	5.9
1960	592,700	63,635	10.7
1970	1,139,400	136,189	12.0
1980	1,981,247	222,096	11.2
1990[b]	2,417,123	242,085	10.0
1995[b]	3,032,430	261,450	8.7

[a]Values through 1980 are constant 1970 dollars calculated at purchasing power parity exchange rates, drawn directly from Bulmer-Thomas.

[b]Values for 1990 and 1995 are extrapolated from Bulmer-Thomas's 1980 base, based upon growth rates drawn from growth rates reported by the IADB.

sour ces: Victor Bulmer-Thomas, *The Political Economy of Central America Since 1920* (Cambridge: Cambridge University Press, 1987), tables A1 and A9; Inter-American Development Bank (IADB), *Latin America After a Decade of Reforms: Economic and Social Progress in Latin America, 1997 Report* (Baltimore: Johns Hopkins University Press, 1997), tables B-1 and B-18.

TABLE A.7   Attitudes and Participation, Urban Costa Rica, 1995

Variable	Voting	Campaign	Contact	Communal	Group	Overall Participation
Interpersonal trust						
Low	1.68	1.24	.28	1.64	1.06	5.90
Medium	1.76	1.26	.46	2.02	1.13	6.57
High	1.77	1.00	.45	1.80	1.75	6.74
Significance[a]	NS	NS	**	*	**	NS
Life satisfaction						
Low	1.80	1.04	.41	1.37	1.06	5.66
Medium low	1.71	1.33	.42	1.83	1.01	6.31
Medium high	1.74	1.26	.36	1.75	1.26	6.33
High	1.72	1.07	.38	1.98	1.30	6.39
Significance[a]	NS	NS	NS	NS	NS	NS
Diffuse support						
Low	1.59	.97	.39	2.12	1.21	6.27
Medium low	1.73	1.27	.37	1.60	1.36	6.32
Medium high	1.74	1.31	.45	1.85	.90	6.20
High	1.82	1.01	.27	1.77	1.52	6.37
Significance[a]	*	NS	NS	NS	*	NS
Anticommunism						
Low	1.64	1.10	.55	2.00	1.20	6.48
Medium	1.70	.98	.32	1.76	1.42	6.17
High	1.78	1.36	.38	1.77	1.05	6.30
Significance[a]	NS	**	*	NS	NS	NS
Democratic norms						
Low	1.67	1.33	.42	1.84	.76	6.02
Medium low	1.75	1.16	.38	1.73	.88	5.85
Medium high	1.73	1.12	.37	1.84	1.02	6.03
High	1.75	1.40	.39	1.81	1.81	7.03
Significance[a]	NS	NS	NS	NS	***	**
Left-right ideological orientation						
Far left	1.75	1.09	.33	1.54	1.54	6.22
Center-left	1.72	1.12	.45	1.92	1.46	6.67
Center-right	1.73	1.30	.42	1.87	1.39	6.67
Far right	1.74	1.18	.33	1.70	.87	5.79
Significance[a]	NS	NS	NS	NS	**	*
Support radical change?						
Radical change	1.58	1.58	.75	2.42	1.75	8.08
Reforms	1.74	1.25	.36	1.81	1.30	6.43
No change	1.70	.95	.39	1.71	.71	5.43
Significance[a]	NS	*	NS	NS	**	**

[a]Significance of difference of means (analysis of variance): * = .05, ** = .01, *** = .001, NS = not significant.

source: 1995 survey.

TABLE A.8   Intercorrelations Among Modes of Political Participation, 1973

	Group Activism	Communication	Contacting	Communal Activism	Party Activism
Group activism	–				
Communication	.33	–			
Contacting	.30	.30	–		
Communal activism	.25	.12	.27	–	
Party activism	.30	.35	.25	.15	–
Voting	.18	.15	.08	.02	.14

sour ce: John A. Booth, "Democracy and Citizen Action in Costa Rica: The Modes and Correlates of Popular Participation in Politics," Ph.D. dissertation, University of Texas at Austin, 1975, p. 134.

TABLE A.9   Intercorrelations Among Modes of Political Participation, 1995

	Contacting	Group Activism	Communal Activism	Voting	Campaigning
Contacting	–				
Group activism	.16	–			
Communal activism	.35	.20	–		
Voting	−.01	.08	.05	–	
Campaigning	.17	.09	.21	.01	–

sour ce: 1995 survey.

Index

Acción Alajuelense Democrática. *See* Alajuelan Democratic Action
African Costa Ricans, 86–87
Age
  antidemocratic attitudes and, 145–146
  political participation and, 108, 113
Agencies. *See* Bureaucracies
Agrarian movements and protests, 115–116
Agriculture, 20, 23, 26, 115. *See also* Banana industry; Coffee industry
Alajuelan Democratic Action (Acción Alajuelense Democrática), 69
Alliance for Progress, 23, 180
Amparo, right of (assistance), 58
Anderson, Leslie, 122
Anticlericalism, 41, 42, 58, 89, 90
Anticommunism, 114, 132, 143
  in foreign policy, 184–185
Antidemocratic attitudes, 142–146
Arbenz, Jacobo, 22
Arias Sánchez, Oscar, 29, 69, 89, 120, 164, 179
  peacemaking policy of, 188–191
Aristocracy, 34–39. *See also* Elites; Upper and upper middle classes
Aristotle, 3, 6
Armed extremist groups, 119
Atlantic Railway, 41
Attitudes
  political participation and, 114
  See also Political culture; Support
Authentic Confederation of Democratic Workers. *See* Confederación Auténtica de Trabajadores Democráticos

Authoritarian methods, justification or support for, 140–142, 144, 145, 152*n*
Authoritarian values, democratic values versus, 134–137

Banana cartel, 182
Banana industry, 20, 21, 38, 41, 42, 182
Banana workers, 43, 116
Banking, state monopolies in, 180
Banks
  Costa Rican, 164
  international, 163
Belize, 21
Biesanzes (Karen Zubris de, Mavis Hiltunen de, and Richard), 82–84, 99, 130, 153
Birch, Anthony, 5
Blacks, 16*n*, 34, 38, 86–87, 118
Book publishing, 91
Budget deficit, 159–160, 164, 165
Bureaucracies, autonomous (decentralized), 63–64
Bush, George, 25, 191
Business organizations, 96–97

Cabildos (municipal councils), 35, 38–39, 54
CACM. *See* Mercado Común Centroamericano
Cafetalero elite. *See* Coffee grower (*cafetalero*) elite
Caja Costarricense de Seguro Social (Costa Rican Social Security Institute; CCSS), 59
Calderón Fournier, Rafael Angel, 68, 188, 191

Calderón Guardia, Rafael Angel, 43–44,
    46–47, 52, 68, 89, 156, 165, 197
Campaigning (campaign activism), 75,
    111–113, 124, 199
Campaigns, electoral, 72–76
Candidates, political, 72–76
Carazo Odio, Rodrigo, 61, 63, 179, 183,
    184
Caribbean Legion, 179
Carrillo Colina, Braulio, 39
Cartago, 33, 35
Carter, Jimmy, 183, 184
Carthaginian Agricultural Union. *See*
    Unión Agrícola Cartaginesa
Carvajal Herrera, Mario, 147, 148
CATD. *See* Confederación Auténtica de
    Trabajadores Democráticos
Catholic Church. *See* Roman Catholic
    Church
Catholics, 108, 131
    political participation by, 114
Catholic Union Party (Unión Católica), 42,
    68, 89
CCSS. *See* Caja Costarricense de Seguro
    Social
CCTD. *See* Confederación Costarricense de
    Trabajadores Democráticos
CCTR. *See* Confederación de Trabajadores
    de Costa Rica
Center for the Study of National Problems,
    47, 49
Central America
    commonalities between Costa Rica and,
        26–27
    contemporary, 22–26
    differences between Costa Rica and the
        rest of, 28–29
    historical background, 17–22
    political participation in, 110
Central American Common Market. *See*
    Mercado Común Centroamericano
Central American Federal Republic, 19, 39
Central American Theological Institute. *See*
    Instituto Teológico de America
    Central
Central Intelligence Agency (CIA), 22, 92

CGT. *See* Confederación General de
    Trabajadores
Chamorro, Violeta Barrios de, 25, 191
Children, constitutional provisions on, 58
Chinese Costa Ricans, 88
Chinese immigrants, 38
CIA. *See* Central Intelligence Agency
Civic League (Liga Cívica), 43
Civil disobedience, support or tolerance
    for, 140, 141, 152*n*
Civil Registry, 71
Civil society, 122–124
Civil war (1948), 44, 47–48
Classical theory of democracy, 3–4, 6
Class structure, 83
Clinton, Bill, 26
CNT. *See* Confederación Nacional de
    Trabajadores
CODESA. *See* Corporación Costarricense
    de Desarrollo
Coffee cartel, 182
Coffee grower (*cafetalero*) elite, 55*n,* 156,
    198
    in the nineteenth century, 36, 39, 41,
        44
Coffee industry, 20, 36–39, 42, 82–83, 170
Cohen, Carl, 4, 5
Colón, devaluation of, 51, 165
Colonial era, 33–35
Columbus, Christopher, 32, 33
Comisión Nacional de Asuntos Indígenas
    (National Commission for Indian
    Affairs; CONAI), 87–88
Communalism. *See* Community
    improvement
Communications media, 91–93
Communism/communists, 22, 120, 121,
    132
    See also Anticommunism; Partido
        Vanguardia Popular
Communist Party, Costa Rican. *See* Partido
    Vanguardia Popular
Community improvement, 105, 107–110,
    112, 124
    authoritarian methods and, 141, 145
Compañía Bananera de Costa Rica, 116

CONAI. *See* Comisión Nacional de Asuntos Indígenas
Confederación Auténtica de Trabajadores Democráticos (Authentic Confederation of Democratic Workers; CATD), 102n
Confederación de Trabajadores de Costa Rica (Confederation of Costa Rican Workers; CTCR), 43, 46
Confederación de Trabajadores de Costa Rica (Confederation of Workers of Costa Rica; CCTR), 120n
Confederación Costarricense de Trabajadores Democráticos (Costa Rican Confederation of Democratic Workers; CCTD), 102n
Confederación General de Trabajadores (General Confederation of Workers; CGT), 43, 45, 102
Confederación Nacional de Trabajadores (National Workers Confederation; CNT), 102n
Confederación Unitaria de Trabajadores (Unitary Confederation of Workers; CUT), 102n
Confederation of Costa Rican Workers. *See* Confederación de Trabajadores de Costa Rica
Confederation of Workers of Costa Rica. *See* Confederación de Trabajadores de Costa Rica
Confrontational political methods, 202
Consejo de Gobierno. *See* Council of Government
Consejo Permanente de los Trabajadores (Permanent Council of Workers; CPT), 102n
Conservatives, 19
in the nineteenth century, 35, 38, 39
Constitution of 1949, 48, 56–66, 78, 198, 199
executive branch under, 61–64
general provisions of, 56–57
judiciary under, 64–66
Legislative Assembly under, 59–61

personal and political rights under, 57–58
political parties under, 66
social rights and guarantees under, 58–59
Constitutions, 6, 93
1821–1847, 39, 93
1869, 93
1871, 40
Contadora Group, 185
Contras, Nicaraguan, 25, 27, 92, 120, 162, 178, 179, 185, 189, 191
Coronado, Juan Vázquez de, 33
Corporación Costarricense de Desarrollo (Costa Rican Development Corporation; CODESA), 160, 164
Cortés Castro, León, 47
Corte Supremo de Justicia (Supreme Court of Justice; CSJ), 60, 63, 65
Costa Rican Confederation of Democratic Workers. *See* Confederación Costarricense de Trabajadores Democráticos
Costa Rican Development Corporation. *See* Corporación Costarricense de Desarrollo
Costa Rican Electrical Institute. *See* Instituto Costarricense de Electricidad
Costa Rican Social Security Institute. *See* Caja Costarricense de Seguro Social
Council of Government (Consejo de Gobierno), 62
Coups d'état, 40–41
1838, 39
1917, 45
Courts, 65, 66. *See also* Corte Supremo de Justicia
CPT. *See* Consejo Permanente de los Trabajadores
CSJ. *See* Corte Supremo de Justicia
CTCR. *See* Confederación de Trabajadores de Costa Rica
Cultural homogeneity, myth of, 30, 34, 86, 94, 99
Currency devaluation, 51, 165

Currency exchange rate. *See* Exchange rate
CUT. *See* Confederación Unitaria de Trabajadores

Dealy, Glen, 2, 129
Debt, foreign. *See* Foreign debt
Demilitarization, Costa Rica's, 48, 57, 178, 179
Democracy, 195–196
  classical theory of, 3–4, 6
  consolidation and survival of, 8–12
  definition of, 3–4, 195
  measuring, 4–5
  problematic aspects of, 5–7
Democracy in Costa Rica, 1, 2
  changes in recent decades, 205–206
  external strains and, 203–205
  lessons of, 206–208
  myths about, 29–30
  prospects for, 206
  stability of support for, 146–147
Democracy in Latin America, 1–2
  stability of, 10
Democratic Party (Partido Demócrata), 47
Democratic values, authoritarian values versus, 134–137
Democratization, 7–8, 196–198
  peacemaking via, 187–191
Department of State, U.S., 59
Dictatorships, 41
  civilian, 20
  military, 20, 22–23, 40, 45
  See also individual dictators
Diffuse support for the political system, 132–134, 137
  by elites, 147–148
DINADECO. *See* Dirección Nacional de Desarollo de la Comunidad
Dirección Nacional de Desarollo de la Comunidad (National Community Development Directorate; DINADECO), 97, 125*n*
Direct participation, 4
Distribution of income, 28, 29, 83–86

Echandi, Mario, 49
Economic aid, U.S., 24, 25, 162, 164
Economic crisis of the 1980s, 95, 98–99, 115, 116, 203
  attitudes and, 146
Economic growth, 50
Economic inequality, coffee boom and, 36
Economic policy
  foreign, 179–183
  See also Political economy
Economy of Costa Rica, 26, 28
  1821–1905, 36–38
  after World War II, 50
  See also Political economy; *specific topics*
Education, 28–29, 41, 93–95
  higher, 94–95
  spending on, 168
  See also Literacy; Schools
EEC. *See* European Economic Community
Elections, 10, 199
  1889, 41
  1905, 44
  1909, 44
  1913, 44
  1944, 47
  1948, 22, 47
  1948–1998 (table), 67
  1953, 49
  1998, 46, 69, 75–76, 200
  administration of, 71–72
  campaign finance, 73
  campaigns and, 72–76
  constitutional provisions and laws, 39, 40, 45–47, 48
  direct presidential, 44
  stability of democracy and, 10
  See also Voter turnout
Elites, 6
  coffee grower *(cafetalero)*, 36, 39, 41, 44, 55*n*, 156, 198
  political culture of, 147
  See also Aristocracy; Upper and upper middle classes
Elite settlement, 49, 197
  stability of democracy and, 8–9
Elite theories of democratization, 8
El Murciélago military base, 187

El Salvador, 20, 25, 27, 189
  historical background, 23, 24
Encomiendas, 33
Environment, natural, 172
European Economic Community (EEC),
  182
Exchange rate, 180
Executive branch, 200
  constitutional provisions on, 57,
  59–64
  decrees and regulations issued by, 63

Family, constitutional provisions on, 58
Farabundo Martí National Liberation
  Front. *See* Frente Farabundo Martí
  para la Liberación Nacional
Figueres Ferrer, José, 22, 47–50, 52, 75,
  156–157, 178, 179, 194*n,* 197
Figueres Olsen, José Maria, 76, 92, 165,
  166, 191
Fiscal crisis of the 1980s, 95
FMLN. *See* Frente Farabundo Martí para la
  Liberación Nacional
Foreign aid. *See* Economic aid, U.S.;
  Military aid, U.S.
Foreign currency reserves, 155, 181
Foreign debt, 26, 155
  neoliberal political economic model
  and, 163–168
  social democratic development model
  and, 159, 160–161, 163
  See also Economic crisis of the 1980s
Foreigners in Costa Rica, 88
Foreign investment, 181
Foreign relations and policy, 12, 177–193,
  204–205
  economic policy, 179–183
  general characteristics of, 178–179
  geopolitics and, 183–190
  universalization of, 183
Forum for Peace and Democracy, 185
Foundation myth, Costa Rica's, 35–36,
  196–198
Free Costa Rica Movement. *See*
  Movimiento Costa Rica Libre

Frente Farabundo Martí para la Liberación
  Nacional (Farabundo Martí National
  Liberation Front; FMLN), 25
Frente Sandinista de Liberación Nacional
  (Sandinista National Liberation
  Front; FSLN), 24, 120
Fruit companies, 38
FSLN. *See* Frente Sandinista de Liberación
  Nacional

GATT. *See* General Agreement on Tariffs
  and Trade
GCE. *See* Gran Consejo Electoral
General Agreement on Tariffs and Trade
  (GATT), 164, 182
General Confederation of Workers. *See*
  Confederación General de
  Trabajadores
Geopolitics, 183–190
German Costa Ricans, 88
Gómez, Miguel, 146
González Flores, Alfredo, 44
González Víquez, Cleto, 44
Government
  attitudes toward, 132–134
  size and scope of, neoliberalism and,
  166–168
  See also Executive branch; Judiciary;
  Legislative Assembly
Governmental structures, stability of
  democracy and, 10
Gran Consejo Electoral (Grand Electoral
  Council; GCE), 45, 47
Grand Electoral Council. *See* Gran Consejo
  Electoral
Grupo Soberania. *See* Sovereignty Group
Guardia Gutiérrez, Tomás, 40
Guatemala, 189, 198
  historical background, 17, 19, 20, 22–24
Gudmundson, Lowell, 29
Guerrillas (rebels), 24

Hacienda system, 19, 34, 35, 53
Hamilton, Alexander, 6
Haya de la Torre, Victor Raúl, 43, 49
Homogeneity, myth of, 30, 34, 86, 94, 99
Honduras, 189

historical background, 20–23
Honey, Martha, 92, 130
Housing, spending on, 168
Housing movements, 117–118
Human rights, 199
    perception of the government's respect
      for, 134
Huntington, Samuel, 10

IADB. *See* Inter-American Development
    Bank
ICE. *See* Instituto Costarricense de
    Electricidad
IMF. *See* International Monetary Fund
Immigration, 11, 33, 38
Import substitution industrialization (ISI),
    50, 158, 180
Income and wages, 28
    neoliberalism and, 169–170
Income distribution, 11, 28, 29, 83–86,
    200
Indians (indigenous people), 17, 19, 32–34,
    87–88
Industry, 23, 28
Infant mortality, 27, 28
Inflation, 165
Infrastructure, government investment in,
    168–169
Inglehart, Ronald, 7, 129–130, 150
Instituto Costarricense de Electricidad
    (Costa Rican Electrical Institute;
    ICE), 169
Instituto Nacional de Vivienda y
    Urbanismo (National Urbanization
    and Housing Institute; INVU), 168
Instituto Teológico de America Central
    (Central American Theological
    Institute; ITAC), 89–90
Insurance, state monopolies in, 180
Inter-American Development Bank
    (IADB), 163, 165, 166
Inter-American Reciprocal Assistance
    Treaty, 193*n*
International Monetary Fund (IMF), 163,
    165–166

International relations. *See* Foreign
    relations and policy
Interpersonal trust, 7, 114, 122, 124,
    130–131
Intervention by Great Britain, 21
Intervention by the United States, 20, 21,
    25, 26
Investigatory commissions, Legislative
    Assembly, 61
Investment on infrastructure, by
    government, 168–169
INVU. *See* Instituto Nacional de Vivienda y
    Urbanismo
Iran-contra scandal, 189
ISI. *See* Import substitution
    industrialization
ITAC. *See* Instituto Teológico de America
    Central

Jamaicans, 38, 86, 90
Jefferson, Thomas, 3–5, 14*n*
Jews, 33, 88
Jiménez Oreamuno, Ricardo, 44, 45
John Paul II, Pope, 90
Judicial review, 63, 65
Judicial Investigation Organism. *See*
    Organismo de Investigaciónes
    Judiciales
Judiciary, 199
    constitutional provisions on, 64–66
    See also Corte Supremo de Justicia
Junta of 1948–1949. *See* National
    Liberation movement and junta

Labor
    constitutional provisions on, 58
    shortage of, 34, 36
    See also Workers
Labor unions, 43, 44, 47, 49, 89, 97
    confederations of, 102*n*
La Familia (the Family), 121
La Nación, 92
Latin America
    democracy in. *See* Democracy in Latin
      America
    political culture of, 129–130
Law of the Sea Treaty, 182

Laws, promulgation of, 60
Leftist parties, 69
Leftists, Costa Ricans identified as, 143–144
Legislative Assembly, 57, 200
    constitutional provisions on, 59–61, 63
Liberals, 19, 35
    in the nineteenth century, 38, 39, 42
    political economy and, 156
Life satisfaction, 114, 131–132
Liga Cívica. *See* Civic League
Limón, 87, 118, 165
Literacy, 23, 27–29, 94

Manufacturing. *See* Industry
Mauro, 93
MCRL. *See* Movimiento Costa Rica Libre
Media, 91–93
Mercado Común Centroamericano
    (Central American Common Market;
    CACM) 23, 24, 26, 50, 157, 178,
    180–181
Mestizos, 11, 17, 19, 34, 35
Mexico, 19, 183
Middle class, 41, 49, 83–86
Migration
    within Central America, 26–27
    See also Immigration
Militarism, 36
Military, 19–20, 41
    1889 elections and, 42
    prohibition of a standing army, 48, 57,
    178, 179
Military aid, U.S., 24, 25
Military intervention by the United States,
    20, 21, 25, 26
Military rule (military dictatorships), 20,
    22–23
    1917–1919, 45
    nineteenth century, 40
Mill, John Stuart, 3
Minerals, absence of, 26, 33
Minimum wage, 47
Minorities, 11, 86–89
    See also specific minorities
Missionaries, Protestant, 90

Monge Alvarez, Luis Alberto, 97, 120, 162,
    179
    foreign policy of, 184–187
Mora Fernández, Juan, 39
Morazán Quesada, Francisco, 39
Movimiento Costa Rica Libre (Free Costa
    Rica Movement; MCRL), 120
Mueller, John, 6
Myths, national, 29–30, 52
    of classlessness and homogeneity, 82, 99
    foundation myth, 35–36, 196–198

NAFTA. *See* North American Free Trade
    Agreement
National Commission for Indian Affairs.
    See Comisión Nacional de Asuntos
    Indígenas
National Community Development
    Directorate. *See* Dirección Nacional
    de Desarollo de la Comunidad
National Electoral Tribunal. *See* Tribunal
    Nacional Electoral
National Liberation forces, 47, 197, 198
National Liberation movement and junta
    (1948–1949), 22, 29, 49, 50, 156–157
    See also Civil war (1948)
National Liberation Party. *See* Partido de
    Liberación Nacional
National Union Party. *See* Partido Unión
    Nacional
National Urbanization and Housing
    Institute. *See* Instituto Nacional de
    Vivienda y Urbanismo
National Workers Confederation. *See*
    Confederación Nacional de
    Trabajadores
Natural environment, 172
Neoliberalism (neoliberal development
    model), 158, 162–174, 203–204
    democracy and, 172–174
    export promotion and, 170
    government investment and, 168–169
    natural environment and, 172
    policy implications of, 166–172
    size and scope of government and,
    166–168

structural adjustment programs and, 163–166
taxation and, 169
urban population growth and, 170–172
wage policy and, 169
Neutrality, 184–187
News of the Continent radio station (Radio Noticias del Continente), 120, 128*n*
Newspapers, 91
Nicaragua, 39, 97
Costa Rican policy toward, 179, 183–186
historical background, 20–24
peacemaking via democratization policy and, 187–192
Sandinista government of, 25, 92, 162, 188
Sandinista revolution in, 120, 178, 183–184
Somoza regime, 179, 183–184
Soviet Union and, 25
Nicaraguan contras, 25, 27, 92, 120, 162, 178, 179, 185, 189, 191
Nicaraguans in Costa Rica, 88–89
North American Free Trade Agreement (NAFTA), 182–183
Nuñez, Benjamín, 89

OAS. *See* Organization of American States
O'Donnell, Guillermo, 129
Oduber Quirós, Daniel, 63, 148
OIJ. *See* Organismo de Investigaciónes Judiciales
Oil prices, 181
Older citizens
political participation and, 108
See also Age
OPEN. *See* Organización para Emergencias Nacionales
Organización para Emergencias Nacionales (Organization for National Emergencies; OPEN), 120–121
Organization of American States (OAS), 179, 183, 193*n*
Organization of Banana Exporting Countries, 182

Organization for National Emergencies. *See* Organización para Emergencias Nacionales
Organizations and associations, 95–96
Organismo de Investigaciónes Judiciales (Judicial Investigation Organism; OIJ), 61

Pacifists, 187–188
PAEs. *See* Programa de ajuste estructural
Panama, 25, 30
Panama Canal, 21
Paramilitary groups, 120–121
Paris Club, 163, 165, 166
Participation. *See* Political participation
Partido de Liberación Nacional (National Liberation Party; PLN), 11, 48–49, 52, 61, 66, 68, 70, 157, 165, 199, 197
Partido Demócrata. *See* Democratic Party
Partido Republican. *See* Republican Party
Partido Unidad Social Cristiana (Social Christian Unity Party; PUSC), 68, 73, 165
Partido Pueblo Unido (United People's Party; PPU), 69
Partido Reformista (Reformist Party; PR), 68
Partido Unión Nacional (National Union Party; PUN), 44, 47, 48
Partido Vanguardia Popular (Popular Vanguard Party; PVP), 22, 43–44, 46, 47, 49, 69, 157
Party activism, 105
Party system. *See* Political parties
Peace accord, Central American, 164, 179, 191, 204
Peacemaking policy, 187–190
Peasants, 83, 98, 99, 115, 116, 122
Peeler, John, 54*n*, 70, 208*n*
Pentecostals, 90–91
People's Revolutionary Party, 69
Permanent Council of Workers. *See* Consejo Permanente de los Trabajadores
Picado, Miguel, 90
Picado Michalski, Teodoro, 22, 44, 47
PLN. *See* Partido de Liberación Nacional

Pluralist-elitists, 6, 14*n*, 15*n*
Political capital, 122–124
Political culture, 129–154, 201–203
  antidemocratic elements in, 142–146
  attitudes toward government, 132–134
  correlates of, 137–142
  democratic values versus authoritarian
    values, 134–137
  elite, 147–149
  general, 130–132
  Latin American, 129–130
  stability of democracy and, 9–10
  stability of support for democracy,
    146–147
Political culture theories of
    democratization, 7, 198
Political economy, 154–175
  democracy and, 172–174
  evolution of, 155–165
  foreign economic policy, 179–183
  in Liberal era, 156
  See also Neoliberalism; Social
    democratic development model
Political participation, 4, 9, 103–128, 200,
    201–203
  1973 national survey of, 104–108,
    125–126*n*
  1995 urban survey of, 108–114,
    125*n*
  age and, 108, 113
  agrarian movements and protests,
    115–116
  in campaigns, 74
  concentration of, 105, 107, 110, 112
  correlates of, 107–108, 112
  levels of, 105, 108–109
  in other Central American nations, 110
  perceived efficacy of, 134
  perceived freedom to participate index,
    133
  religion and, 108, 113–114
  socioeconomic factors and, 107–108,
    112
  structure of, 105, 109–110
  unconventional, 114–121
  urban protests, 116–118

  violent, 118–121
  by women, 108, 112
Political parties (party system), 10, 66–71,
    78, 199
  alternation of power between, 70
  constitutional provisions on, 66
  leftist, 69
  regional, 68–69
  stability of democracy and, 10
  See also specific parties
Political refugees, 26–27, 88
Political rights
  constitutionally guaranteed, 6–7
  under constitution of 1949, 57–58
Popular Vanguard Party. *See* Partido
    Vanguardia Popular
Population growth, 27
  urban, 170–171
Poverty, 23, 27, 85
PPU. *See* Partido Pueblo Unido
PR. *See* Partido Reformista
Presidential candidates, nomination of,
    72–73
Presidential form of government, 10
Presidents of Costa Rica, 40
  See also Executive branch; *specific
    presidents*
Press, the, 65, 91–92
Process theories of democratization, 7, 198
Programa de ajuste estructural (structural
    adjustment programs; PAE),
    163–166, 181
Protestantism, 7, 90–91
Protestants, 131
Provinces, 57
Public employees, 64, 165
Publishing, 91
PUN. *See* Partido Unión Nacional
PUSC. *See* Partido Unidad Social Cristiana
Putnam, Robert, 9, 122
PVP. *See* Partido Vanguardia Popular

Racial bias (discrimination), 34, 38, 88
Racial homogeneity, myth of, 82, 99
Radical left, 12
Radio, 91

Radio Noticias del Continente. *See* News of
the Continent radio station
Railroads, 38, 41
Reagan, Ronald, 24, 25, 185, 189, 191
Recessions
1970s, 23, 51, 159, 161, 162
1980s, 26, 28
early twentieth century, 42–43
See also Economic crisis of the 1980s
Reform Party, 68
Reformist Party. *See* Partido Reformista
Refugees in Costa Rica, 26–27, 88
Religion, 89–91
constitutional provisions on, 58
political participation and, 108,
113–114
See also Anticlericalism; Roman Catholic
Church
Religious fundamentalism, 131
Representative democracy, 4–5
Republican Party (Partido Republicano),
22, 43, 44
Retirees, foreign *(pensionados),* 88
Rightists, Costa Ricans identified as,
143–144
Rights
citizens' (constitutionally guaranteed),
6–7
human, 134, 199
political, 6–7, 57–58
Rioting, 118
Rodriguez, José J., 42
Rodriguez, Miguel Angel, 66, 76
Rodriguez Quirós, Carlos Humberto,
90
Rojas, Yolanda, 95
Román Arrieta, Alajuela, 89
Roman Catholic Church (Catholicism), 41,
49, 89–90, 105
conservatism of, 90
constitutional provisions on, 58
Roosevelt, Theodore, 21
Rousseau, Jean-Jacques, 3, 6
Rovira, Jorge, 95
Rural Guard, 119
Sanabria Martinez, Victor, 43, 89

Sandinista National Liberation Front. *See*
Frente Sandinista de Liberación
Nacional
Sandino, Augusto, 20
San José, 33, 35, 170–171
San Juan River, 185, 193n
Schools, 93, 94
Self-government, 35
Seligson, Mitchell, 146
Slaves, 34
Social capital, 122
Social Christian Unity Party. *See* Partido
Unidad Social Cristiana
Social classes, 83
Social democratic development model,
155–162, 164
crisis of, 158
emergence of, 157
Social Democratic Party, 47,
49
Social equality, 11
Socialist Party, 69
Social rights and guarantees, under
constitution of 1949, 58–59
Social security law (1941), 46–47
Social spending, 168
Social structure, 82–91
income distribution and, 83–86
social classes, 83
Socioeconomic factors
democratic stability and, 11–12
political participation and, 107–108,
112
Sojo, Carlos, 184
Solidarismo (solidarity associations), 90,
97
Somoza Debayle, Anastasio, 183
Somoza family, 22
Somoza García, Anastasio, 20, 178, 193n
Sovereignty Group (Grupo Soberania),
69
Soviet Union, 25
Spanish rule, Central America under, 17,
19
Squatters, urban, 116, 118
Stability
of democracy, 8–12

of support for democracy, 146

Standing army, prohibition of (demilitarization), 48, 57, 178, 179

State, the, stability of democracy and, 10–11

Strikes, 38, 43
  of banana workers (1934), 43
  of banana workers (1984), 116
  right to, 44

Structural adjustment programs. *See* Programa de ajuste estructural

Structural theories of democratization, 7–8

Support
  for civil disobedience, 140, 141
  for democratic principles, 137, 140
  for the political system, diffuse, 132–134, 137, 147–148

Supreme Court of Justice. *See* Corte Supremo de Justicia

Supreme Electoral Tribunal. *See* Tribunal Supremo de Elecciones

Tariffs (import taxes), 180, 181
  GATT and, 182

Taxation, neoliberalism and, 169

Teachers, 94–95

Television, 91

Thiel, Bernardo, 89

Tinoco Granados, Federico, 43, 45

TNE. *See* Tribunal Nacional Electoral

Tourism, 164

Trade, 37, 38. *See also* Agriculture; Tariffs

Trade balance, 155

Tribunal Nacional Electoral (National Electoral Tribunal; TNE), 47

Tribunal Supremo de Elecciones (Supreme Electoral Tribunal; TSE), 48, 49, 65, 75, 199

TSE. *See* Tribunal Supremo de Elecciones

Tuna war, 182

Turnout rates, 46, 48. *See also* Elections

UAC. *See* Unión Agrícola Cartiginesa

Ulate Blanco, Otilio, 22, 47–49, 157, 197

Unión Agrícola Cartaginesa (Carthaginian Agricultural Union; UAC), 68–69

Unión Católica. *See* Catholic Union Party

Unión de Pequeños y Medianos Agricultores (Union of Small and Medium Farmers; UPA-Nacional), 116

Unión Generaleña (Valle del General Union), 69

Unions. *See* Labor unions

Union of Small and Medium Farmers. *See* Unión de Pequeños y Medianos Agricultores

Unitary Confederation of Workers. *See* Confederación Unitaria de Trabajadores

United Fruit Company, 21, 38, 43

United People's Party. *See* Partido Pueblo Unido

United States
  1940s–1950s Central American policy, 22
  Central American peace accord and, 164
  Costa Rican policy toward, 178, 183
  intervention by, 20, 21, 25, 26
  Iran-contra scandal in, 189

Unity coalition, 68

Universidad de Costa Rica, 94

Universidad de Santo Tomás, 93

UPA-Nacional. *See* Unión de Pequeños y Medianos Agricultores

Upper and upper middle classes, 83–85

Urbanization, 170–172

Urban protests and movements, 116–118

U.S. Agency for International Development, 164, 166, 186

USAID. *See* U.S. Agency for International Development

Valle del General Union (Unión Generaleña), 69

Valverde, Bosco, 92

Vesco, Robert, 65

Violence, political, 118–121

Volio Jiménez, Jorge, 43, 45, 89

Voter turnout, 46, 48

Voting, 105

Voting procedures, 76
Voting requirements, 72

Wages. *See* Income and wages
Wiarda, Howard J., 129
Women, political participation by, 108, 112
Workers (working class), 83
    constitutional provisions on, 58–59
    in the nineteenth century, 36–38,
      42–43
    See also Labor; Labor unions; Strikes

World Bank, 162, 163
World War II, 21

Yashar, Deborah, 54*n*, 55*n*,
    208*n*
Young people
    antidemocratic attitudes and, 145–146
    political attitudes of, 141